CHINESE CULTURE
ITS HUMANITY AND MODERNITY

CHINESE CULTURE
ITS HUMANITY AND MODERNITY

QIAN SUOQIAO

Newcastle University, UK

World Scientific

NEW JERSEY · LONDON · SINGAPORE · BEIJING · SHANGHAI · HONG KONG · TAIPEI · CHENNAI · TOKYO

Published by

World Scientific Publishing Europe Ltd.

57 Shelton Street, Covent Garden, London WC2H 9HE

Head office: 5 Toh Tuck Link, Singapore 596224

USA office: 27 Warren Street, Suite 401-402, Hackensack, NJ 07601

Library of Congress Cataloging-in-Publication Data
Names: Qian, Suoqiao, author.
Title: Chinese culture : its humanity and modernity / Suoqiao Qian, Newcastle University, UK.
Description: New Jersey : World Scientific, [2021] | Includes bibliographical references and index.
Identifiers: LCCN 2020027890 | ISBN 9781786348999 (hardcover) | ISBN 9781786349057 (paperback) | ISBN 9781786349002 (ebook for institutions) | ISBN 9781786349019 (ebook for individuals)
Subjects: LCSH: China--Civilization. | China--History. | China--Politics and government. | China--Social life and customs.
Classification: LCC DS721 .Q2485 2021 | DDC 951--dc23
LC record available at https://lccn.loc.gov/2020027890

British Library Cataloguing-in-Publication Data
A catalogue record for this book is available from the British Library.

Copyright © 2021 by Suoqiao Qian

All rights reserved.

For any available supplementary material, please visit
https://www.worldscientific.com/worldscibooks/10.1142/Q0263#t=suppl

Desk Editors: Britta Ramaraj/Michael Beale/Shi Ying Koe

Typeset by Stallion Press
Email: enquiries@stallionpress.com

Printed in Singapore

To Jimmy Siqi Qian

Contents

Preface viii

1 Chinese Cultural Identity: History and Language **2**
A People with a Long History 2
Chinese Language 18

2 *Pax Sinica*: The Chinese Model of Government **28**
Family-State: The Legalist and Confucian Convergence 29
The Examination System and Civil Rule 36
Government for the People 43

3 Three Religions as One: Confucianism, Taoism, and Buddhism **56**
Confucian Self-Cultivation 56
Taoist Self: Being One with Nature 65
Chinese Buddhism: The Taming of Monkey 74

4 A Poetic Culture: An Aesthetics of Life **84**
Poetic Expression of Heart and Mind 85
Detachment and Freedom 97

5 The Rise of Modern Chinese Nationalism **110**
Opium and Missionaries 111
Arise! Ye Who Refuse to Be Bond Slaves! 120

6	**Embracing the World: Cosmopolitan Visions**	**136**
	Evolution and Great Union	137
	Chinese Renaissance	150
7	**Radical Revolutions to a Super-State**	**164**
	Taiping Communism	164
	From Restoration to Revolution	170
	Yan'an Talks and Its Shadows	183
8	**The Rise of China and Its Cultural Challenge**	**192**
	The Rise of China and Its Cultural Factors	193
	To Be or Not to Be a Chinese: Where Is China's Soft Power?	202
	Works Cited	218
	Suggested Further Readings	222
	Chinese Character List	224
	Index	230

Preface

This book is a critical overview of Chinese culture intended for college students as well as for general readers interested in the topic.

The terms "culture," "Chinese" and "critical," however, all need a bit of explanation here. "Culture," or "*wenhua*" in Chinese today, is a modern neologism — a newly coined term in Chinese often via Japanese translation of Western terms when the classical Chinese gave way to vernacular Chinese. It does not mean that classical Chinese does not have a notion for "culture." On the other hand, after more than a century of usage, the Chinese have pretty much taken these new loanwords for granted as their own. That also means that when the Chinese today talk about "culture," its connotations are not that different from its usage in the West.

We basically have two approaches toward "culture." The more dominant one is the anthropological and sociological approach. Ever since Franz Boas (1858–1942), the father of cultural anthropology in the United States, "culture" is taken as something "objective," referring to the material or non-material products of a group of people. Many disciples of Boas offer further elaborations and interpretations of culture in the twentieth century. Most famously, Kroeber and Kluckhohn reviewed over 160 definitions of culture in 1952. And since then, there have been more schools and perspectives such as structuralist, post-structuralist, cultural studies, and so on. But some of the basic assumptions remain the same. They claim to be "objective" and "progressive": anti-racist, anti-elitist, appreciating "cultural difference" based on cultural relativism. Starting from its anthropological gaze upon Native American cultures, this approach has been adopted universally including in interpreting Chinese culture. "Chinese culture" through this lens is seen in terms of Chinese Arts and Crafts, Chinese Kung Fu, Chinese Painting, Chinese Architecture, Chinese Clothing, Chinese Furniture, and Chinese Music among others.[1] The Chinese themselves are also approaching culture in this light with introductory books on Chinese culture focusing on its various aspects such as Chinese Bronze, Chinese Characters, and so on. There is a little irony here. While the anthropologist attempts to look at the other culture objectively appreciating their difference, there is an inevitable Nationalist tone (Look, what we have got!) when the Chinese apply them. Furthermore, while the anthropologist attempts to be objective and tries to get rid of prejudices against other cultures, this seems to be precisely the problem when looking at Chinese culture in this light. If a college student outside China reads, say, "Chinese Clothing" or "Chinese Furniture," thinking she knows something about how the Chinese wear or sit, she would feel cheated when she goes to China for the first time and sees the Chinese wear nothing like she has read or sits on pretty much the same furniture as back home. I think that is the last thing I want for any reader having read this book.

There is another approach to "culture" that is still prevalent in the West, and perhaps more so in the Chinese context. When the Chinese invoke "culture," more often than not it is in the context of referring to someone as "cultured," which generally entails a set of qualities not necessarily related to one's degree, although a college education today would be a part of it. These qualities normally mean the possession of broad knowledge related to China and the world (to be able to recite traditional Chinese cultural knowledge alone is hardly an admirable quality), as well as a style of embodying them in good manners. There is certainly traditional legacy here echoing the Confucian preoccupation with moral self-cultivation and proper behavior (good manners). But it is also definitely a result of modern transformation of Chinese culture through translation and borrowing from Western sources. After all, before the anthropological notions of culture

---

[1] These are some of the titles in the recent 30-volume *Introductions to Chinese Culture* by Cambridge University Press.

became predominant reference points to discourses on culture, European Romantics (particularly German and British thinkers) had a lot to say about "culture." Immanuel Kant, for instance, invokes the German notion of *Bildung* by defining Enlightenment as a process or event for mankind to achieve maturity, "to dare to know, to have the courage, the audacity, to know." Perhaps the most well-known nineteenth-century cultural critic was Matthew Arnold who saw "culture being a pursuit of our total perfection by means of getting to know, on all the matters which most concern us, the best which had been thought and said in the world." Culture in this sense is very close to what we understand as "civilization." Gu Hongming, a noted modern Chinese cross-cultural critic heavily influenced by Matthew Arnold, had this to say in trying to bring out what he interprets as the "spirit of the Chinese people":

> In order to estimate the value of a civilisation, it seems to me, the question we must finally ask is not what great cities, what magnificent houses, what fine roads it has built and is able to build; what beautiful and comfortable furniture, what clever and useful implements, tools and instruments it has made and is able to make; no, not even what institutions, what arts and sciences it has invented: the question we must ask, in order to estimate the value of a civilisation — is, *what type of humanity*, what kind of men and women it has been able to produce.[2]

My approach to "culture" in this book is more in accordance with Arnold-Gu Hongming's line of critical thinking, but with two major modifications. Gu Hongming believes that the key to understanding Chinese culture is through an exposition of "Chinese men and women" (sometimes he uses the now-racially-condemned term "Chinamen"), not in terms of their "characteristics" but through an interpretive look into their "spirit." But the "Chinese" Gu was presenting at the beginning of the twentieth century was already a dying species when, as he himself admits, a new type of humanity was already arising to replace the old one. The guiding question

---
[2] Gu Hongming (Ku Hung-Ming), *The Spirit of the Chinese People*, p. 1.

for my book here is this. When a college student goes to China today for the first time, say, for a year abroad to study the Chinese language, and she wants to make a Chinese friend, what can she learn beforehand about "Chinese culture" in general terms, as may be embodied in the Chinese individual she is likely to make friends with? Focused as such, one immediately recognizes that an emphasis on such topics as Chinese Kung Fu, Chinese clothing, or even calligraphy is really off the point. The Chinese friend the college student may establish a relationship with is really the product of "the new type of humanity" as a result of the dramatic modern transformations that have been going on in the past one hundred and fifty years or so, and still very much ongoing. To think of "Chinese culture" in terms of "kung fu" or "Confucius" would be very misleading indeed. The New Culture Movement in the latter half of the 1910s, which in many ways ushered in the Chinese culture as we know it today, including, for instance, the very Chinese language we speak and write nowadays, was radically iconoclastic or anti-Confucian. So was the Communist ideology that reigned in China during much of the twentieth century. But that does not mean the traditional culture has been totally wiped out. Transformation is not replacement. Despite suffering from deconstructive attacks and all-out political campaigns, many elements of traditional culture still linger on, for better or worse. It does mean, though, in my opinion, that a century and half or so modern experience of transformation outweighs the several-thousand-year-old traditional legacy when we think of the effects on the formation of Chinese culture as we know it today. In that light, this book is very different from what one usually gets out of a survey course on "A History of China" or "A History of Chinese Civilization." It does not offer a chronological account, dynasty by dynasty, of important events and achievements in Chinese history. Rather, it focuses on those elements that matter most to Chinese culture as we know it today, as may be embodied in a Chinese individual one way or another. It means an emphasis on the cross-cultural transformations in the modern epoch. When it does deal with traditional cultural resources, history is seen in a backward way, or as "history of the present" — if I may use a term by the French philosopher Michel Foucault. In other words, I look at those traditional elements as still contributing to Chinese culture today, as living legacies instead of as museum treasures.

If to apply the Arnoldian notion of culture as "the best which had been thought and said in the world" in the Chinese context is to exalt Chinese cultural achievements in a nationalist tone, which underlines much of the impulse to talk about "Chinese culture" in today's China, I am least interested. Modern Chinese nationalism has its own historical *raison d'être,* which will be the focus of discussion in one chapter in the book. But the issue also needs to be considered critically. In fact, to be "critical" is to inherit another Arnoldian legacy, for to Arnold, "the best that is known and thought in the world" can only be achieved through unprejudiced and impartial criticism by trying to "see the object as in itself it really is," as he put it in his famous essay "The Function of Criticism at the Present Time." In an essay of the same title (coincidental or intentional?), though it was originally written in Chinese and later translated into English by himself, the modern Chinese cross-cultural critic Lin Yutang further elaborated on the preeminence of criticism as regards to modern Chinese cultural transformation. To Lin, criticism is the defining feature of modern culture as distinct from traditional cultures East and West, in that the authority of sages can no longer hold sway, and it is critics such as Nietzsche, Schopenhauer, Ibsen, Shaw, and Tolstoy who are our greatest thinkers. In fact, we cannot rely on these great thinkers entirely either. We ought to think for ourselves and arrive at our own individual judgment on the myriad things of modern life, so "the center of gravity has shifted from these men of intellectual eminence to the intellectual proletariat." For Chinese culture to reach maturity out of modern transformation, each one of us ought to develop critical faculties in the face of changes and challenges to our morals, customs, and institutions. For we live in a global age and modern culture is necessarily transnational and all-encompassing: "This culture does not belong to any one nation, but to the modern world as a whole, in which all nations are members of the world republic of letters and thought."[3] A critical introduction of Chinese culture follows this Arnoldian-Lin Yutang critical disposition in identifying such key issues as history, language, governmentality, self-cultivation, aesthetics of life, nationalism, cosmopolitanism, communism, the rise of China, and its soft power for our

---

[3] Lin Yutang, "The Function of Criticism at the Present Time", p. 6.

critical reflection. The last thing I want my readers to get out of this book is to still regard Chinese culture as somehow an Other, perhaps even a better Other, an alternative to all the ills some self-proclaimed "progressives" take to define their own culture. The real progressive thing to do is to take Chinese culture seriously as "a member of the world republic of letters and thought."

I just hope that, as Chinese culture continues to evolve, critical issues explored in this book will prove to be outdated in a couple of decades when my son goes to college, and he will not be reading this book.

Chapter 1

Chinese Cultural Identity:
History and Language

Currently, there are 7.5 billion people inhabiting the earth. China, Europe, and the United States each occupy similar geographical areas — about 10 million square kilometers. however China has a population of 1.4 billion, Europe half of that (0.7 billion), and the United States a further half (0.35 billion). In other words, if we take a family photo of the world, we will see approximately one Chinese person every five individuals. This leads to the question: what are these Chinese like? What are the cultural features that constitute them as a people and distinguish them from other members? Let us first approach the question from two essential perspectives: history and language.

A PEOPLE WITH A LONG HISTORY

The Chinese are a people with a long pedigree, so to speak. The Chinese are Chinese because they have a shared history — a history of continuity from a common ancestry to the present. That is quite unique among the members of the world family. The Chinese call themselves "sons and daughters of the Yellow Emperor" and are generally proud of such reference to cultural genealogy. Apart from its apparent nationalist exultation, the statement is nevertheless true in that *Huangdi*, or the Yellow Emperor, was recorded in some of the earliest historical documents as the founding father of a political entity governing all the people

Figure 1: Yellow Emperor

Figure 2: Sima Qian

under heaven — whom nowadays we call "Chinese." By the Han Dynasty, there emerged a great historian called Sima Qian (c. 145–85 BC), whose *Records of the Grand Historian*, which begins with a biography of the Yellow Emperor, offers a panoramic and authoritative account of the Chinese history to date and has been regarded as a grand masterpiece in the collective consciousness of the Chinese people. The Chinese have understood the value and power of history from very early on and have been conscious and conscientious historians. Confucius, the greatest teacher of Chinese culture, for instance, is known for many things, of course, but perhaps most importantly as a historian who compiled *The Annals of Spring and Autumn*, which merely records the happenings of the state of Lu in a matter-of-the-fact style. Yet, when the *Annals* was completed, "patricides and regicides were scared." The power of history continues to affect contemporary life and politics. When the Great Leap Forward, initiated by the Communist Leader Mao Zedong in 1958, resulted in the Great Famine, Liu Shaoqi, the No. 2 person in the CCP leadership, was scared and challenged Mao in a moment of frustration and revelation: "Now that we have a wide-spread famine where cannibalistic activities are rampant. We will all be recorded in history!"[1]

What kind of effects then has such sense and sensibility of history produced in shaping some paramount features of a Chinese cultural identity? To answer that question, it requires an understanding of Chinese history itself. To highlight the continuity of Chinese history is not to underestimate its changes. In fact, change is constant, as the Chinese philosophical wisdom goes. But looking back upon the continuous line of China's history to date, we can identify a couple of moments of gigantic

---

[1] Mao then backed down for a while, only to re-emerge later to launch the more destructive Cultural Revolution in which Liu was persecuted to death. Mao did not seem to be scared of "history" and perhaps that is why many in China today purport to believe that Mao was not even an "emperor," but a god, and therefore beyond history.

changes and paradigmatic shifts that rechanneled historical development and made a huge impact upon the formation of Chinese culture. There are in fact two such moments and Chinese history can be lined up into three epochs accordingly: the Classical Era, which begins with the times of the Yellow Emperor to the Warring States period when the classical order breaks down; the Dynastic Era, when the First Emperor of the Qin Dynasty unified the warring states and established a new order, to be followed by a series of dynasties challenging, modifying but ultimately maintaining that order down to the last dynasty of Qing; and the Modern Era, which began with the Opium War of 1840 when western gunboats brought China into a family of nations, which had until then functioned and regarded itself, by and large, as a civilization.

The Classical Era includes the antiquity period and times of its breakdown — the former refers to the times of the Five Emperors (starting with the Yellow Emperor and ending with Emperor Yao and Emperor Shun) and Three Dynasties (Xia, Shang, Zhou). The Zhou Dynasty was founded in 1046 BC, but after about 300 years, the classical order began to break down and China entered into a period (about 500 years) of first, hundreds of smaller states (called the Spring and Autumn period) and then, about half a dozen larger states (called Warring States period) competing and constantly at war, until China was unified again under the Qin Dynasty in 221 BC. The classical order was as important in Chinese cultural tradition as classical Greek culture was to Renaissance Europe, except that there was not a millennium of Christendom in between. On the other hand, Chinese culture and society in the Classical Era share some similar features of medieval Europe in that it is marked by a feudal social structure and the prominence of religiosity in one's lives to the extent that state and religion are inseparable. In fact, when Christianity was introduced to China in modern times, "God" was translated, quite aptly, into "Shangdi" by invoking the native Chinese term found in ancient texts referring to religious life in Chinese antiquity. However, the classical order in terms of both religious and socio-political life broke down and China was in a civilizational crisis. The crisis proved to be an occasion for rejuvenation as well. Out of the ruins of war and treachery emerged a cultural renaissance to define Chinese culture for millennia to come. Not only was the breakdown period a time of competing warring states, it was also a time of competing ideas — a time when "a Hundred Schools of Thought" flourished. And out of these "Hundred Schools of Thought," three schools of teaching will prove to be of paramount importance for the shaping of Chinese culture: Confucianism under the teachings of Confucius and Mencius, Taoism under the teachings of Laozi and Zhuangzi, and Legalism under the teachings of Han Fei. About a millennium later, Chinese culture will face the challenges of the spread of Buddhism from the "West," and begin a process of assimilation and incorporation of Buddhism as another leg of its cultural fabric.

It is quite important to appreciate that Chinese antiquity precedes the Chinese renaissance of the "Hundred Schools of Thought." In other words, Chinese culture already had approximately 2500 years of history before Confucius, and a further 2500 years after Confucius. Were it not the case, a renaissance would be out of the question, for Confucius' lifetime mission was to restore the classical order, or to recover "the rituals of Zhou," so as to rectify the moral degradation and warring chaos of competing states. But Confucius failed in his lifetime: when Confucianism was institutionalized in the Dynastic Era, it was a different kind of order. Nevertheless, the classical order was a major source of reference and standard for the dynastic order. Rather than eschatological, Chinese culture used to be always primordial: looking back to the golden era under the sage kings of Huangdi, Yao, and Shun. Huangdi, and particularly Yao and Shun, have been heralded as cultural heroes with long-lasting impact.

Sima Qian's *Records of the Grand Historian* begins to trace the beginning of the Chinese people. Interestingly, we do not find any "Genesis" story. Rather, the first chapter of the book is a biography of the "Five Emperors," from which we can have a glimpse of what kind of qualities are attributed to Huangdi, Yao and Shun as cultural heroes. Huangdi is said to be "perspicacious" at birth, and "as an infant, he was able to speak, as a boy, he was quick, as a youth, he was industrious, as an adult, he was intelligent." Huangdi is mainly credited with unifying the land by fighting off feudal lords and bringing peace and harmony through able government. In Huangdi's time, there was a rebel feudal lord called Chi You who was considered to be "the most tyrannical." Huangdi drilled an army, called in troops for the feudal lords and fought with Chi You, and captured and killed him in the end. "The feudal lords all honoured Huangdi as the Son of Heaven...[and] he set up the Left and Right Grand Superintendents to superintend the myriad states. The myriad states were harmonious, and their sacrifices to spirits, to mountains and rivers are considered to be the most frequent." Here Huangdi is described as an able leader for his military prowess as well as his governmental skills to keep myriad states in harmony. In addition to human affairs, he also has a duty to the "spirits" and "mountains and rivers."

The emphasis of the chapter, however, is obviously on the lives of Yao and Shun, more well-known as cultural heroes in the Chinese tradition. The Grand Historian's introduction of Yao was full of lavish praise: "His benevolence was as that of Heaven. His intelligence was as that of spirits. Drawing near to him, he was like the sun. Gazing on him from afar, he was like the clouds. He was rich, yet not arrogant, noble, yet not contemptuous. He made his cap yellow, his silk gown black, his carriage vermillion and his horses white. He was able to glorify those of good virtue and thereby to harmonize the relations between the nine generations." However, the greatest virtue of Yao lies in enabling Shun to succeed him. When Yao was getting old and the country was faced with the crisis of serious flooding, Yao consulted his chiefs on who could manage the affairs of the state. The chiefs recommended Yao's heirs one by one, and Yao rejected each one of them on the grounds of inability and flaws of character. In the end, the chiefs suggested that Yao could at least *try* one of the heirs and see if he could do the job. So Yao listened to them and put one of his heirs in position. But after nine years, the job of managing the floods was not done. Yao summoned his chiefs again and said: "I have been on the throne for seventy years, now you can take over!" The chiefs all replied they couldn't possibly do the job. "Then recommend to me from all those under the Heaven, whether nobles or commoners, who can take the job!" Yao replied. The chiefs then recommended a bachelor among the people called Shun: "He is the son of a blindman. His father is obstinate, his mother is mean, his younger brother is presumptuous, and he is able to keep harmony among them by filial love. He graciously keeps them in order, lest things end up in evil." Yao then tried Shun by marrying two of his own daughters to him and observed Shun's deeds with respect to them and his ability in administering state affairs for twenty years. Then Yao completely stepped back from his duties and entrusted the state affairs in the hands of Shun. The Grand Historian comments: "Yao knew that his son was not worthy and was not good enough to give him the world. Thereupon, he gave Shun the world. Giving it to Shun, the people of the world would have the benefit of it and his son would be displeased. If he gave his son the world, then the people of the world would be displeased and his son would have the benefit of it. Yao said, "In the final analysis, I will not displease the people and benefit a single person."

Shun was not merely a filial son but an extraordinarily filial son. His mother died early and his father, the "blindman", remarried and had another son, and he favored the second son. This second son was "presumptuous." The whole family were not just "mean" to Shun, but tried to kill him. Unlike Harry Potter who has magical powers and can escape to the magical world, Shun had no magical powers but a tremendous capacity for love and tact: he loved them all and served them well: "when they wanted to kill him, they were not able to find him. But when they needed him, he was always around." When Yao married his two daughters to Shun, he managed to have them behave properly toward his family, not daring to appear haughty in front of them despite their noble status. But that was not enough. His father, step-mother, and younger brother still conspired to kill him. Once his father made Shun climb up the granary to plaster and mend it, then he set the base on fire to burn down the granary. Using two large bamboo rain-hats as an umbrella, Shun jumped safely to the ground and simply left. Another time, Shun was asked to dig a well, and while digging it deep, he built an extension that led to an exit. While Shun was down in the well, his father and brother filled up the well with dirt. They were so happy in their belief that they had succeeded in killing him and started to claim Shun's property as their own. His younger brother went to Shun's house and attempted to take Yao's two daughters as his own when Shun appeared unexpectedly again much to his surprise. Despite all this, Shun forgave them all and continued to serve his father and to love his younger brother more attentively.[2]

That is how Chinese culture puts emphasis on the prominence of "family virtues" or "filial piety." Confucianism believes that social fabric and governing of the state are parallel to family governance, and it is not surprising that Yao and Shun are canonized — chiefly in the hands of Confucius — as "sage kings" and serve as exemplary "cultural heroes" for the Chinese people. In terms of "cultural heroes," though, no one is more influential and prominent than Confucius himself. Born 551 years before Jesus Christ, Confucius has been revered in Chinese history not as someone who brought religion, but as someone who taught culture to the Chinese people. Confucius was a scholar and teacher. As a scholar, he was a generalist and cross-disciplinary, in today's terms, excelling in philosophy, history, literature, art, music, anthropology, political science, physical education, and so forth. As a teacher, he practiced the liberal policy of "education to all" (*you jiao wu lei*) by accepting students regardless of their class background (of noble and common family backgrounds alike). He gathered around him seventy-two noted disciples plus hundreds of other students. "Culture" in the Zhou Dynasty refers to the "Six Arts" — Rites, Music, Archery, Carriage-driving, Reading and Writing, and Mathematics. Confucius lived at a time when the Zhou Dynasty had collapsed and its court was hanging on in name only. The six arts, particularly rites and music, were forgotten, ignored or lost. Born of a humble family origin but of nobility in his heart and blood, Confucius studied these arts, especially rites and music, from early on and established himself as an authority. Confucius' attitude in his study would probably still surprise many students today. Once, when Confucius was in the state of Qi, he happened to come across a lost piece of music from ancient times, and he immediately plunged himself into studying the piece; he was so engrossed in his study that he lost the taste for meat for three months. But Confucius did not study rites and music merely for academic purposes. He had great ambitions. He wanted to save the world with his learning. By restoring and promoting proper manner (rites) and fine music

---

[2] The above quoted translations are from William H. Nienhausser, Jr. edited, *The Grand Scribe's Records*.

Figure 3: Confucius

of ancient times (the times of Yao and Shun, and the subsequent Three Dynasties of Xia, Shang and Zhou), Confucius hoped to bring order and good government based on humaneness (*ren*) and justice to a world of chaos and wars and moral degradation. Confucius spent many years of his adult life in exile, traveling with his devoted disciples through myriad states, preaching proper manners and fine music as a means to good governance to a host of heads of states, very eager to serve and put his ideas into practice. Sometimes those dukes and barons were interested in listening to him, but not really in employing him. Sometimes they employed him for a while and then sacked him due to pernicious attacks from others. Sometimes they refused to see him outright. Sometimes they attempted to kill him. Sometimes they employed him but were not following the principles he preached, so Confucius quit and left with his disciples. Throughout his career, though he served his premiership very shortly (for three months) in his home state of Lu, and some of his disciples also served in other states, he could hardly arouse ripples of attention from those in power, let alone save the world. In his later years, Confucius devoted all his time to scholarly pursuits, compiling such classics as *The Book of Poetry*, *The Book of Change*, and his favorite history book *The Annals of Spring and Autumn*. One of his disciples commented that precisely because Confucius did not serve in the government, he could devote his time to scholarly pursuits and became most accomplished. But Confucius himself cared very much about serving in this world, sometimes even bending his principles for such an opportunity. For his failure to realize his great ambitions for government service, Confucius sometimes had a sense of humor:

> Confucius went on to the state of Zheng and the Master and disciples lost track of each other. While Confucius stood alone at the East Gate of the outer city, the natives reported to Zigong: "There is a man at the East Gate whose forehead is like that of Emperor Yao, whose neck resembles that of an ancient minister Gaoyao, and whose shoulders resemble those of Zichan; but from the waist down, he is smaller than Emperor Yu by three inches. He looks crest-fallen like a homeless, wandering dog." Zigong told Confucius this story (when they met) and Confucius smiled and said: "I don't

know about the descriptions of my figure, but as for resembling a homeless, wandering dog, he is quite right, he is quite right!"

But more often than not, he was in sorrow. Seven days before his death, one of his disciples came to visit him.

Confucius was just then walking slowly around the door, supported by a walking stick, and said to him: "Ah Sze, why do you turn up so late?" Confucius then sighed and sang a song:

"Ah, the Taishan (Mountain) is crumbling down!
The pillar is falling down!
The philosopher is passing out!"

He then shed tears and said to Zigong: "For a long time the world has been living in moral chaos, and no ruler has been able to follow me."

Upon Confucius' death, his disciples gathered, and they all observed the orthodox ritual of three years of mourning as he himself had taught them, and then dispersed. But they did not disappear. On the contrary, these Confucianists, the followers of Confucius, who in others' eye were a group of eccentric cultural experts insisting on proper rituals such as burial rites and fine music, spread and grew all the way to the present day. The Grand Historian, who lived about three hundred years after Confucius, concluded his biography of Confucius with the following comments: "There have been many kings, emperors and great men in history, who enjoyed fame and honor while they lived and came to nothing at their death, while Confucius, who was but a common scholar clad in a cotton gown, became the acknowledged Master of scholars for over ten generations."[3] This comment is applicable 2200 years later. Despite the twists and turns of history, despite its compromises and own shortcomings, Confucianism essentially teaches a philosophy of humanity, a human way of life and

---

[3] The above quoted translations are from Lin Yutang, *The Wisdom of Confucius*.

a humane way of governance. In other words, Confucianism survives because it speaks humanity to power.

Confucius was lucky that he died some 330 years earlier. Were he alive when China was finally unified in 221 BC under the First Emperor of the Qin Dynasty, he would have been buried alive, as the First Emperor, who followed the Legalist philosophy to build a super-state, believed in thought unification and put it into practice by burning the books of Hundred Schools of Thought and burying Confucian scholars alive. The establishment of the Qin Dynasty successfully put an end to the period of chaos and wars amongst feudal lords and set a new political order built upon military prowess — but this was an order that would have been abhorrent to Confucius and was indeed condemned by Confucianists throughout the centuries for its cruelty and despotism. The "First Emperor" was self-named thus because he imagined his dynasty would last for ten thousand generations starting with him as the first. In reality, Qin's rule proved to be so rigid and cruel that the dynasty was overthrown shortly after his death by peasant rebellions. It was not until several generations after the successive Han Dynasty was established that rulers began to appreciate the value of Confucian teachings in upholding stability and order by way of humane and moral government. In the meantime, the Han Confucians at the time made compromises to accept much of the de facto practices in governance that had originated from Legalist and other teachings. When Confucianism was instated as the "dominant philosophy" in the Han Dynasty and remained so throughout the Dynastic Era, many would argue that it was no longer quite the same as the original teachings of Confucius. In any case, during the long Dynastic Era starting from 221 BC when the First Emperor founded the Qin Dynasty to 1840 when British gunboats opened up the shores of China during the Opium War, Confucianism served, by and large, as a guiding principle for Chinese personal, social, and political life. It would grow and undergo changes and transformations, particularly later on under the influence of Buddhism.

During the two-millennia-long Dynastic Era from 221 BC to 1840, dynasties rise and fall and each dynasty carried its own distinctive features, but Chinese cultural development would rely upon the resources of the

Hundred Schools of Thought, particularly Confucianism and Taoism, except in the second millennium when it assimilated Buddhism. Although the First Emperor's rule was notoriously dictatorial and short-lived, his unification of China was highly significant and shaped the future development of Chinese culture. For some 500 years during the Spring and Autumn period and the Warring States period, the Zhou Court lost central authority and China became a land of many states. Not only were there different measuring systems and other local customs, but different writing systems emerged in different states. Were it not unified under Qin, China would have developed very much along the line of post-Renaissance Europe with its myriad states and languages. But the First Emperor unified everything. When the Han Dynasty succeeded Qin, it basically inherited all of the Qin policies related to unification. In the long Dynastic Era, there emerged a pattern: whenever dynasties fell, the population shrank due to war-related depravity. Usually, after a short period of chaos, China reunites again under a new dynasty. Unification has always been the cultural consensus. Nobody advocated for the peaceful coexistence of smaller states. One may argue that is perhaps why the Dynastic Era lasted for too long without breakthroughs in China's historical development. But China's history dictates that unity outweighs disunity, and the urge and anxiety for unification has become a major cultural trait, and more so in modern times when a traditional sense of dynastic unity is coupled with modern nationalism.

Chinese dynastic rule was further marked by two distinctive interrelated features: secular rule developed in a bureaucracy run by scholar/officials from the Civil Examination (*keju*) system. To think of the long Dynastic Era as "The Middle Ages" would be quite misleading. The Chinese feudal system died upon the Qin unification, and ever since, there has been a marked decline of the aristocratic class in China. In the Han Dynasty, the aristocracy was still a significant factor in Chinese culture and society. But with the instigation of the Civil Examination system in the Sui and Tang dynasties, fully developed in the Song Dynasty and followed up in the Ming and Qing dynasties, the scholar-gentry class became unquestionably the dominant ruling class in Chinese society, and Chinese culture also centered around Confucian scholars. Much of Chinese literature and other arts were made *by the scholars*, *of the scholars*, and *for the scholars*. The Civil Examination system was fundamentally a democratic institution intended for the imperial court to identify and gather all the talents under heaven to serve the government through selection. Selection was done through examinations (mainly on Confucian classics) open to all (or, more accurately, all men). Candidates went through three levels of examinations — at the county level, the provincial level, and the national level — and once passed, they were awarded with three different titles, very similar to a modern bachelor's degree, master's degree, and doctoral degree. And they became officials serving at different levels of government. The Examination system was abolished in 1905 in the Modern Era, but contemporary College Entrance Examination very much inherited the spirit of the Civil Examination system in terms of its fair access to all, regardless of your class background. Given such a historical legacy, no one should be surprised at Chinese families' emphasis on education.

The two-millennia Dynastic Era was a long period, perhaps too long. It showed that the Chinese culture was very conservative, and while it demonstrated a stamina for sustenance and revival, it lacked the vitality to make breakthroughs. It almost did in two points of time in China's history: one in the Song Dynasty and the other in the late Ming Dynasty. But they both failed. The breakthrough took place when the British Empire extended its global reach to the farthest place on earth — the "Far East" (obviously a Eurocentric angle) in 1840, when, to protect its opium trade with Chinese merchants, she sent gunboats to China and blew up China's coastal fortresses. China was forced to take note and the Chinese had to open up their eyes to the reality of the new world and were alarmed to find themselves in "an unprecedented crisis since Confucius's time." China entered the Modern Era and is still very much in it today. Even though the Modern Era is less than 200 years old, its impact upon shaping Chinese culture as we know it today is as significant, if not more, as the previous two periods added together. Chinese culture has gone through tremendous changes during the last 150 years or so. If Chinese culture is deficient in many ways today, the one thing it does not lack is vitality.

Despite its long history, Chinese culture may appear to be entirely new and modern. Visitors to major, and not so major, Chinese cities will notice the McDonald's, the Starbucks, and the 7-Elevens dotted over a city landscape of high-rise buildings. In China today, one can hardly find any hundred-year-old buildings. Chinese high-tech industries are reinventing Chinese ways of life, sometimes one step ahead of their counterparts in the West. Perhaps more than ever before, an Orientalist traveler bent on discovering an old exotic China would be more than disappointed. Chinese culture today is very much a mixed culture, a hybrid culture, of both old and new, of both ancient and modern, the synthesis of which is still very much an ongoing process. Despite its fluidity, however, we can outline some key features of Chinese modernity.

Chinese modernity is an interplay of three forces — nationalism, cosmopolitanism, and communism — and an interplay between these three forces and traditional cultural legacies.

It is true that modernity was forced upon Chinese by way of western gunboats. But along with the gunboats also came the missionaries, military professionals, modern technologies, and all kinds of ideas originated in the West such as evolutionism, nationalism, romanticism, anarchism, socialism, and so forth. In other words, a whole new world was opened up to the Chinese, and indeed, was aggressive in penetrating into the Chinese world. The keyword for the Chinese reaction to this aggression is not resistance or confrontation, but rather self-reflection and assimilation. The Chinese adopted an intellectual attitude of cosmopolitan translation, engagement, and assimilation. Such an approach is largely Confucian by nature. The Confucian worldview has always been cosmopolitan, a system of teaching not meant for "Chinese" as such, but for "all under heaven." Even in Confucius's time, there were minority "barbarian" peoples living on the peripheries of China proper. Not only did Confucius accept all students regardless of their class or racial background, but his moral philosophy very much subverts the civilized and barbarian dichotomy. In Confucian teaching, you are civilized and a gentlemen when you follow moral principles and behave properly even though you may come from a "barbaric" region; on the other hand, you will be a barbarian and "a small man" if you don't follow proper manners or listen to coarse music, no matter how noble your family. Once in a moment of frustration, Confucius said to his disciples that he would rather go to a far-away "barbaric" place, and one of his disciples remarked that the region was rough and coarse. Confucius' reply was: "where a gentleman dwells, how can there be barbarity?" In other words, when the western aggression of technology and ideas came, there was no native ground for "resistance" as alien and Other. Instead, the Chinese abolished the Examination system (of learning Confucian classics) and sent hundreds and thousands of students abroad to study western learning. After their return, they launched the New Culture movement calling for "Mr. Democracy" and "Mr. Science" — two most powerful keywords for Chinese modernity.

To be a cosmopolitan embracing western learning in science and technology and advocating liberal democracy in modern China does not mean one is not a nationalist. The nationalist urge to save China from being colonized or disintegrated was overwhelming across the board. When the Chinese were forced to open their eyes to the world, they found themselves in a most precarious situation, faced with hungry powers in the world intent on grabbing a piece of China, if not all of it, for their resources and capital investment. Even though China was never colonized *in toto* it was very much a semi-colonial situation. Dr. Sun Yat-sen, father of Chinese nationalism, however, thought the Chinese were kidding themselves by calling it "semi-colonial." He called China a "hyper-colony" in that the Chinese had to serve multiple masters, while colonials in a colony only served one master. In the modern Chinese context, nationalism was very much about resistance against colonial encroachment, about national freedom and independence. For the Chinese, the twentieth century began with the Eight Allied Powers (British, French, German, Austrian, Italian, American, Russian, and Japanese) looting Beijing after they defeated the Boxer's Rebellion — a scene of humiliation ingrained in the modern Chinese mind. More humiliation came when the Japanese attempted to eat up China, committing tremendous atrocities during China's fourteen-year War of Resistance (1931–1945) such as the Rape of Nanking. It was during the War of Resistance that Chinese nationalism reached its full-blown stage and the Chinese people obtained their national identity as a modern nation.

Politically, twentieth-century China saw the partisan feud between Nationalists and Communists. Both groups were revolutionaries, though with quite different ideologies. The Nationalists founded the Republic of China (ROC) in 1912, the first republic in Asia. During the tumultuous years of modern China, the two parties collaborated twice — during the Great Revolution of 1927 and the War of Resistance against Japan — and fought each other for over two decades. The Communists eventually beat the Nationalists — who retreated to the island of Taiwan — and established the People's Republic of China (PRC) in 1949. The Nationalist objection to Communism was its international allegiance — to Soviet Russia, and its promotion of a class revolution. The Chinese Communist Party (CCP) was established in 1921 under the direct assistance of the Communist International, and throughout its growth period it could not have survived without financial, personnel, and military assistance from Soviet Russia. But to regard them as unpatriotic fifth-column activists would be only telling the half-truth. The Chinese Communists started out as revolutionary cosmopolitans. Just as Chinese liberal cosmopolitans who wanted to see an independent China endowed with universal liberal values, the Communists also wanted to see an independent China, albeit under a "proletarian dictatorship." The problem is, however, to a liberal democrat, both were authoritarian and dictatorial, although the Communists far surpassed their rivals in that direction. The irony is that the Nationalists eventually began the program of democratization after they retreated to Taiwan and ceased One-Party Rule when the indigenous Taiwan independence movement was on the rise. While in the Mainland, Deng Xiaoping advocated reform and opening-up and the Communist ideology of class struggle was somewhat replaced by, alas, patriotism and nationalism.

In short, Chinese cultural identity is a long history in the making. A deep historical sense is at the core of its consciousness. Yet its short, tumultuous modern history is as important as tradition in the formation of such an identity. While traditional Confucianism has always emphasized maintaining a harmonious order and stability, and the current Communist regime has also put all its military might and economic resources to preserve such stability, both the Chinese state and culture are very much evolving, unstable to say the least, and in the process of combining the old and the new, the ancient and the modern.

Nowhere is this unique combination of continuity and modernity more amply demonstrated in the Chinese language itself.

CHINESE LANGUAGE

The Chinese language is certainly one of the essential elements constituting the Chinese cultural identity. The Chinese language as practiced today is both a classical and a modern language, combining historical continuity and modern transformation. On the other hand, it reflects both the homogeneity and diversity of the Chinese people, in terms of both its writing style and speech. Written Chinese consists of *wenyan* (classical style) and *baihua* (vernacular style), as well as simplified and complicated characters. Though *wenyan* is rarely used today, it is still taught in middle schools and constitutes part of the College Entrance Exam for the Chinese subject in China, which amounts to say that to be really educated as a Chinese person, you need to have a certain level of understanding of classical Chinese. The simplified characters are used in mainland China, while complicated characters are used in Taiwan and Hong Kong. A standardized Romanization system called *pinyin* for Chinese characters has been in use in mainland China and worldwide, while some varied versions of the old Wade-Giles system are still in use in Taiwan and Hong Kong. In terms of speech, the Chinese people can now finally celebrate the triumph of a national speech: the *Putonghua* (common speech) as it is called in mainland China, or *Guoyu* (national speech) as called in Taiwan, or otherwise called Mandarin speech, which has successfully become the *lingua franca* for all Chinese, whether in the Mainland, Taiwan, or even most recently in Hong Kong, while various dialects still coexist, and will certainly continue to coexist for a long time to come, with the national speech.

Written Chinese in the form of "characters" is uniquely Chinese. The creation of Chinese characters is usually credited to Cang Jie, an imperial recorder at Huangdi's court. It is said that when Cang Jie created the characters modeled upon the signs and traces of nature, the spirits cried at night for fear of the expansion of man's intelligence and power. The earliest extant Chinese writing, as we can see today, is called *jiaguwen*, writings on oracle bones and animal skins of various kinds in the Shang

Dynasty. These were discovered in Anyang, Henan province in modern times and indicate a quite developed and mature system of writing. On bronzes from the Shang and Zhou dynasties, we also find early characters. Early Chinese characters are apparently pictorial, modeling upon images from nature. This feature of the Chinese language gives a lot of imagination to western cultural critics who take this characteristic of Chinese language as a point of departure to criticize the logocentrism and phonocentrism of the western languages. In the early twentieth century, the great modernist poet Ezra Pound discovered Ernest Fenollosa's unfinished paper "The Chinese Written Character as a Medium for Poetry," edited it and published it, and launched the Imagist Movement in modern poetry and thought. The Chinese character thus facilitated an important critical tradition in modern western culture, which certainly has its own merits and significance. Its take on the Chinese character is not entirely false, either, as the Chinese character certainly has a strong visual quality, even as it is practiced today. And for that matter, the Chinese have cultivated a unique form of art based on the characters: calligraphy, which serves as the foundation for traditional Chinese art and has its own aesthetic principles. However, to think of Chinese characters as merely pictorial is wildly misleading. This would have put the Chinese language at its early primitive stage, fixated and static ever since. In fact, as far as the Chinese language is concerned, who created the Chinese characters is less important than how they have developed over a long period of time. In its expansion and development, the pictorial function has been significantly decreased, while one of the major principles for the creative expansion of characters is actually "phonetic loans," that is, to combine a significant element and a phonetic element to form a new character. A large majority of Chinese characters are formed in such a manner, so much so that, according to the Chinese saying: "if you don't know how to pronounce a particular character, you may guess by merely pronouncing half of the character."

The development of the Chinese language goes hand in hand with the blossom of Chinese writing, and the foundation of Chinese writing is laid during the Spring and Autumn and Warring States period when "The Hundred Schools of Thought" flourished and there appeared an impressive body of works, including the Confucian classics as well as a great number of works belonging to other schools. The Confucian classics originally refers to Six Classics: *Book of Poetry* (*Shijing*), *Book of Documents* (*Shangshu*), *Book of Rites* (*Liji*), *Book of Changes* (*Yijing*), *Spring and Autumn Annals* (*Chunqiu*), and *Book of Music* (*Yuejing*).[4] In the Song Dynasty, the Confucian classics were re-canonized as The Five Classics and Four Books, the Four Books being *Great Learning* (*Daxue*), *Doctrine of the Mean* (*Zhongyong*) (both excerpts from *Book of Rites*), *Analects* (*Lunyu*), and *Mencius* (*Mengzi*). More well-known texts from other schools include *Dao De Jing* (*Laozi*) and *Zhuangzi* of the Taoist school, *Hanfeizi* of the Legalist school, *Mozi* of the Moist school, and *The Art of War* (*Sunzi bingfa*) of the Militarist school.

Just as Chinese writings flourished, the characters themselves were undergoing changes, and due to the long period of disunity, variations of the characters began to emerge in different states. When China was finally unified under Qin, the First Emperor of Qin (Qin Shihuang) did two extraordinary things — one constructive and the other destructive — that would have a long-lasting impact upon Chinese culture. First, aided by his Prime Minister Li Si, he unified the writing system by standardizing 3000 characters in the form of *xiaozhuan* (Small Seal), which laid the basis for later expansion of Chinese characters and ensured the unity and stability of Chinese characters. The standardization of Chinese characters allows for the continual development of Chinese characters on an integral path, which makes the Chinese writing system the single most important factor in sustaining the continuity of Chinese culture. Second, he ordered to "burn all the books" of competing schools of thought to purify and unify thought under his imperial rule. Luckily for Chinese culture, the Qin Dynasty was short-lived, and the First Emperor did not yet have modern technology of surveillance and could not really burn *all* the books. Nevertheless, this anti-cultural act cast a perpetual shadow over the question of the authenticity of canonical texts. When Confucianism became the orthodox teaching in the early Han Dynasty, a tremendous amount of effort was taken in recovering and discovering lost texts and new editions of the canonical texts emerged. On the other hand, allegedly pre-Qin texts were unearthed, which were not quite consistent, and they sometimes even contradict with

---

[4] Since the last one is lost, it is also called The Five Classics.

the new editions in certain passages. Thus began a long line of debate between the so-called Ancients and Moderns, with those in favor of the "Ancients" usually getting the upper hand. It is through constantly coming back to the "Ancient" writings — pre-Qin texts — that writers in successive dynasties get their inspiration and develop their styles and characteristics, nominally by modeling upon the "Ancients." In other words, it was along with this controversy that a continuous tradition has developed all the way to the Modern Era. Amid this controversy, the Han Dynasty also produced the first great Chinese philologist Xu Shen (ca. 58–148), who compiled the first authoritative Chinese dictionary called *Shuowen jiezi* (Explaining and Analysing Characters), explaining the structure and rationale and etymology of the characters. By examining the evolution of characters in detail, Xu attempts to bridge the gap between old and new texts and offers his own balanced interpretation based on philological studies. Its influence lasted all the way to the modern era.

By late nineteenth and early twentieth centuries, China entered the Modern Era when tons of new ideas and terminologies inundated the Chinese language. In accordance with a new world opened up to western cultural ideas and knowledge sources, Chinese classics and traditional texts were no longer able to function as the only resources and points of reference. Translation played a transformative role in reshaping the knowledge structure, and Chinese writing was also significantly transformed. The New Culture Movement of 1917 started with the "Literary Revolution," which at its core consists of the call for the replacement of *wenyan* — the classical style of writing from the ancients to the twentieth century — with the modern vernacular style of writing, or *baihua*, which has become the standard in modern Chinese today. The New Culture intellectuals were able to achieve their goal just in a matter of a few years largely due to the fact that the vernacular Chinese writing had actually been in practice for almost a thousand years. While *wenyan* may very well correspond to speech in Confucius's time (*Analects* was mainly a recording of his conversations with his disciples), it had already ceased to be the case by the Tang Dynasty, even though Chinese scholars adhered to the style of writing for another thousand years as authoritative and orthodox. On the other hand, starting with the translation of Buddhist texts, and later also flourishing in popular drama and fiction writings, there developed a subcultural line of vernacular writing, but they were regarded as "lowly" and "vulgar." The New Culture Movement elevated the vernacular writing into the orthodox and reestablished the principle of "writing as you speak." Therefore, modern Chinese is very much a hybrid product, inheriting the vernacular tradition (while incorporating the classical *wenyan* tradition as well, since there is no clear binary cut between the classical and the vernacular) but also expanding on a large scale with loanwords and new terminologies through the translation of western ideas and cultures. In that sense, despite its vitality and creativity, and despite its large volumes of output compared to the classical tradition, modern Chinese writing is still very young and is still struggling to achieve maturity by striking a certain balance between transforming the traditional and assimilating translation novelties.

Nowadays, when you walk on the streets of Beijing or Shanghai, or on the streets of Taipei and Hong Kong, you will see two somewhat different sets of Chinese characters on display as part of the city landscape. That is because a system of simplified characters is used in Mainland China today, while complicated (or orthodox) characters are still being used in Taiwan and Hong Kong. Sometimes this becomes a political issue highlighting the political division of today's China. But it is more helpful to understand this division as part of the legacy of modern China. Language reform was at the center of the New Culture Movement to bring Chinese culture onto the modern path, which, for many radical Chinese intellectuals at that time, meant total westernization to catch up with the West in all aspects of culture. In the evolutionary scheme of things, Chinese characters were thought to be signs of China's cultural backwardness, and one of the high-sounding revolutionary ideas was to abolish the Chinese characters altogether and to replace them by creating a phonetic writing script like western languages. To promote the vernacular as the standard, modern Chinese was initially used merely as an interim compromise. Were it to be implemented, Chinese culture would indeed take on an entirely new departure. The fact of the matter is, even under the "proletariat dictatorship" during its craziest period — the Cultural Revolution — to create a brand-new phonetic writing script to replace Chinese characters simply proved unworkable and the idea is now all but dead. It simply would not happen. Culture, after all, has its own means of defiance.

But after the establishment of the PRC, the Communist government did successfully put forward a new "simplified characters" system, which is now in practice in Mainland China. Whether this measure will prove to be as historically significant as the First Emperor of Qin's standardization of Chinese characters, history will tell. Before we jump into conclusions, however, it is important to understand some historical facts. While the scheme was institutionalized under the PRC government, the reform of Chinese characters and the attempt to simplify them had been pushed by progressive intellectuals across the political spectrum, left or right, in modern China. In the 1930s, for instance, several popular journals had already tried to print simplified characters. The rationale for putting forward simplified characters is to raise the educational level of the masses more easily. The current scheme only modified a limited number of characters and hardly constituted a radical break from traditional characters. Though some character simplifications are controversial, a majority of those simplified characters have already been in use unofficially by the public (such as shop-owners, business people, and professional calligraphers) for a long time, just like the vernacular style of writing has been in use but not recognized as a respected and dignified way of writing. It does not take much effort for an educated Chinese to read and understand both simplified and complicated characters. Furthermore, when most writing is typed on a computer nowadays, the switch between the complicated and the simplified is just a matter of a click away. Perhaps Chinese culture is big enough to tolerate the coexistence of both sets of Chinese characters.

In Chinese speech, diversity is more self-evident and widespread. In Chinese language programs taught outside China, it is customary to emphasize they are teaching "Mandarin," as if diversities amongst the Chinese are so distinct that the term "Chinese" is not appropriate to refer to a common speech shared by the people. This is no longer the case. In China today, one can speak one form of Chinese speech — *putonghua* (common speech), or *guoyu* (national speech) as called in Taiwan — and be understood. This is a very recent phenomenon, as a result of just over a hundred years of the progression of modernity but more importantly of the social development of the last four decades. During the Republican period, the effects of the government's efforts to standardize national speech were limited. After the Nationalist government retreated to Taiwan, however, it took drastic measures to enforce rigid rules of teaching *guoyu* in schools, which proved to be overwhelmingly successful — much to the displeasure of independence-minded local residents. There was no comparable rigid implementation of *putonghua* in mainland schools under the Communist regime, and the current unquestionable dominance of *putonghua* is very much a result of the large internal migration of people and socio-economic development of the last four decades. Shenzhen is a typical Reform-era city, and during the late 1980s, for instance, Cantonese was still the lingua franca as most migrants came from the Guangdong province, and many job ads would indicate a preference for Cantonese-speakers. That period is gone. Several years ago, in Guangzhou, there was a popular "defending Cantonese" movement, which would have been unthinkable before. In my hometown city Changzhou, a second-tier city in Jiangsu province, I grew up only speaking the Changzhou dialect in the 1960s and 1970s. Nowadays when I go back visiting the city, more often than not, I find myself having to speak *putonghua* when I go out shopping or dining. A mere statistic would perhaps explain why: in the 1960s and 1970s, the population of the city was about three hundred thousand, now it's more than three million with a large migrant population.

In that respect, China has finally become a nation-state with a national language (speech) intelligible to a vast majority of the people. The varieties of Chinese speech in terms of its dialects have always been a problem in the nationalist agenda of modern China. Like Chinese characters, Chinese sound and pronunciation have also had a very long and complicated historical development. By the early twentieth century, the linguistic map of the Chinese has a clear division between the North and the South, just as in other aspects of Chinese life. In the North, which goes from Northeast all the way to the Southwest, it is the Mandarin region. It is called "Mandarin" (*guanhua*, or official speech) because, by Ming and Qing dynasties, the educated scholar/officials and businessmen already spoke a certain kind of common speech among themselves, which served as a kind of lingua franca, but it was by no means standardized and institutionalized on a massive scale. Within the North Mandarin region, there are still regional differences and distinctions, some variations larger and some smaller, but by and large, their speeches are intelligible to one another. This pre-modern critical mass of linguistic uniformity is rather striking. In the South, however, there are hundreds of "dialects" which are usually grouped into several major dialect regions such as Wu, Min, and Yue (Cantonese). Were there not the standard writing system in place, these "dialects" could have developed into different languages with their own writing systems. Chinese historical development favored unification, and in modern times the demand for unification became more urgent under the influence of nationalism from the West. To modernize China and to transform China into a modern nation-state like the European powers, modern Chinese intellectuals realized that China must have a unified "national language (speech)." To achieve that, you need to devise a phonetic script system standard to all. But the great variety of dialects made it a challenging task without some political will. Apparently, the logical way was to devise a system based on Northern Mandarin speech. But it met a lot of resistance because that would, in a way, make Southerners "second-class citizens" linguistically. Actually, western missionaries were the first to devise phonetic scripts for Chinese, and some simply based on some dialects to print a translated Bible. The most commonly used script in the West until the late last century was the so-called Wade-Giles system, produced by Thomas Wade (1818–1895) and completed by Herbert Giles (1845–1935), which is currently used in Taiwan and Hong Kong with variations. Zhao Yuanren (Yuen Ren Chao, 1892–1982), the most influential Chinese linguist in modern times, led a team of Chinese linguists to first devise a Chinese Romanization system, which was never put into serious practice. Since the ultimate goal of modern Chinese intellectuals was to devise a phonetic script system to replace Chinese characters altogether, their system tends to show "Chinese characteristics" by being novel, distinctive, and too professionalized for practical usage. It was not until the 1950s under the PRC government, a group of linguists devised the standard Romanization scheme called "pinyin", which has now been gradually accepted worldwide. Now this system does not have any "noble" goal to replace Chinese characters altogether but remains merely as a supplementary system for scripting Chinese for international usage.

Last but certainly not least, the Chinese language is quite unique in its aesthetic value. Perhaps no language in the world has developed an aesthetic quality like the Chinese through the art of calligraphy. Chinese calligraphy is an art of Chinese characters. It is also the foundation of the art of Chinese painting. The development of calligraphy is closely related to the development of the characters and has a long history in the making. There are basically five major aesthetic styles of calligraphy. *Zhuanshu* (Seal Style) distinguishes itself by modeling upon the ancient characters inscribed on the bronzes in Shang and Zhou dynasties while *Lishu* (Official Style) was first developed in the Qin Dynasty, originally practiced by clerks and officials in writing documents, later developed into a distinct aesthetic style. The most common style is called *Kaishu* (Regular Style) noted for its inflexible regularity of design and beginners are usually advised to start practicing this style first. If you are of a more romantic temperament and want to express your individuality, you may be attracted to *Xingshu* (Running Style), most wellknown as the style of the great calligrapher Wang Xizhi (303–361), and *Caoshu* (Random Style, or Dancing Style), in which the characters themselves are hardly recognizable. A great calligrapher, just like a great artist, always develops his own distinctive style. Calligraphy in China used to be, and still is, a mark of "Culture" and distinction. In traditional times when the scholar/official was the ruling class, it would be unimaginable that a scholar/official was not at the same time a calligrapher. An official can be very corrupt and bad, but if he can produce a style of calligraphy with great distinction, he would still be regarded as at least "cultured." Emperor Huizong of the Song Dynasty, for instance, was really a "bad" emperor on all accounts — not only losing the state to the northern invaders but himself ending up as a prisoner. Yet, he was a great artist and calligrapher who developed his own elegant "slender style," which is still regarded as a great contribution to Chinese culture. Nowadays when Chinese people are using computers to type out characters (most commonly using the *pinyin* input system), calligraphy is still widely practiced and appreciated, perhaps as much as before. The legacy continues. School children are still taught that, even if they do not practice calligraphy with ink and brush, they at least need to develop a good handwriting style with a pen. I must mention here that beautiful calligraphy still carries much prestige and social status in Chinese society. For a foreign student learning Chinese and planning to go to China, if she can learn to become a calligrapher and demonstrate the art, her Chinese friends, or the not-so-very-friendly Chinese, would immediately "rub their eyes and give her a second look" with great respect and appreciation, and count her as one of their own. There is one caveat, though — it takes years of regular practice to be a good calligrapher.

Chapter 2

Pax Sinica:
The Chinese Model of Government

For a period of 2,000 years from the Qin Dynasty to the late Qing Dynasty, dozens of dynasties had come into succession, but almost all of them had adopted a Confucian model of government. Governmental institutions would change and expand in successive dynasties as social and economic situations developed, but the basic structures and principles would remain consistent over the two-millennia-period despite the cyclical change of dynasties. This was not a continuous period of peace and stability, but rather a cycle of peace and turmoil. Major dynasties (the Han, Tang, Song, Ming, and Qing) would last about 300 years each, followed by shorter periods of bloody violence, usually marked by a sharp decrease in population when dynasties fell, as rebellions devastate the whole country, and then "heroes" would emerge to establish a new dynasty. But overall, when dynasties stood, the Chinese people enjoyed peace and stability, and even prosperity, sometimes called *Pax Sinica*.

More than religion, political governance was at the core of Chinese culture as Confucianism consists of two interrelated principal components — *neisheng* ("being sage" inside via moral cultivation) and *waiwang* ("being kingly" outside in governance). In Chinese culture, the issue of separation of state and religion never really occurred. The model of government that lasted throughout the two-millennia Dynastic Era had always been a secular rule, though governance relied heavily on moral indoctrination and penetration, and in the late imperial period when Confucianism was influenced by Buddhism, Confucian moralism can be viewed as reaching the level of being quasi-religious.

When democratic governance became the norm in the West and exerted its impact upon the rest of the world, including China, the Chinese in modern times would grapple with the two-thousand-year legacy of its own political culture, which had apparently developed along its own distinctive route. Western modernity came out of a millennium-long Christian theocracy and feudalism with the gradual advance of the separation of state and religion. Enlightenment ushered in a secular society and paved the way for the democratic model of government with an emphasis on citizen's rights and equalities. In China, on the other hand, feudalism faded away two millennia ago and a secular rule under a centralized government became the norm, but it never brought about a democratic model of governance. What is the nature of this Chinese model of government that underlies the so-called *Pax Sinica*? Is it antithetical to democratic values and institutions?

FAMILY-STATE: THE LEGALIST AND CONFUCIAN CONVERGENCE

When we talk about the Confucian model of government throughout the Dynastic Era, it is very important to remember that the imperial order established out of the chaos of Warring States was not Confucian, but Legalist. The Confucians did not win the debate among the "hundred schools of thought," but the Legalists did. It was by implementing Legalist ideas and measures that the state of Qin rose to become a super-state and eventually unified China. Only in the subsequent Han Dynasty was Confucianism recognized as the orthodox principle for government. But Han Confucianism did not replace Legalism. Rather, Confucianism harmonized the harshness and rigidity of the Legalist penal code, and on the other hand, accepted and incorporated some core ideas of Legalism into its own. As a result, there has always been tension among Confucians themselves in regard to this, one can almost call the "original sin" of their complicity with the Legalists.

The basic principle for the Confucian model of government is called "Three Fundamental Obediences and Five Constant Virtues" (*sangang wuchang*): officials (ministers) must be obedient to the ruler (Emperor), (just as) son must be obedient to father and wife to husband; and five constant virtues are humaneness (*ren*), justice (*yi*), propriety (*li*), wisdom (*zhi*), and integrity (*xin*). This basic principle was propounded by the Han Confucian scholar Dong Zhongshu (179–104 BC) and Confucianism was consequently elevated to the official status of imperial ideology ever since. Throughout the Dynastic Era afterward, this basic principle had served as the cornerstone for Confucianism, so that one is hardly reminded that the "Three Fundamental Obediences" was in fact not Confucian, but Legalist in origin.

Legalism was one of the influential schools of thought among the "hundred schools of thought." The Legalists advocated "rule of law," but it would be gravely mistaken to associate it with the Western democratic tradition, in fact the opposite is true. While the "rule of law" is central to the idea of democracy, Western democratic tradition was developed, particularly in the English tradition, in the struggle against the monarchical power, usually led by feudal lords and barons. The "rule of law" means everybody is equal before the law — particularly between the monarch and the aristocratic class. The Legalists, however, advocated "rule of law" for the sake of securing absolute power for the ruler/Emperor and the monarch, so that their rule can last for centuries and millennia — perpetual peace. In other words, the "rule of law," which basically involves severe penal code and system of punishment, should be equally applicable to "all" — feudal lords and ordinary subjects alike (thereby weakening the feudal aristocratic class), so that absolute power resides only in the hands of the Emperor, the son of Heaven. In Western political science jargon, the Legalists are sometimes called "realists." For like the "realists," the Legalist emphasis was on practical means of governance to amass wealth and power for the imperial state and to achieve order, security, and stability under the imperial rule. And most of all, just like the "realists," the Legalists abhorred the moral teachings of Confucianism on government. To the Legalists, the Confucian teachings of a moral benevolent rule by way of "rites" and "music" were not only opaque and impractical, but harmful and dangerous in its obstinacy in citing the alleged golden era under the sage rulers Yao and Shun as veiled criticism of contemporary government.

Han Fei (280–233 BC), the chief Legalist philosopher, condemned the "scholars praising the ways of the former kings and imitating their

Figure 4: Han Fei

benevolence and righteousness" as "the vermin of the state." This is because, as Han Fei argued, "those who attempt to use the ways of ancient kings to govern the people today will all prove to be silly and laughable just like the farmer of the state of Song waiting for the rabbit."[1] The Confucians praised the ancient kings for their universal love of the world, as they believed the ancient kings loved the people just as father loved his son and whenever they heard some punishment had been administered, all musical performances would be canceled, and whenever a death sentence had been passed on someone, they would shed tears. But that leads neither here nor there in terms of effective government. Han Fei believed that fatherly love is indeed a universal thing, but what happens if the son still becomes a crook? What if the father continues to show love and the son still becomes unruly? The love of the ancient kings was no greater than the fatherly love, and if such love could not prevent children from becoming unruly, how could it bring the people to order and what would be the use of shedding tears? Han Fei offered a tougher alternative to achieve order and stability in a hegemonic state:

> In the state of an enlightened ruler, there are no books written on bamboo slips; law supplies the only instruction. There are no sermons on the former kings; the officials serve as the only teachers; there are no fierce feuds of private swordsmen; cutting off the heads of the enemy is the only deed of valor...
>
> Therefore, in times of peace the state is rich, and in times of trouble its armies are strong.[2]

---

[1] Han Fei tells a story here that has become a proverb in Chinese, still popular and in use today: There was a farmer in the state of Song, and one day a rabbit, racing across his field, bumped into a stump and dropped dead. Thereafter, the farmer quit farming and took up watch by the side of the stump for more rabbits — to no further luck. The Chinese proverb is called "*shou zhu dai tu*."
[2] Burton Watson trans. *Han Fei Tzu*, p. 111.

To Han Fei, the virtuous acts of the ancient kings Yao and Shun are precisely the root of disorder. King Yao, instead of acting like a king by extending his monarchical line, yielded the world to his "subject" Shun. Shun, as a minister/official, instead of serving the royal family of Yao, made himself the king and ruled the world. If Confucians eulogized Yao and Shun as sage kings and cultural heroes, how can there be loyalty and filial piety in the world? Therefore, Han Fei put forward the basic principle for establishing imperial order for the family-state: officials/ministers must be obedient to the ruler/Emperor, (just as) son to father, and wife to husband. Only with these three obediences will come the order and stable government of the world; without them there will be disorder.

The Legalists were not mere "philosophers," but men of action who proposed practical means to strengthen monarchical power. Shang Yang (390–338 BC) first instituted a series of reforms in the state of Qin, then a relatively weak and impoverished state among the Warring States, and helped to strengthen Qin into a dominant power. Shang Yang's reform measures included centralization of the power in the hands of the king and standardization of the penal code so as to make it applicable to "all under the Emperor," thus stripping away the privileges of feudal lords. Unlike Confucians, who preached that human nature is good, the Legalists believed human nature to be evil and selfish, and the best way to rule over the people was to enforce strict punishment, even over little offenses. For instance, those found throwing out dust onto the street would be subject to the punishment of body-tattooing — marking characters on their faces to indicate their offense — for the sake of instigating shame. Under the First Emperor of Qin, it was his Prime Minister Li Si (280–208 BC), a noted Legalist — who advised the First Emperor to take the measure of "burning books and burying Confucian scholars alive." In his memorial to the First Emperor, as recorded in *Shiji*, we read the following:

> Your servant suggests that all books in the imperial archives, save the memoirs of Qin, be burned. All persons in the empire, except members of the Academy of Learned Scholars, in possession of

the *Book of Poetry*, the *Classic of Documents*, and discourses of the hundred philosophers should take them to the local government and have them indiscriminately burned. Those who dare to talk to each other about *Poetry* and *Documents* should be executed and their bodies exposed in the marketplace. Anyone referring to the past to criticize the present should, together with all members of his family, be put to death. Officials who fail to report cases that have come under their attention are equally guilty. After thirty days from the time of issuing the decree, those who have not destroyed their books are to be branded and sent to build the Great Wall. Books not to be destroyed will be those on medicine and pharmacy, divination by the turtle and milfoil, and agriculture and arboriculture. People wishing to pursue learning should take the officials as their teachers.[3]

A dynasty that exercises such a policy could not last, even though it may achieve hegemonic status. Legalist measures were a disaster for the Chinese civilization, but it also provided a valuable lesson for future dynasties — actually more than just a lesson, it laid down a chilly foundation for the dynastic order to follow, or *Pax Sinica* as we may call it. Soon after the death of the First Emperor of Qin, riots erupted in the construction sites of the Great Wall, and the dynasty was overthrown — Qin's royal palace was burned down and totally destroyed. Given its notorious harsh and cruel measures toward the people and its swift downfall, ensuing dynastic rulers would never again dare to claim Legalism as their guiding principle of governance.

Enter the Han Confucianism. The Han Confucian scholar Dong Zhongshu was instrumental in promoting Confucianism as the official ideology of the imperial state. But, alas, this is very much a "realistic" version of Confucianism. For in his efforts to promote Confucianism to be the "sole orthodox line of teaching" for the dynastic rule, Dong inherited Han Fei's idea of the three principles of obediences and made it a cornerstone for

---

[3] The translation is from Wm Theodore de Bary, *Sources of Chinese Tradition*, p. 210.

Confucianism — the so-called *sangang*, or "Three Fundamental Principles." In other words, Han Confucianism harmonized much of the harshness of Legalist laws, but at the same time inherited the basic institutional structure as well as the Legalist ideology supporting that very structure, in such a way the name "Legalism" has retreated to the background while everything is now done in the name of Confucianism as the "orthodox ideology." As such, the imperial order set up in the Han Dynasty and followed up for two millennia, was a Confucian order nominally, but was in fact a combination of Legalist and Confucian ideas and practices.[4]

This Confucian order, which sustained itself for two millennia despite dynastic changes, can be characterized as a family-state through a civil administration by means of a moral rule.

This "family-state" model consists of two interconnected aspects: the whole state is family-owned by the royal family, and essentially run like a family. In other words, "All under heaven" belongs to a hereditary absolute monarch. To establish a new dynasty is called "to obtain all under heaven" and the ultimate aim of running this state is also to keep the royal blood running for endless generations to come. The state is the private ownership of the royal family, no more no less. *Shiji* records an anecdote of the founding Emperor of the Han Dynasty Gaozu, which is the most revealing of the all-embracing sense of ownership of the "state enterprise." Since the grandiose royal palace of the Qin Dynasty was burned down during the uprising, a new palace was to be built after the establishment of the new Han Dynasty to symbolize its new authority and grandeur:

> When the building project of the magnificent royal palace was completed, Emperor Gaozu held a big banquet at the front hall with his ministers and lords for celebration. Holding a jade wine cup in hand, Gaozu rose and walked to his father, expressed best

---

[4] It would also be fair to say that Dong Zhongshu did not get Confucianism all wrong, for a key to Confucius' reinterpretation of the classics lies in his emphasis on "loyalty to the King" (*zhong jun*), as, for instance, highlighted in Gu Hongming's interpretation. See Chapter 8 for further discussion.

wishes for his longevity, and then said: "When I was young, you my honourable father often thought of me as a good-for-nothing rascal, incapable of any accomplishment in terms of wealth and property, and much inferior to my elder brother. Now look at the enterprise I've accomplished, how does this compare to my elder brother's?" Ministers and lords in the hall all burst into laughter, hailing "Long Live Emperor Gaozu!"[5]

In this model, to call the Emperor "Head of State" would be misleading because he is the state. He exercises direct rule over the Chinese people as if they are all his children. Nominally, the legitimacy of the imperial rule derives from the mandate of Heaven and the Emperor rules as son of Heaven. In practice, the legitimacy was obtained by force through rebellions and uprisings, just as in the case of the founding Emperor of the Han Dynasty. The mandate of Heaven could theoretically be revoked, but in practice only by means of violent uprisings and bloody civil wars, which would inadvertently cause widespread devastation and significant decrease of population; the combination of Legalist and Confucian ideology and institutions was precisely designed to maintain the imperial-monarchical rule. The effect of moral indoctrination through the Three Fundamental Principles of Obediences meant that it would be violating one's moral instinct to think of disobedience and revolt. Moral education was to start from the family, and family ethics and the Three Principles was to be strictly enforced. There was no division between private and public spheres. One's behavior and even psychology were very much matters of government. Precisely because the moral rule was very effective and deep-seeded in one's psyche, it would take an unbearable degree of corruption and crisis for a revoke of the mandate to take place, and then even more devastation and bloodshed to complete a dynastic change. This cycle did not happen once or twice, but dozens of times in the long Dynastic Era. Amazingly, the model sustained itself and lingered on, with somewhat different distinctions of each dynasty, until the modern times — the late Qing period. One of the reasons for its longevity lies perhaps in the

---

[5] Sima Qian, *"Gaozu benji"* (Biography of Emperor Gaozu), p. 215. Translations in this book are all mine unless otherwise noted.

creation of an elite class that served as a buffer zone between the monarch and the people — the scholar-official class, or the literati class.

THE EXAMINATION SYSTEM AND CIVIL RULE

Unlike the medieval feudal social structure in Europe or in Japan, the long Dynastic Era in China was characterized by the gradual rise of the scholar-gentry class as the ruling class of society, so that by the late imperial period (Ming and Qing dynasties), the four social strata of "scholar-officials, farmers, craftsmen, and merchants" was well established. This was sustained by the institutionalization of the Examination system beginning from the Sui and Tang dynasties till the late Qing period, when it was abolished in 1905. It was essentially a democratic system for social upward mobility based on merits instead of blood and was grounded in the assumed importance of education. It had tremendous effects on the Chinese culture as a whole, but most of all, it brought about a secular and civil administration for Chinese polity, in which the function of the literati service went in both ways: on the one hand, the Emperor, as the supreme examiner for all candidates, was able to recruit "all of the brightest and the most talented under the heaven" to serve the monarch with devoted loyalty, but on the other hand, his power could also be significantly checked by a huge bureaucracy of scholar-officials headed by a prime minister.

There are, of course, some caveats to say that the Examination system was essentially a "democratic" one. Women, for instance, were never part of the scholar-official class, even though quite a few women were educated at home by the late imperial period and there were several illustrious Empresses in history — one of them, Wu Zetian (624–705), was actually instrumental in promoting and institutionalizing the Examination system. But the point is, we can see a clear line of historical progress from more blood-based aristocracy to merit-based scholars in terms of the composition of the ruling class. As early as in the Han Dynasty, under the reign of Emperor Wu, a national academy was set up to promote Confucian learning, and along with it, imperial examinations came into existence as promoted by leading Confucian scholars such as Dong

Zhongshu. But in the Han Dynasty, entrance into officialdom was largely done by recommendations within the aristocratic class. It was not until the Sui Dynasty that an examination system was first instituted in AD 605 explicitly to recruit talents to serve the monarch. Even though the Sui Dynasty was short-lived, the system was adopted by the ensuing Tang Dynasty and developed into a considerable degree. Under the Song Dynasty the system was fully developed, and all the way to the late Qing, it played a major role in Chinese cultural and political life. Candidates from all corners of the empire coming to the capital periodically for the Examination occupied a unique phenomenon of Chinese cultural landscape. Chinese culture was essentially an elite culture, produced by an educated class, all of whom spent their childhood and youth preparing for the Exam.

It was in fact a series of exams held at the local, provincial, and national levels. Local exams were held in counties accessible to teenage individuals. Those who passed were called "*xiucai*" (learned men). They were not yet eligible for officialdom but would be eligible to enter the exam at the provincial level. Even if they failed at the provincial level, they would constitute a part of the larger educated literati class, enjoying some social privileges such as exemption from statute labor and participating in local village governance. Another popular profession for them was to become tutors for children. Those who passed the provincial exam were awarded the "*juren*" (recommended men) degree. They would be now eligible to serve in provincial and local governments and to sit in the national exam. There were two parts of the national exam. Candidates from all provinces first came to the capital to take part in the national exam, and those who passed would further sit for a palace exam administered by the Emperor himself (usually through his proxy, though), after which usually all of them would be awarded the "*jinshi*" (advanced scholar) degree, but further categorized into three classes: the first class (consisting of three candidates ranked No. 1, No. 2, and No. 3 only in the exam), the second class, and the third class.

The subjects for the exam varied somewhat in different dynasties. Normally they followed the Confucian "six arts," which may include archery, poetry, rituals, and understandings of Confucian classics. In the late imperial period, however, it was narrowed down to an exegetical exercise of Confucian "Four Books and Five Classics" by composing a rigidly structured treatise (the so-called eight-sectioned essay). In any case, the Chinese elites achieved their "reputation" through successful examinations by way of a moral and literary education as morality and literature were two fundamental elements in the exams. The civil administration, engendered by the Examination system, was supposed to be a moral rule, a literary rule.

The Examination system was devised to be fair and accessible to all. To ensure fairness, strict measures were adopted during the exam to avoid nepotism and corruption. Examiners were incarcerated for several days during the exam period to avoid any possible contact with candidates. And candidates took their exams in "Examination cells" — tiny cubicles under close scrutiny to avoid any contact among themselves. The question papers could be changed at the last minute to avoid any possible leaks and be directly ordered by the Emperor himself. The candidates were identified by numbers rather than by their names, and their answer papers were hand copied by third-party clerks because one's calligraphy may very well reveal his identity.

Historians today may tell us that, despite its noble claim, and women's exclusion aside, only a small group of people were privileged to receive an education and a very small number of elites ever obtained a "*jinshi*" degree. And they tended to be overwhelmingly from the landed gentry class, merchants, or those with aristocratic lineages. While that is of course true, it would have missed the point of the historical progressiveness of the system. Very much in line with Confucius' own practice of "education to all," the Examination system was designed to attract "all talents under the heaven" to serve and create a powerful aspirational culture in Chinese society over the ages. While the imperial throne was hereditary (unless the Mandate was revoked during revolutionary times), it was possible for everybody to step into the elite ruling class through diligent study. If a kid from a poor or less privileged background can demonstrate a good potential in his studies, it was not uncommon for the village community to pool resources together to support his study, in the hope that one day when he does achieve fame and glory by passing the exams, the fame and glory would belong to the whole village community as well. The Examination system flourished and matured in the Song Dynasty and there were many examples of high-achieving scholar-officials from a humble family background. Take the case of Fan Zhongyan (989–1052). Fan came from a low-ranking provincial official family, but his father died when he was one year old, leaving the family in a dire state. His mother had to remarry, and Fan also had to change his surname. It was precisely against such adverse circumstances, however, that Fan was determined to turn his fortune around by means of passing through the exam system, devoting himself to studies with extreme diligence. Eventually Fan obtained the *"jinshi"* degree, brought his mother home in his care, and served in various governmental posts reaching all the way to the top post of a vice premier. Fan was known as an upright Confucian statesman, often offering daring and critical opinions to the Emperor. His most well-known legacy is the couplet from his famous prose "Memorial to the Yueyang Tower" (*Yueyang lou ji*), which epitomizes the Confucian ideal of a moral rule:

> Be the first to feel the pain and hardships of the people,
> And the last to enjoy the pleasures and comfort of the world.

Su Dongpo (1037–1101), perhaps the most illustrious scholar from the Song Dynasty — some will say the best all-round personality in Chinese cultural history as a whole — also came from a commoner's family background in the remote southwestern part of China. His father started to focus his attention to study only later in life. He accompanied his two sons (Su Dongpo and his brother) to the capital for the Examination and socialized with the leading literati class. Not only did he prove himself to be a talented writer and win appreciation among leading literati scholars in the capital, his two sons also obtained the *"jinshi"* degree at the same time. "The Father-and-Sons Trio" would be known in Chinese literary history as three of the "Eight Greatest Essayists of Tang and Song Dynasties." Su Dongpo, in particular, earned his name during the palace exam. Ouyang Xiu (1007–1072), chief examiner and leading savant of the time, was so amazed with the talent Su demonstrated in his writing that he passed around his piece after the exam, telling everybody to look out for this new rising star as he was convinced that he would outshine him in the future. But since the marking was done anonymously, Ouyang very much suspected that it must be from one of his disciples; so to avoid potential accusation of nepotism, he ranked the candidate only second in the palace exam. In fact, another anecdote for the exam showed that Su's "talent" almost made his judges very uncomfortable:

He was developing the theme that in giving rewards one should rather err on the side of generosity, and in punishment one should give every benefit of the doubt to an offender lest an innocent man be killed. In the time of the Emperor of Yao, he wrote, a man was about to be condemned to death. "Three times the minister of justice said, 'Let him be killed!' and three times Emperor Yao said, 'Let him be pardoned!'" The dialogue read very well, and it seemed to support an authentic story that the sage emperor was willing to use a bad man and give him a chance to prove his talent. The judges read the story, but dared not question it, because it amounted to their admitting not having read it somewhere in one of the obscure ancient texts. So Su Tungpo [Su Dongpo] was passed. After the examinations one day Mei Yaochen, one of the judges, said to him:

Figure 5: Su Dongpo

"By the way, where does that story occur about Emperor Yao and the minister of justice? I can't quite recall where I read it."

"I invented it," the young scholar confessed.

"You did!" said the old judge.

"Well, that was what the sage would have done, wasn't it?" replied Su Tungpo.[6]

Even though Su Dongpo was ranked second in the palace exam, which gave him instant national fame, he had to start his official career as a county clerk, moving from the very bottom in the bureaucracy upward. Throughout his life career, however, Su went through ups and downs several times, from an influential state advisor to being banished to remote "barbarian" places, as far as, for instance, the island of Hainan. Su's tumultuous career can serve as a mirror to the functioning of the civil bureaucratic rule as enhanced by the Examination system. Song emperors were much less despotic in general and they tended to work with the bureaucracy for governance. During Emperor Shenzong's reign, the Song State found itself short of revenues and the Emperor adopted the "New Policies" put forward by Prime Minister Wang Anshi (1021–1086). Wang Anshi's Reform, as it is historically known, included a series of measures in the areas of state finance, security, and education aimed at enhancing state control and power. But they proved to be very controversial, meeting resistance from a large cohort of the literati class including a host of renowned scholar-officials such as Ouyang Xiu and Su Dongpo. In other words, the scholar-gentry class was split into two opposing camps, and this contention ran throughout the dynasty, even after the generation of Wang Anshi and Su Dongpo had passed. Looking back upon this controversial reform today, it would be pointless to lay blames on either side. Lessons must be drawn, however, about the nature of the "Chinese model of government" as such. Reform measures were debated in court and opposing voices were heard. There even appeared a neologism to

---

[6] Lin Yutang, *The Gay Genius: The Life and Times of Su Tungpo* pp. 39–40.

describe the phenomenon: *dangzheng* (party contention). However, instead of developing into a democratic system of checks and balances of power, of open debates and public opinion, and of negotiating and respecting dissenting voices, "party contention" was considered to be totally negative in the sense of creating chaos and obstacles. After all, the civil administration was a totalitarian rule, as the supreme power lies in the hands of the Emperor. The ups and downs of reformers (like Wang Anshi) and opponents (like Su Dongpo) often depended on the whims of emperors. Ironically, some emperors would really rather not to be in that position and were genuinely uninterested in the business of governing. The (in)famous Emperor Huizong of Song, for instance, was an extremely talented artist and calligrapher who fashioned his own "slender style," and preferred to stay in the world of art and calligraphy, instead of running an empire and losing it. He ended up living in captivity for life among the "barbarian" invaders.

The phenomenon of "party contention" gives us an idea about the kind of tolerant culture that totalitarian civil rule had produced in the Song Dynasty. In other words, despite the totalitarian nature of the family-state, the secular bureaucratic rule of the scholar-gentry class in the Song Dynasty did demonstrate a remarkable legacy of tolerance — the hallmark of a democratic culture. There is no doubt that fighting between two opposing parties can be fierce and often results in persecutions. But the issues were openly debated in court. The Emperor listened to both sides and he had to make decisions. Some of the criticisms were directed right in the face of the Emperor, for instance, consider this one from Su Dongpo on one of the economic reform measures:

> "If the people of the country are rich, does a ruler ever have to worry about his private wealth? ... I do not know, when Your Majesty speaks about enriching the country, whether you are speaking about enriching the people or enriching your own purse."[7]

---

[7] This quote from Lin Yutang (*The Gay Genius: The Life and Times of Su Tungpo*, p. 110) is somewhat a liberal translation of the original "Letter to the Emperor" by Su Dongpo.

Under a despotic regime like that of the First Emperor of the Qin Dynasty, Su Dongpo would have been buried alive. The harshest punishment Su was handed down was banishment, not once, but several times. Yet, even in exile, Su Dongpo was able to make his dissent voices heard by writing poetry of protest. Every time Su wrote a new poem, it was immediately copied and recopied and circulated throughout the empire just in a matter of weeks, contributing to the emergence of a powerful public opinion, at least among the educated class. And despite their heated differences over the reform, Wang Anshi and Su Dongpo could still keep a cordial gentlemanly relationship with mutual respect, at least as poet-friends. When Wang also lost favor in the court and retired to live in Nanjing, Su went to visit him and the two spent days together discussing poetry and Buddhism. It takes *culture* for opponents to differ and yet to be gentlemanly toward each other.

GOVERNMENT FOR THE PEOPLE

"Party contention" in the Song Dynasty did not produce a healthy mechanism of checks and balances of power. Instead, in the ensuing dynasties of Ming and Qing, it was taken as a negative example and there appeared much tighter control upon the literati-gentry class. The Chinese model of government lasted for 2,000 years without a breakthrough despite failures of dynastic rule that resulted in the succession of dynasties. From historical hindsight, it really demonstrates the paucity of Chinese political thought, that is, Confucianism, as it served as the guiding political ideology. Under this scheme, there is no concept of "rights," either for individuals or groups, by which individuals or groups of people can defend against the government. It is definitely a top-down totalitarian rule, aimed at maintaining stability and the obtainment of "all under heaven" by the royal family. The emergence of the civil bureaucratic administration brought about by the Examination system was a double-edged sword. On the one hand, the monarch attempted to bring all the talent under the heaven to serve and strengthen the family-state. The fact that the system was first significantly enhanced and improved under one of the cruelest and most despotic rulers — the Empress Wu Zetian — was revealing.

But on the other hand, the system enabled the existence of an educated class who may very well have their own thoughts or own interpretations of Confucianism. When Su Dongpo questioned the Song emperor whether his reform measures were benefiting his own family (perhaps in the name of the state) or the people, he was invoking an alternative vision of Confucianism, particularly through Mencius, that is, the ideal of government for the people. Indeed, there has always been tensions within Confucianism between orthodox Confucianism upholding the Three Principles of Obediences vis-à-vis the Mencian line of Confucianism, which advocated the Mandate of Heaven (and the lack of it) and the ideal of the government for the people. Throughout the ages, Confucian scholars relied on the interpretation and reinterpretations of this Confucian line to advocate their dissent and launch their resistance movements. It is this legacy that will prove to be the most valuable resources for us today.

As we noted before, it was Confucius who eulogized the transferring of power between Yao and Shun based on virtue not on heredity. Confucius advocated order, a hierarchical order for that matter through loyalty to the king, but not necessarily the absolute top-down monarch where officials must be totally obedient to the ruler to the point where "you must die whenever your ruler demands." *The Analects* records a conversation as follows: once Duke Ding asked how a king should employ his ministers, and how ministers should serve their king. Confucius replied, "A king should employ his ministers in good manner; ministers should serve their king with loyalty." Clearly, the king's attitude and treatment of the minister is stated here as the condition for ministers' loyalty. In other words, the relationship between the king and the minister is a reciprocal one of propriety and loyalty. In fact, an important tenet of Confucianism is the obligation of the subordinate "to speak truth" to the superior. *The Book of Filial Piety*, one of the Confucian classics, records the following dialogue:

> Zeng Zi says: "Now I understand the meanings of parental love, deference, caring for the parents, and honouring the family name. May I ask: to be obedient to your father, is that filial piety?"

Confucius says: "What are you talking about! What are you talking about! In the past, the Emperor had seven ministers specifically designated to speak the truth, so that even if the Emperor was not following the Way, the empire could still be maintained. The kings had five ministers specifically designated to speak the truth, so that even if the kings were not following the Way, the kingdom could still be maintained. The barons kept three ministers specifically designated to speak the truth, so that even if the barons were not following the Way, the fiefdom could still be maintained. The scholars also had bosom friends who would speak truth to him when they made mistakes, so that their name and honour could be upheld. When a father has a son who would speak truth to him, he is likely to find himself in the wrong. Therefore, whenever injustice occurs, a son must speak truth to his father, and a minister must speak truth to his ruler. You must speak truth against injustice. How can it be filial piety if you are only obedient to your father?" (Chapter 15)

In the Confucian tradition, Mencius has been credited as the Second Master after Confucius. In his conversation with King of Qi, Mencius elaborates more on the ruler/minister relationship and offers, some would argue, an almost revolutionary view:

Mencius said to King Xuan of Qi, "If the King treats his ministers as his bosom friends, they will treat him likewise; if he treats them as servants, they will treat him as a stranger; if he treats them as garbage, they will treat him as an enemy."

"According to the rules of propriety," said King Xuan, "a minister wears mourning when he leaves the service of the King. Under what circumstances will this be observed?"

Mencius replied, "A minister ought to speak truth to the King and the King listens to his advice, so that blessings will descend on the people. And for some reason the minister leaves the country, the King ought to send a messenger beforehand to prepare for the way and then an escort to accompany him beyond the boundaries. When he has been gone for three years and does not return, only then does the King take back his land. This is known as the 'three courtesies'. If the King behaves this way, then it is the minister's duty to wear mourning for him. Nowadays, a minister's honest words not listened to, his advice not followed and people's welfare totally ignored. As such, the minister has reason to leave, and yet the King arrests him and puts him into prison, and tries by all means to damage his opportunities in the country he intends to go; or, when the minister does manage to leave, the King confiscates his land the day he leaves. This is called the behaviour of an 'enemy'. What mourning is there for an enemy?"[8]

It is in *Mencius* that we find the unambiguous Confucian ideal of the government for the people, as Mencius explicitly put the people above the ruler in a hierarchical order:

"The people are of supreme importance; the altars to the gods of earth and grain come next; the last comes the ruler."[9]

In this dictum, the ultimate aim of governance is for the benefit of the people. If somehow the ruler's behavior endangers the spirits of the land and grain, he should be changed; and if all proper sacrificial services have been made to the gods, yet draught or flood ensue, then make sacrificial services to a different god.

It was this Mencian line of "government for the people" that served as the moral basis for Confucian dissent voices and even resistance movements. There have been a host of upright and honest ministers who dared to "speak the truth" to the Emperor, such as the famous Wei Zheng (580–643) of the Tang Dynasty, who proclaimed that the right way of governance is to consider the benefit of the people as the ultimate goal, as

---

[8] Mengzi, *Mencius*, pp. 88–89, translation modified.
[9] Ibid, p. 159.

the people, like the boat, can carry the family-state, but can also overturn them. And along with the rise of the scholar-gentry class prompted by the Examination system, there had also been student-led resistance movements throughout different dynasties, which, by the late imperial period, developed into cultural movements for moral revival that eulogized and worshipped the intellectual independence and uprightness (*guqi*) as the very identity of a Confucian scholar.

As early as the Han Dynasty, there occurred a protest incident involving Imperial Academy students. At the request of the Han Confucian scholar Dong Zhongshu, the Imperial Academy was set up during the reign of Emperor Wudi to promulgate Confucian learning and to train elite scholars for imperial service. Not long after its establishment, however, a protest incident occurred. In the year 2 BC, the then prime minister was running a business errand in the royal cemetery, and he allowed his subordinates to travel on the "Emperor-only path" there. It so happened that Bao Xuan, the police chief of the capital city, who was known for his uncompromising uprightness, came to inspect the cemetery and saw the PM staff making use of the royal path at will. He scolded the staff, had them arrested, and confiscated their carriages. The PM was quite offended, understandably. The next day, he ordered the imperial court police to Bao's house, demanding the release of his men and carriages. Amazingly, Bao shut his door and would not even see them. Now he was accused of violating the imperial order and disrespecting the court, hence eventually arrested and put into prison awaiting a death sentence. The news spread out and caused uproar among the Imperial Academy students. One of them, by the name of Wang Xian, took up the cudgel, calling upon fellow students: those who are with me on the side of truth and justice, line up behind my banner. And more than a thousand imperial students followed! The next morning, they gathered by the side of the road the PM would have to pass on his way to the court, stopped the PM's carriage, protested, and demanded the release of Bao Xuan. Then they went to the square outside the imperial court and knelt down on the ground, appealing to the Emperor directly for the release of Bao. They argued that Bao was merely following the imperial edict in the first place and should not deserve the death penalty at all. Out of pressure, the Emperor eventually decided not to grant the death penalty and executed some minor measures of punishment instead. This was a significant victory on the part of the protesting Academy students. By kneeling down in collective protest, Confucian scholars were able to "speak truth" and uphold justice in defiance of the Emperor's will, and the Emperor himself had to bow down to the pressure and change his mind. And this incident had taken place two years before Jesus Christ was born.

In the Song Dynasty, students' petitions and protests became an important part of its political life due to a number of reasons. Both culture and commerce had reached significant heights during the Song Dynasty, but throughout this period, it was under constant threat from Northern nomadic peoples. It was under national crisis that Confucian scholars were called upon to defend the Confucian civilization by demonstrating defiant moral character. And along with the mature development of the Examination system, there also emerged intellectual channels for public opinion. During Wang Anshi's Reform, as we have seen, new policy measures were debated and opposing voices were heard. Scholars like Su Dongpo heralded the importance of listening to public opinion, warning that "once solicitation of public opinion has vanished, then even the greatest hero will be unable to rise…when the emperor will stand alone, the system will collapse, and anything may happen."[10]

During the most critical moments of the Song Dynasty, a hero did emerge — Chen Dong (1086–1127), a scholar who rose to the times and led a patriotic student movement. The Song Dynasty was under constant threat from the northern Jurchens, and during the reign of Emperor Huizong their army approached the Song capital in 1126. As we have seen, Huizong was a very talented artist but a very lousy ruler, to say the least. He indulged in luxurious lifestyle and relied on corrupt ministers to run the country, causing widespread resentment among the people — which, incidentally, served as the political background for the well-known novel *Water Margins* (*Shuihu zhuan*) describing popular uprisings and rebel heroes. At this critical juncture of foreign invasion, Huizong simply handed the throne to

---

[10] The translation is from Wm Theodore de Bary, *Sources of Chinese Civilization*, p. 641.

his son Qinzong and tried to flee to the South. Chen Dong, a common student at the imperial academy at the time, rallied the support of his fellow students and presented a petition to Qinzong to impeach and execute six notoriously corrupt ministers serving Huizong as the first step to rectify the wrongs of governance under Huizong. It was a bold petition but won overwhelming support from both the officials and the populace. Under huge pressure and attempting to consolidate his new power, Qinzong had to accept most of the demands of the petition, either executing or banishing the corrupt ministers in Huizong's reign. But he still had to deal with the most critical issue of the Jurchen invasion. After temporary retreat, the Jurchen army encircled the capital again, making humiliating demands including royal hostages, ransom, and land cessations. To resist or to appease, Qinzong was indecisive. The veteran general Li Gang insisted on protracted resistance to wear out the Jurchens' supplies, while other ministers like Li Bangyan would much prefer "peace" at any cost. Qinzong accepted both: letting Li Gang prepare for the defense while secretly negotiating peace with the invaders. When the resistance suffered a tactical battle, Qinzong immediately sacked Li Gang and was ready to accept the Jurchen demands wholesale. At this critical moment, Chen Dong rose again. Together with hundreds of imperial academy students, they knelt down in front of the imperial court and presented another emergency petition to the Emperor himself, demanding the return of the general Li Gang to lead the resistance. This time, the protesting students also won popular support from the urbanites in the capital who gathered around the students' call for resistance. The carriage of the appeaser Li Bangyan was stopped by protesters, barely escaping the wrath of the vigilantes. Afraid of collapse before the foreign invasion, Qinzong had to call back General Li Gang who went to the streets in person to assure the angry crowd that he would lead the resistance.

But Chen Dong's win was short-lived and did not prevent the dynasty from collapse. As soon as the Jurchens retreated from the capital, controversies arose as to whether to reprimand the "mob rebels" led by Chen Dong. The appeasers wanted to execute him for breaking imperial order while his supporters argued for selfless courage and patriotic character. In the end, Qinzong restored an official post for Chen who nevertheless declined and retired to his hometown. And Qinzong further sacked both camps and found himself "standing alone." The Jurchens grasped the opportunity, swiftly conquered the capital, captured both Huizong and Qinzong, and took father and son to the North as hostages. Months later, Qinzong's son Gaozong set up the throne in the South (beginning of the Southern Song in history) and immediately recalled Li Gang as the premier, as well as Chen Dong for service at the court. Again, Chen Dong called for all-out resistance and petitioned that Gaozong lead the expedition army himself to save his grandfather and father. But Gaozong had other ideas: if Huizong and Qinzong were really saved and brought back, he would have to concede the throne. Eventually, under some false pretext, Gaozong had Chen Dong killed to pave way for his conciliatory peace deal with the Jurchens. Chen probably knew this could very well be the consequence of his outspoken character. His self-sacrificing uprightness inspired later generations of scholars in Southern Song who continued to be engaged in resistance movements against the more powerful tendency for appeasement with the North. In the celebrated struggle between General Yue Fei (1103–1142) and the appeaser premier Qin Hui (1090–1155), even though Qin had an upper hand in court politics and had Yue killed in the end, the public opinion was overwhelmingly in favor of the patriotic general Yue Fei who has been lionized in Chinese cultural history as the exemplary figure of loyalty and patriotism, while Qin Hui as the ultimate image of the traitor.

During the late Ming Dynasty, Confucian dissent voices again took center stage in the political scene. The Donglin Confucians' fight against the eunuch premier Wei Zhongxian (1568–1627) in the late Ming Dynasty was one of the most spectacular and tragic events in Chinese intellectual history. The Donglin party refers to a group of literati officials who gathered around the Donglin Academy in Jiangsu province in the late Ming. Through their regular academic conferences, the Donglin scholars advocated a revival of Confucian moralism and were noted for their blunt criticism of contemporary court politics. This was indeed a very strange period in China's dynastic history when Emperor Wanli refused to run the government and did not go to the court for three decades. His grandson who eventually succeeded him was in love with carpentry work, leading to the power being concentrated in the hands of the eunuch premier Wei Zhongxian. The Donglin Confucians' open dissent against the autocracy of the eunuch Wei Zhongxian resulted in purges and counter-purges, often rather bloody and deadly. It was under extreme political circumstances in the late Ming that there developed a special cult for moral uprightness (often bluntly) and steadfast loyalty (often blindly). It is interesting that two modern Chinese intellectuals, Chen Yinke and Lin Yutang, both chose famous courtesans (talented prostitutes) of this period to exemplify the intellectual uprightness (*guqi*) in the late Ming.

Liu Rushi (1618–1664) was one of the so-called "Eight Famous Courtesans of Nanjing." The courtesan culture was an important phenomenon in Chinese literary culture. A courtesan plays an alternative role to the traditional woman. A famous courtesan is highly sought after for her talent in the arts and for her character. In other words, the literati men go to courtesans to find their equals in literary and intellectual companionship (in addition to sexual relationships). After she broke up with Chen Zilong, Liu Rushi disguised herself as a man and took the initiative to approach Qian Qianyi (1582–1664), a leading man of the letters at the time, with her own poem. Qian was so impressed with the poem that he was immediately won over. When later Liu revealed her identity and wrote another poem hinting at her willingness to accompany Qian for life, Qian immediately built a house for her and married her. But it was a time of national crisis. As a leading member of the Donglin party, Qian was deeply involved with the twists and turns of the late Ming court politics. Eventually, the Ming Dynasty collapsed, and the Manchu army encircled the provisional capital of Nanjing. At this juncture, Liu urged her husband to commit suicide while attempting to jump into the river herself. Yet, Qian thought otherwise. He led a team of ministers and officials of the Ming court at the city gate, knelt down and opened the gate, and surrendered to the Manchu army. He was appointed a senior post in the Qing court in Beijing, and Liu Rushi refused to accompany him there. A couple of years later, however, partly due to Liu's persuasions, Qian quit the job and went home, devoting himself to the resistance movement to restore the Ming. It was a risky and dangerous endeavor. Once Qian was implicated in the anti-Qing activity and put into prison, it was thanks to Liu's daring and delicate maneuvers that Qian was eventually released. He was fighting a losing battle, spent all his financial resources, and died due to illness in 1664. Thirty-four days later, unable to suffer the humiliation of being chased for the family debt, Liu Rushi hanged herself at the age of forty-six. In the 1950s and 1960s, against the onslaught of the totalitarian regime, the celebrated modern Chinese historian Chen Yinke wrote his masterpiece *A Biography of Liu Rushi*, praising the late Ming courtesan as "embodying the spirit of independence and freedom of the Chinese people."

Li Xiangjun (1624–1653) was also one of the "Eight Famous Courtesans of Nanjing." Thanks to her artistic talent and upright character, Li became a coveted courtesan among the circles of literati-officials. At the age of 16, she found her true love in Hou Fangyu (1618–1654), another leading figure of the late Ming scholars associated with the Donglin party. However, when another high-ranking official tried to take her by force, Li struck her head against the wall, splashing her blood onto a fan given to her by Hou. Li's heroic act became legendary when dramatized by the playwright Kong Shangren (1648–1718) in *Peach Blossom Fan* (*Taohua shan*). The well-known modern Chinese writer Lin Yutang regarded Li as embodying the untamed spirit of intellectual integrity, and handwrote the following poem onto the scroll painting "Portrait of Li Xiangjun":

> Xiangjun was a woman,
> Whose blood dyed a fan with peach blossoms.
> Her righteous courage shines through history,
> Subjecting men to shame.
>
> Xiangjun was a woman,
> Whose personality was that of an untamed spirit.
> Hung on the wall of my study,
> [Her portrait] shows me what accomplishments a person is capable of.

> Nowadays among the men of the world,
> Who still remains untamed?
> Everyone changes his allegiance between sunrise and sunset,
> What kind of attitude is this!
>
> In our present world,
> There are only peddlers and liars.
> I miss the ancient beauty,
> To keep my heart in the right place.[11]

Of course, intellectual integrity in the tumultuous years of the late Ming was demonstrated not only through courtesans. After the debacle of the Donglin struggle and the fall of the Ming Dynasty, there emerged a real critical reflective voice of the entire Confucian polity by Huang Zongxi (1610–1695). An heir to the Donglin intellectual movement, Huang was a leader of the scholar-gentry class during the transitional period from Ming to Qing. He joined the resistance movement and became the confidant of Qian Qianyi in his later years. When the resistance movement failed, he hid himself in the mountains and focused on his scholarship. Despite several invitations from the Qing court for his service, he remained unmoved and refused to serve the new dynasty. The crown accomplishment of his scholarship was his political treatise *Ming yi dai fang lu*, or *Waiting for the Dawn*, a path-breaking book in Chinese intellectual thought. Retrieving the Mencian tradition of "government for the people," the book offers a scathing attack upon the system of family-state rule, pitting the selfishness of the royal family sharply against the benefits and well-being of the people. As Huang put it:

> In ancient times the people were considered the master, and the Emperor was the tenant. The Emperor spent his whole life working for the people. Now the Emperor is the master, and the people are tenants. That no one can find peace and happiness anywhere is all on account of the Emperor. In order to get whatever he wants, he

---

[11] Shi-yee Liu, *Straddling East and West: Lin Yutang, a Modern Literatus*, p. 39.

maims and slaughters the people and breaks up their families — all for the aggrandizement of one man's fortune. Without the least feeling of pity, the Emperor says, "I'm just establishing an estate for my descendants." Yet when he has established it, the Emperor still extracts the very marrow from people's bones and takes away their sons and daughters to serve his own debauchery. It seems entirely proper to him. It is, he says, the interest on his estate. Thus, he who does the greatest harm in the world is none other than the Emperor. If there had been no rulers, each man would have provided for himself and looked to his own interests. How could the institution of governance have turned out like this?[12]

Unfortunately, under the notoriously cruel censorship system of the Qing Dynasty, the book only had very limited circulation during Huang's time. It was not until 200 years later when the Qing Dynasty began to crumble that Huang's book re-emerged and became inspirational for a new generation of revolutionary modern Chinese intellectuals determined to overthrow the Qing Dynasty and the family-state autocracy once and for all.

In conclusion, the Chinese model of government for the long Dynastic Era was certainly not a government *of the people and by the people*, for that would require "the people" be taken as individuals with unalienable rights. While Confucianism practices a governance based on the principle of a family-state in which the imperial reach ostensibly covers "all under heaven," it does contain a Mencian line that specifically promotes the idea of a government "for the people" as the foundation for the Mandate of Heaven. The Imperial Examination system was an important institutional invention that inspired for a secular and moral rule. Along with the literati culture, there also developed a long tradition of Confucian dissent voices of "speaking truth to power." In the end, however, Confucian knees bend too easily. In any case, this Confucian model eventually collapsed under the challenge of Western modernity. Since the late Qing period and the twentieth century, this Confucian model of government has been severely

---

[12] Huang Zongxi, *Waiting for the Dawn*, p. 92, translation modified.

challenged and discredited by almost all schools of modern Chinese intellectuals. The Communist revolutionaries used to be the most radical critics of the Confucian model.

But the Chinese model of government proved to be resilient. After more than a century of modernity experience since the collapse of the dynastic rule, China is still yet to find a way out. Nowadays, this Confucian model has been rekindled to provide native resources in alignment with the grand ambition of setting up a new *Pax Sinica* for the world for centuries and millennia to come. It should be noted that the reason why the Confucian model sustained itself despite cyclical dynastic succession was not merely a matter of paucity in Chinese intellectual thought. In fact, it would be wrong to assume that Chinese culture developed along a singular and enclosed environment. Rather, it was a result of constant contentions between the Confucian agrarian civilization and the Northern nomadic civilizations. On many occasions, China, or parts of it, was colonized by Northern nomadic peoples. In the end, however, the colonizer was by and large colonized by the Confucian culture. Likewise, if the democratic model originated in the West crumbles by itself (as it went through major crises in the twentieth century through two world wars), the Confucian model of government may very well retain its potency in the centuries to come. In that scenario, we need to at least understand its implications and be prepared for its consequences.

Chapter 3

Three Religions as One:
Confucianism, Taoism, and Buddhism

Chinese immigrants are sometimes asked, or even requested to fill in a form, with the question: what is your religion? This is a rather embarrassing question; surely, there are many Muslims and Christians in China today, but majority of the Chinese hardly identify themselves with any religious sect as commonly recognized in the world today. So to answer that question, you have to tick "none" or "other," which, however, may carry the connotation that you are a "pagan," or not religious, or do not have spirituality, none of which is appealing at all.

It would be a gross mistake to think of Chinese culture as in want of a spiritual life. In the Chinese cultural tradition, one talks about "three religions as one." The Chinese term for "religion" here is "*jiao*," or teachings. The Chinese have been indoctrinated with not one, but three "teachings" in their cultural history, in which these competed and struggled against one another, but by the late imperial period, had already integrated into "one." These "teachings" offer the Chinese a philosophy of life, both secular and spiritual in nature, while each "teaching" prioritizes different orientations toward one's selfhood — Confucian emphasis on moral self-cultivation, Taoist focus on natural self, and Buddhist universal compassion out of belief in and practices of "non-self."

CONFUCIAN SELF-CULTIVATION

Generally speaking, Confucianism consists of two interrelated dimensions: *neisheng* (internal sagehood), or self-cultivation to moral perfection, and *waiwang* (external kingship), or moral governmentality for universal peace and harmony, the latter of which was the focus of our discussion in the last chapter. While Confucianism was very much a this-worldly political philosophy, it was also a spiritual philosophy grounded upon very ancient metaphysical understandings of the world. After the Song Dynasty, heavily influenced by Buddhism (or challenged by the sophistication of Buddhist teachings), the so-called Neo-Confucianism took on a very distinct religious outlook, as self-cultivation became very much involved with the rituals of Buddhist meditation techniques. Nevertheless, the basic ideas already existed in the Confucian classics. We focus our discussion here on one of the most important and popular classics: *Lunyu*, or *Analects* — a collection of discourses and sayings of Confucius; as well as conversations and dialogues, and questions and answers between Confucius and his disciples; or sometimes sayings of his disciples, or their comments on Confucius and his sayings.

Confucian self-cultivation is about how to become a "gentleman," or *junzi*. A Confucian gentleman must have a threefold quality: first, he must have a moral and compassionate character; second, he should be an ethical person, namely, a socially deferential person in dealing with relations with his family and with friends; and third, he ought to be an educated person, wise and knowledgeable.

First, what is then "a moral and compassionate character"? Central to the Confucian philosophy is the notion of *ren*, which has been translated as benevolence, compassion, humaneness, or morality; perhaps it can be simply translated as "humanity." To Confucius, it is that which defines human beings in an elemental sense. But perhaps precisely it is so fundamental, it does not mean it is easily attainable. "In clever words and pretentious appearances, you'll seldom find moral character," Confucius warns us. [1:3][1] Once a disciple asks Confucius: "A man with whom ambition, vanity, envy and selfishness have ceased to act as motives —

---

[1] Here I mainly follow the translations by Gu Hongming (Ku Hung Ming) with some modifications. References in brackets indicate chapters first and then paragraphs in *The Analects*. See Ku Hung Ming, *The Discourses and Sayings of Confucius*.

may he be considered a moral character?" "What you suggest," answered Confucius, "may be considered as something difficult to achieve; but I cannot say that it constitutes a moral character." [14:2]

Obviously, Confucius sets a very high standard to what he considers as constituting a moral character. It is well known that Confucius had seventy-two close disciples, but he would not even regard some of his most well-known disciples as possessing a moral character. Zilu, for instance, was one of the ablest and accomplished disciples, and we do not know what he would think if he heard the following comments from the Master:

> Once a man from a noble family in Confucius' native State asked Confucius: "[Among your disciples], is Zilu a moral character?" "I cannot say," answered Confucius. But on being pressed, Confucius said, "In the government of a State of even the first-rate power, he could be entrusted to lead the army. But I cannot say if he could be called a moral character." [5:7]

If his own disciple could not be called a moral character, who can? Confucius did give clues as how to achieve moral character. First, one needs to be conscious of the difficulty in cultivating a moral character. "A man who wants to live a moral life must first be conscious within himself of a difficulty and has struggled to overcome the difficulty: that is the definition or test of a moral life," [6:20] says Confucius. Indeed, so long as one wants to have a moral character, one can overcome the difficulty and achieve it because moral desire is of innate quality. As Confucius puts it, somewhat cryptically here:

> "Is moral life something remote or difficult? If a man will only wish to live a moral life — there and then his life becomes moral." [7:29]

And Confucius does have an exemplary figure of a gentleman — his favorite disciple Yan Hui: "For months he could live without deviating from a pure moral life in thought as in deed. With other people, the utmost is a question of a day or a month." [6:5] So to Confucius, the key to a moral life is to be able to cling to it by way of self-cultivation. To be a gentleman, it is not good enough to perform one good deed now and then. A moral character is something that is within you, cultivated in such a way that has become part of your being.

> Confucius remarked, "Riches and honours are objects of men's desire; but if I cannot have them without leaving the Way, I would not have them. Poverty and a low position in life are objects of men's dislike; but if I cannot leave them without departing from the Way, I would not leave them.
>
> A gentleman who leaves his moral character is no longer entitled to the name of a gentleman. A gentleman never for one single moment in his life loses sight of a moral life; in moments of haste and hurry, as in moments of danger and peril, he always clings to it." [4:5]

Furthermore, Confucius also gives clues and examples in terms of what kind of deeds and actions constitute the abode of a moral character. For a gentleman, "whatever things you do not wish that others should do unto you, do not do unto others." [12:2] This may be seen as a minimal standard. In cultivating his own self, a gentleman ought to benefit others as well: "A moral man in forming his character forms the character of others; in establishing himself, he helps to establish others." [6:28] And Confucius believes in the power of examples. On one occasion when asked by one of his disciples to define what constitutes a "moral character," Confucius answered in two characters: "loving people." [12:22] On another occasion, Confucius further elaborates that "A man who can carry out five things wherever he may be is a moral man." These five things are:

> Earnestness, consideration for others, trustworthiness, diligence, and generosity. If you are earnest, you will never meet with want of respect. If you are considerate to others, you will win the hearts of the people. If you are trustworthy, men will trust you. If you are diligent, you will be successful in your undertakings. If you are generous, you find plenty of men who are willing to serve you. [17:6]

And when his favorite disciple Yan Hui enquired about what constituted a moral life, Confucius' answer was most revealing: "Renounce yourself and conform to the ideal of decency and good sense." [12:1] For, if self-cultivation eventually comes down to renouncing one's self, the Taoists and the Buddhists would have a lot to say on that, as we will see later.

Second, a gentleman is an ethical person in that he understands the ritual proprieties governing human relationships and behaves appropriately. A gentleman is a good son at home and a good citizen in society. Under Confucian scheme, morality and governance start from home, and indeed, the concept of "filial piety" is considered as the "foundation of a moral character." [1:2] *The Analects* records a very lively conversation between Confucius and one of his disciples on the question of what counts as "being filial":

> A disciple of Confucius enquired about the period of three years' mourning for parents, remarking that one year was long enough.
>
> "For," said he, "if a gentleman neglects the Arts and usages of life for three years, he will lose his knowledge of them; and if he put aside music for three years, he will entirely forget it. Again, even in the ordinary course of nature, in one year the old corn is mown away to give place to new corn which springs up, and in one year we burn through all the different kinds of wood produced in all the seasons. I believe, therefore, that after the completion of one year, mourning may cease."
>
> Confucius answered, "If, after one year's mourning, you were to eat good food and wear fine clothes, would you feel at ease?"
>
> "I should," replied the disciple. "Then," answered Confucius, "if you can feel at ease, do it. But a good man during the whole period of three years' mourning, does not enjoy good food when he eats it, and derives no pleasure from music when he hears it; when he is lodged in comfort, he does not feel at ease: therefore, he does not do anything of those things. You, however, since you feel at ease, can, of course, do them."

> Afterward, when the disciple had left, Confucius remarked, "What a man without moral feel he is? It is only three years after his birth that a child is able to leave the arms of his parents. Now the period of three years' mourning for parents is universally observed throughout the Empire. As to that man, — I wonder if he was one who did not enjoy the affection of his parents when he was a child!" [17:21]

In our contemporary reading, we would inevitably feel much more sympathetic to the disciple who seemed much more reasonable on the issue (nobody nowadays really observes the mourning even for one whole year!). On the contrary, Confucius appeared to be rather "diplomatic" even to his disciples and would turn around and criticize them sarcastically behind their back! But on the other hand, it goes to show how profoundly family ethics is rooted in the Chinese psyche, which continues to exert influence upon Chinese lives even today.

One of the five cardinal ethical relationships in Confucianism is that among friends, and a gentleman cherishes a visit of a friend from afar. [1:1] Confucius advises that making friends should be a good means of enhancing one's moral character, and "have no friends who are not as yourself." [1:8]. He teaches that "a gentleman is agreeable with an identity whereas a snob conforms with identicalness." [13:23] A gentleman is broad-minded and embraces brotherhood "within the corners of the Earth":

> A disciple of Confucius was unhappy, exclaiming often: "All men have their brothers: I alone have none." Upon which another disciple said to him, "I have heard it said that Life and Death are pre-ordained, and riches and honours come from God. A gentleman is serious and without blame. In his conduct towards others he behaves with earnestness, and with judgment and good sense. In that way he will find all men within the corners of the Earth his brothers. What reason, then, has a gentleman to complain that he has no brothers in his home?" [12:5]

On the other hand, a gentleman does not shun away from solitude as he is confident that his moral character is resourceful and all-encompassing:

> On one occasion Confucius said he would go and live among the barbarous tribes in the East. "You will there," remarked somebody, "feel the want of refinement."
> "Where a gentleman resides," retorted Confucius, "how can there be want of refinement?" [9:13]

Last but certainly not least, a Confucian gentleman ought to be an educated person. That, of course, does not simply refer to the possession of knowledge, much less to the passing of exams. Rather, it refers to a *cultured* person with a well-rounded personality. On one occasion, Confucius talked about the disposition of an educated gentleman in terms of specific comportment in food, dwelling, speech, work ethic, and ways of making friends:

> "A gentleman, in matters of food, should never seek to indulge his appetite; in lodging, he should not be too solicitous of comfort. He should be diligent in work and careful in speech. He should seek for the company of men of virtue and learning, in order to profit by their lessons and example. In this way he may become a gentleman of real culture." [1:14]

And in this remark: "A gentleman will not make himself into a mere machine fit only to do one kind of work," [2:12] Confucius sounds like a modern prophet in foreseeing the specialization and compartmentalization of our modern education. In later times of the Dynastic period when the Examination system flourished and prevailed, the image of a Confucian scholar/official was often cast in the figure of a very cultured and sophisticated weakling, devoid of physical strength and agility, very much in contrast to a heroic knight in Europe or a samurai in Japan. But that was not the ideal image of a gentleman for Confucius:

> Confucius remarked, "When the natural qualities of men get the better of the results of education, they are rude men. When the results of education get the better of their natural qualities, they become effete.

> It is only when the natural qualities and the results of education are properly blended, that we have the true gentleman." [6:16]

Here it is clear Confucius also foresaw the defects of over-, or bookish, education and affected culture. It is worth remembering that Confucius himself was a very tall man and good at sports (at least in horseback riding). What Confucius calls for is the right combination of *wen* (literariness, embellishment, or "results of education") and *zhi* (substance, rawness, or "natural qualities") for the ideal of a "true gentleman."

As a book, *The Analects* is a random collection of Confucius' sayings with very loose structural division of chapters and paragraphs. But any reader will be familiar with the following lines that constitute the opening paragraph of the first chapter:

> Confucius remarked, "It is indeed a pleasure to acquire knowledge and, as you go on acquiring, to put into practice what you have acquired. A greater pleasure still it is when friends of congenial minds come from afar to seek you because of your attainments. But he is truly a gentleman who feels no discomposure even when he is not noticed of men." [1:1]

These lines are so well known that they have become part of everyday Chinese language and often quoted separately: the first line is often invoked to emphasize learning and particularly the importance of practice along with learning, while the second line is frequently quoted to welcome an old friend coming from afar. In *The Analects* text, however, it is more appropriate to read them together, which indicates clearly Confucius' notion of a "true gentleman" as involving learning and practice, friendly communication of ideas and knowledge, and most importantly, the composure to stand firm and alone in the world even when you are not being appreciated in this world. Perhaps this is also what Confucius implies in the following — one of the most delightful, and more elaborate, episodes in *The Analects*:

> On one occasion four of his disciples were sitting in attendance on Confucius.

Confucius then said to them, "I am only a little older than you, gentlemen. Do not mind that. Now living a private life, you all say that you are not known and appreciated by men in authority; but suppose you were known, tell me now, each of you, what would you be able to do?"

"I could," answered the intrepid Zilu at once, without hesitation, "if I had the conduct of affairs in a State of even the first power which was hemmed in between two States of great power and which was embroiled in the midst of a war, and hence harassed by famine and distress — I could, if I had the conduct of affairs in such a State for three years, make the people brave and, moreover, know their duty."

On hearing this, Confucius only smiled; and turning to another disciple, said, "And you — what do you say?"

"I could," answered the disciple appealed to, "if I had the conduct of the government of a State, say, of the third or fourth power, I could in such a case, after three years, make the people live in plenty. As to education in higher things, I would leave that to the gentlemen who will come after me."

Confucius then turned to another disciple and said: "Now you — what do you say?"

"I do not say," replied the disciple, "that in what I am going to suppose I *could do* what I propose; only, I would *try* to do it. Suppose then there were functions to be performed in any Court, such as public receptions and general assemblies — dressed in an appropriate uniform, I think I could be the vice-presiding officer."

"And now you," said Confucius to the last of the four disciples, "what do you say?"

The disciple, by the name of Dian, then laid aside the harpsichord which he was thrumming, stood up and answered: "What I have in my mind differs entirely from what those three gentlemen have proposed."

"What harm is there in that?" replied Confucius, "we are all only speaking out each his own mind." "Then," answered the disciple, "we will suppose now that we are in the latter days of spring, when we have changed all our winter clothing for fresh, new, light garments for the warmer weather. I would then propose that we take along with us five or six grown-up young friends and six or seven still younger men. We will then bathe in that romantic river; after which we will go to the top of that ancient terrace to air and cool ourselves; and at last we will return, singing on our way as we loiter back to our homes."

"Ah!" said Confucius then, with a sigh, "I agree with Dian." [11:25]

In a peaceful setting at a casual moment, with background music, four disciples and the master had a chat. The master asked the disciples to loosen up and talk about their "ambitions of service." Three of them professed theirs, each with different degrees of grandeur and modesty. Surprisingly, Confucius chooses to go along with Dian, whose ambition is not about governmental service but rather about living a pastoral life in natural beauty. This passage has bewildered many later more orthodox Confucianists who would have liked to uphold an earnest and serious teacher with a noble cause. Confucius himself, however, may actually have a sense of humor, may be much more nature-oriented, much more of "natural qualities" — something the Taoists would have a lot more to say.

TAOIST SELF: BEING ONE WITH NATURE

Taoism was the second most influential school of thought in Chinese culture. Taoism was also a political philosophy but was seldom taken seriously in China's dynastic history, as Confucianism, aided by (or some would say, corrupted by) Legalism, became the orthodox state ideology for monarchical rule. But Taoism remained very influential in the Chinese psyche, as it was appreciated for its metaphysical discourses and aesthetic taste — a ground very much conceded, or even echoed by, the Confucianists. Indeed, a scholar/official can very well be both a Confucian (particularly while at service) and a Taoist in his literary and aesthetic taste (particularly when he is not at service). More than Confucianism, Taoism served as the philosophical and aesthetic foundation for Chinese literature and arts, and for the characteristic poetic lifestyle of Chinese culture.

Figure 6: Laozi

Figure 7: Zhuangzi

Taoism basically refers to the teachings of two masters: Laozi and Zhuangzi. Like Confucius, Laozi was a historical figure; yet unlike Confucius about whom we know quite a lot about his life and character, we know little about the life of Laozi except that, as the founder of the Taoist teachings, he left behind the 5000-character-long *Laozi*, or *Daodejing* (Tao Te Ching), which is perhaps the second most translated text in the world (next to the Bible), certainly the most translated Chinese classical text. As the second master of Taoism, Zhuangzi to Taoism is like Mencius to Confucianism, whose teachings are collected in the text in his name: *Zhuangzi*. Zhuangzi is the most eloquent and philosophical among all Chinese thinkers, and *Zhuangzi* has been traditionally read not merely as a philosophical text but more so as an exemplary piece of fine prose.

Laozi begins with the following lines:

> The Tao that can be spoken of
> Is not the constant Tao,
> The name that can be given
> Is not the constant name.
> The nameless is the primordial of Heaven and Earth
> The named is the mother of myriad creatures.
> Only in a state of desire-less-ness,
> Can one see the wonderfulness of the primordial;
> With constant desire,
> One can see its manifestations.

> The two occurred at the same time in different names,
> Their simultaneousness is a mystery,
> Reaching from mystery into deeper mystery
> Is the gate to the Secret of Life.[2]

This passage is quite well known and may lead to a plethora of interpretations. It is apparent that Taoist teachings are concerned with the fundamental laws of our universe, or with the Truth of Being. It sees it as a dialectical occurrence — acknowledging the "wonderfulness of the primordial" and the inevitability of the "manifestations of desire." If mankind's progress to "civilization" is inevitable, given our linguistic and naming capabilities, not to mention the driving force of human desire, Laozi reminds us not to lose sight of the "primordial" — the nameless, the Tao that had not been said. Laozi understands that to point out that Truth, he has to say it, and say it quite elaborately — in 5000 characters. All Taoist teachings can be understood as a cautionary reverse mechanism toward human civilization, however inevitable its development may be. To pull the legs of human civilization, Taoists emphasize the primordial state of being, or, Nature, and urges us to stick to it as much as possible. While the chief concern of Confucianism is "Man," or "loving man" — compassion, humanity, and morality, the Taoist principal teaching is "being one with nature." In other words, there is no pre-eminence of "Man" among all beings. Instead, "Man," as one among all beings, must fit in and follow the flow — flow like the water. Indeed, one of the most frequently used metaphors for achieving the Tao, or Way, is water:

> The best of men is like water;
> Water benefits all things
> And does not compete with them.
> It dwells in the lowly places that all disdain,
> Wherein it comes near to the Tao.

The problem with Man, however, is that he is an intelligent being. He has a self, with wits and compassions, desires and ambitions. At the center

---

[2] The translation of *Laozi* here is with reference to Lin Yutang, *The Wisdom of China and India* with my own modifications.

of Taoist teaching lies the rejection of Man as the center of all beings and the denial of the self-othering dichotomy. This is called "the transformation of things" (*wuhua*), which is presented in the famous "butterfly dream":

> Once upon a time, I, Zhuang Zhou, dreamt I was a butterfly, fluttering hither and thither, to all intents and purposes a butterfly. I was conscious only of my happiness as a butterfly, unaware that I was Zhou. Soon I awoke, and there I was, veritably myself again. Now I do not know whether I was then a man dreaming I was a butterfly, or whether I am now a butterfly, dreaming I am a man. Between a man and a butterfly there is necessarily a distinction. This is called the transformation of things.[3]

Here Zhuangzi (or Zhuang Zhou) stops short of negating altogether the very existence of Self, acknowledging that there ought to be a "distinction between a man and a butterfly." But it resolutely rejects man as the knowing subject through which all things must be objectified and rejects a self/other dichotomy. In fact, the Taoist philosophy is founded on the "theory of relativity," or "equalization of things" (*qiwu*) — the title of the second chapter of *Zhuangzi*. In other words, if there is a "self" (there ought to be!), then there must be an other, but there is really no self/other dichotomy because the self and the other are taken as mutually inclusive and interchangeable — the ground keeps shifting according to perspectives. Here is Zhuangzi at his most philosophical moment:

> There is nothing which is not *this*; there is nothing which is not *that*. What cannot be seen by *that* (the other person) can be known by myself. Hence I say, *this* emanates from *that*; *that* also derives from *this*. This is the theory of the interdependence of *this* and *that*.
>
> Nevertheless, life arises from death, and *vice versa*. Possibility arises from impossibility, and *vice versa*. Affirmation is based

---

[3] The translation of *Zhuangzi* in this section is with reference to Lin Yuang, *The Wisdom of China and India*, and Burton Watson, *The Complete Works of Chuang Tze* with my own modifications.

upon denial, and *vice versa*. Which being the case, the true sage takes his refuge in Heaven (Nature). For one may base it on *this*, yet *this* is also *that* and *that* is also *this*. This also has its "right" and "wrong," and *that* also has its "right" and "wrong." Does then the distinction between *this* and *that* really exist or not? A state in which *this* and *that* no longer find their opposites is called the "Axis of Tao."

The Taoist theory of relativity as such has a number of implications, both historically and in terms of its relevance in our contemporary life. Very much unlike the Confucian self-cultivation of a moral, ethical, and educated gentleman, the Taoist questions the validity of a right-wrong self and urges us to "take refuge in Nature" and follow the "Axis of Tao." So, what kind of a man is this? *Zhuangzi* offers the answer in a story — the story of Cook Ding:

> Cook Ding was cutting up an ox for Lord Wenhui. At every touch of his hand, every heave of his shoulder, every move of his feet, every thrust of his knee — zip! zoop! He slithered the knife along with a zing, and all was in perfect rhythm — like the dance of the *Mulberry Grove*, like the harmonious chords of the Yao music.
>
> "Ah, this is marvelous!" said Lord Wenhui. "Imagine skill reaching such heights!"
>
> Cook Ding laid down his knife and replied, "What I care about is Tao, which goes beyond skill. When I first began cutting up oxen, all I could see was the ox itself. After three years I no longer saw the whole ox. And now — now I go at it by spirit and don't look with my eyes. Perception and understanding have come to a stop and spirit moves where it wants. I go along with the natural makeup, strike in the big hollows, guide the knife through the big openings, and following things as they are. So I never touch the smallest ligament or tendon, much less a main joint.
>
> "A good cook changes his knife once a year — because he cuts. A mediocre cook changes his knife once a month — because he

hacks. I've had this knife of mine for nineteen years and I've cut up thousands of oxen with it, and yet the blade is as good as though it had just come from the grindstone. There are spaces between the joints, and the blade of the knife has really no thickness. If you insert what has no thickness into such spaces, then there's plenty of room — more than enough for the blade to play about it. That's why after nineteen years the blade of my knife is still as good as when it first came from the grindstone.

"However, whenever I come to a complicated place, I size up the difficulties, tell myself to watch out and be careful, keep my eyes on what I'm doing, work very slowly, and move the knife with the greatest subtlety, until — flop! the whole thing comes apart like a clod of earth crumbling to the ground. I stand there holding the knife and look all around me, completely satisfied and reluctant to move on, and then I wipe off the knife and put it away."

"Excellent!" said Lord Wenhui. "I have heard the words of Cook Ding and learned the way of cultivating for life!"

What Lord Wenhui means by saying that the cook's words contain the truth for self-cultivation is this. First, self-cultivation is a matter of *technique* (or "technology," an art), something beyond mere "skills," or the art of Tao. And second, this is arrived at through perfection of *practice*. In today's terminology, what Cook Ding is saying seems to suggest that the attainment of Tao relies upon "scientific knowledge," in this case, an understanding of the anatomy of the ox. That is in a sense true. Taoist teachings are not contrary to science, although it did not develop a scientific method as we know it today. What Cook Ding emphasizes here is to reach a stage where "perception and understanding have come to a stop" after years of practice. The story itself tells us that it is possible if you practice your self-cultivation, just as Cook Ding practices his butchering of an ox — the Tao lies in the butcher, if you like.

In quoting and commenting on the story of Cook Ding, the prominent American poet-philosopher Gary Snyder likens it to a philosophy of life based on "apprenticeship," as "these stories not only bridge the spiritual and the practical, but also tease us with an image of how totally accomplished one might become if one gave one's whole life up to a work."[4] Indeed, Taoist teachings contain many enlightening ideas applicable to various aspects of our modern life — some may say rather "politically correct" ideas, such as its stance on the environment, on equality and non-discrimination, and a naturalistic/transcendental attitude toward life and death. Here are two more stories, or rather dialogues between Zhuangzi and his famous interlocutor Huizi.

> Huizi said to Zhuangzi, "I have a large tree, called the tree-of-heaven. Its trunk is so irregular and knotty that it cannot be measured out for planks; while its branches are so twisted to match up to a compass or square. It stands by the roadside, but no carpenter will look at it. Your words are like that tree — big and useless, dismissed by everyone alike."
>
> "Have you never seen a wild cat," rejoined Zhuangzi, "crouching down in wait for its prey? Right and left and high and low, it springs about, until it gets caught in a trap or dies in a snare. On the other hand, there is the yak with its great huge body. It is big enough in all conscience, but it cannot catch mice. Now if you have a big tree and are at a loss what to do with it, why not plant it in the Village of Nowhere, in the great wilds, where you might loiter idly by its side, and lie down in blissful repose beneath its shade? There it would be safe from the axe and from all other injury. If you are no use at all, who'll come to bother you?"

Zhuangzi's idea on the "tree-of-heaven" in the "Village of Nowhere" could very well serve as the starting point for a philosophy of deep ecology. The problem with much of contemporary environmentalism is its anthropocentrism, and Taoism would have none of it. The Taoist self can be transformed into a butterfly in one instance and can speak from the perspective of the "useless tree" in another. To see from the perspective of the other is not only readily possible but almost imperative. And seeing

---

[4] Gary Snyder, *The Practice of the Wild*, p. 147.

from the perspective of the other may result in the most unorthodox and radical views, as shown, for instance, in the following:

> Zhuangzi's wife died. When Huizi went to convey his condolences, he found Zhuangzi sitting with his legs sprawled out, pounding on a tub and singing. "You lived with her, she brought up your children and grew old," said Huizi. "It should be enough simply not to weep at her death. But pounding on a tub and singing — this is going too far, isn't it?"
>
> Zhuangzi said, "You're wrong. When she first died, do you think I didn't grieve like anyone else? But I looked back to her beginning and the time before she was born. Not only the time before she was born, but the time before she had a body. Not only the time before she had a body, but the time before she had a spirit. In the midst of the jumble of wonder and mystery a change took place and she had a spirit. Another change and she had a body. Another change she was born. Now there's been another change and she's dead. It's just like the progression of the four seasons, spring, summer, autumn, winter.
>
> "Now she's going to lie down peacefully in a vast room. If I were to follow after her bawling and sobbing, it would show I don't understand anything about fate. So I stopped."

Beating drums and singing over the dead body of your wife, this would be a hilarious act in the eye of a Confucian, and even in terms of our common sense today. But Zhuangzi's point on the nature of life and death may be well taken and provide much food for thought on a number of nagging issues of our contemporary life, such as abortion and assisted termination of one's own life.

Taoism is a very ancient philosophy, but strikingly with very modern connotations. This is because it is primarily a revolt against civilization, and its anti-civilizational critique sometimes reads quite refreshingly in our modern times compounded with civilizational burden. In Chinese history, Taoism has been appreciated for its psychological and aesthetic value, while in social life and political governance, Confucianism prevailed. That does not mean Taoism has nothing to say in that realm. Here is what *Laozi* says about an anti-intellectual and anti-civilizational political ideal, perhaps particularly enticing for totalitarian regimes:

> Do not honor the noble and the worthy,
> And the people won't compete.
> Do not value rare treasures,
> And the people won't steal.
> Do not display the desirable,
> And people's hearts won't be disturbed.
> Therefore, the sagely governance aims to
> Hollow people's minds and fill their bellies,
> Weaken their wills and strengthen their bones;
> Let them be ignorant and desireless,
> And make even the intelligent ones dare not act.
> Do those things that will result in non-action,
> Then nothing will not be in order.

And what kind of world will this lead us to? Laozi offers us a vision of "small-state-small-population," which is exactly an antithesis of what China is like today — some may argue "a big and powerful state" and a "large population" are precisely two core problems facing China today, but I wonder whether even the most radical protesters against globalization would hesitate to endorse the following?

> Let there be a small country with a small population,
> Let the people give up the use of tools.
> Let them take death seriously and not migrate far,
> Even with boats and wagons available,
> They won't use them;
> Even with armor and weapons available,
> They won't carry them.
> Let them again tie ropes for reckoning,
> Let them enjoy their food,
> Wear beautiful clothes,
> Be content with their housing,

> And delight in their customs.
> Even though the neighbouring states are so close by
> That people can see each other
> And hear the sounds of chickens and dogs from the neighbour state,
> People will never cross the border in their entire lifetime.

CHINESE BUDDHISM: THE TAMING OF MONKEY

Buddhism crossed the borders and began to infiltrate Chinese life since the fall of the Han Dynasty (220 AD). At the time of the Ming Dynasty (1368–1644), after more than a thousand years of penetration (resistance, negotiations, and translations), it had become one of the three *jiao* (teachings/religions) of China: Confucianism, Taoism, and Buddhism, and thus integrated into the Chinese cultural landscape.

Buddhism was founded by Gautama Sakyamuni (ca. 563–483 BC), an Indian prince, the son of the king of a tiny state at the foot of the Himalayas. Brought up amidst luxuries and pleasures, he became disenchanted and practiced religious asceticism, and attained enlightenment at the age of thirty-five, and thereafter came to be known as the Buddha. The teachings of the Buddha may be summarized in one sentence: life is suffering. And human suffering is caused by craving, and human desire is the root of all evil. Therefore, desire for sensual pleasures and material possessions must be annihilated. But you don't have a self so as to work on salvation. Belief in a fixed and permanent self is the most deceitful and harmful illusion hampering the path to salvation. It will only breed egoism, craving for existence, pleasure, fame, and fortune. Instead, Buddhism preaches that there is no permanent self or soul in the individual, and that there is only a living complex of physical and mental elements living on the fruits of the individual's acts. This is called "karma": intention plus the bodily action that follows the intention, which produces other actions. Every action is caused by a previous action and leads to the next action. Therefore, human suffering does not end with death, as life is seen as transformative: through death, it is reborn in another life form. So suffering is perpetual with endless rebirths of life. The key to end this suffering lies in breaking or transcending these life cycles. How can this be achieved? Buddhist teachings offer the so-called Eightfold Path to acquire meritorious karma and eventually lead to salvation, namely, through right views, right intention, right speech, right action, right livelihood, right effort, right mindfulness, and right concentration. The religious life involves vegetarianism, celibacy, positive religious practices, and abstinence from alcoholic beverages. Done in perfection, this will lead to Nirvana: the absolute and infinite stage that finally breaks the life cycles when you achieve Buddhahood.

Along its historical development, there emerged two major sects of Buddhism: Theravada, or "lesser vehicle," which literally means doctrine of the elders, spread to Southeast Asia, emphasizes personal salvation by the individual himself and promises salvation only for those who join the monastic order to become monks and nuns. On the other hand, Mahayana, or "greater vehicle," which spread to China and the rest of East Asia, emphasizes love for all fellow men manifested by compassion, charity and altruism, and offers salvation not to a select few but to all sentient beings. The spread of Buddhism to China and all of East Asia was accompanied by a major enterprise of cross-cultural translation at global scale, so much so that Chinese language was significantly enriched — some of the Buddhist translations such as *yuan* or *jingjie* have long become ordinary Chinese words of daily usage that people don't think of their Buddhist origin at all.

It is perhaps necessary to highlight three keywords in the formation of Chinese Buddhism: *Xuanzang, Guanyin,* and *Chan*. *Xuanzang*, known as Tang Monk, was a heroic historical figure credited with bringing Buddhism to the Chinese through an incredulous pilgrimage during the Tang Dynasty, to which I will return shortly below. The religious ideal of Mahayana Buddhism is bodhisattva, or a being destined for enlightenment, who is the epitome of all Mahayana virtues. It is a personification of a particular trait of the Buddha's personality. Since there are a number of traits, there are a number of bodhisattvas. Out of all, however, Bodhisattva Avalokitesvara represents the compassion of the Buddha, and in China, this bodhisattva became a feminine figure (sometimes depicted with a thousand hands) and attained a Chinese name: *Guanyin*, which is immensely popular — actually even more popular than the Buddha himself.

Along with its spread into China, there emerged several indigenous Chinese schools of Buddhism, and the most influential of them was Chan Buddhism (when further spread to Japan, it has been called Zen Buddhism in English). The Chinese word "Chan" translates to "Dhyana," and it refers to the religious discipline aimed at tranquilizing the mind and getting the practitioner to devote himself to a quiet introspection into his own inner consciousness. At the time of its Sixth Patriarch Hui Neng (683–713) in the Tang Dynasty, the Chan School flourished and became the most influential Chinese school. It adopts an iconoclast attitude toward the Buddhas and the bodhisattvas and calls for disregard for literature and rituals. For instance, one Chan master called his disciples to "kill everything that stands in your way. If you should meet the Buddha, kill the Buddha. If you should meet the Patriarchs, kill the Patriarchs. If you should meet the arhats on your way, kill them too." In celebrating such freedom and spontaneity, it advocates complete and instantaneous enlightenment in achieving salvation. By way of instantaneous enlightenment (*dunwu*), you don't need to rely on reading scriptures and following the monastic rules and order. Enlightenment can happen to anyone, anytime, in the most ordinary manner. People can't achieve this precisely because their lives are full of shackles of all kinds, and therefore, the key is to set your mind free from these. How do you achieve this? The Chan master asks us to "meditate" (*dazuo*, sitting in meditation), to calm your mind and have no conscious thought, to purify your mind consciousness, so as to free yourself from conscious efforts — including craving, desire and attachment to external objects, as well as heeding the teachings of the Buddha, reciting the sutras, worshipping Buddha images, or performing the rituals. Chan Buddhism advocates a return to ordinary life practices. They criticize monastic life of monks and nuns as "parasites" of society. Some Chan masters insist they continue to plough the field. One common teaching of Chan Buddhism, for instance, is to say that sweeping the floor is very much a worthy act to achieve salvation.

Chan Buddhism also preaches through "*gong'an*," or questions and answers between masters and disciples, usually designed and practiced to shock the normal reasoning and logical mind/consciousness of the practitioner. To achieve this, the master may shout at his disciple or administer a physical beating to him. At times, the master may pose a riddle or a conundrum to the student, or offer an answer seemingly unrelated to the question, as, for instance, "Who is the Buddha?" answer: "three pounds of flax." In fact, the following passage from *Zhuangzi* is usually cited as a typical case of "*gong'an*":

> Dongguozi asked Zhuangzi: "Where is what you call the Tao to be found?" Zhuangzi replied: "Everywhere." The other said: "Specify an instance of it. That would be more satisfactory." "It is here in this ant." "That's a rather low instance." "It is in this panic grass." "Why, it's a lower instance." "It is in this earthenware tile." "That is even lower!" "It is in that excrement." Dongguozi shut up.

When the Zhuangzian text is employed to illuminate Buddhist teachings, one can see the extent to which Buddhism is "sinicized," or how "three teachings have become one."

Perhaps one way to illustrate Chinese Buddhism is to read the celebrated novel *Journey to the West* (or *Xiyouji*, sometimes also translated as *Monkey*), often deemed as one of the masterpieces of classical Chinese novels. Published in the sixteenth century during the Ming Dynasty,[5] this fantastic tale draws its inspiration from the historical pilgrimage of Xuanzang (602–664) of the Tang Dynasty, who embarked on a pilgrimage journey to fetch the sutras, leaving Chang'an in 629, through Gansu, Qinghai, Kumul (Hami), across the Tianshan Mountains to Turpan, then through today's Kyrgyzstan, Uzbekistan, Afghanistan, finally reaching India in 630; and after thirteen years in India, came back to Chang'an in 646. Then he set up schools and monasteries and engaged in the monumental enterprise of translating the scriptures he brought back from India. Ever since the Tang Dynasty, there appeared various kinds and versions of popular tales related to the Tang Monk's journey, which formed important pre-texts for the novel *Journey to the West* published in the Ming Dynasty as we know it today.

---

[5] The author of the tale is now generally attributed to Wu Cheng'en (ca. 1500–1582). Wu would be absolutely amazed that his posthumous reputation reached worldwide scale due to his authorship of the novel, something that he tried by all means to hide at the time of publication, since it was considered low-class, low-taste and vulgar for a "man of letters" to engage in composing such "small-talk" — as the "novel" is called in Chinese.

The novel is a fantastic tale about the pilgrimage of Tripitaka (*Xuanzang*) to India, accompanied by four disciples: Monkey, Pig, Sha Monk, and the White Horse. The team had to rely on each other and help each other to overcome eighty-one calamities during their trying journey in order to achieve their goal of fetching the scriptures, and in the process, all of them also eventually achieved self-enlightenment, Monkey and Tripitaka achieving Buddhahood, Sha Monk becoming an arhat, and Pig becoming an arhat cleanser. The most striking difference between this fantastic tale and the historical event is that Monkey, instead of Tripitaka, the master, became the hero of the story. Furthermore, Tripitaka is portrayed as some kind of a weakling, easily fooled by all kinds of monsters and yet rather harsh on Monkey.

The novel can be read on many levels: it is a fantasy novel — about ghosts and demons and evil spirits; it is a travel novel about exotic places, and the wonders and travail of the long journey; it is also a humorous novel, not only in terms of the characterization of Monkey, but particularly with reference to Pig and his relation with Monkey. But after all, it is a religious novel with a unique Chinese take on Buddhism. The novel presents a world where "three religions" are very much juxtaposed and integrated despite references to their infighting in various episodes of the narrative. This is most evident through the characterization of Monkey, the protagonist of the novel. If Monkey can be seen as representing Chinese national character, *Journey to the West* presents a fictional narrative of the Chinese engagement with the Buddhist world on their own terms, willy-nilly.

The fact that Monkey, instead of Tripitaka, the Tang Monk, is the hero of the novel is certainly very significant, and the narrative structure reflects that accordingly. The first seven chapters are solely devoted to the story of the Monkey King from his birth to attaining his powers, and then "wreaking havoc in heaven." Chapters 8–12 then introduces the Tang Monk Tripitaka and the origin of the mission. Chapters 13–100 cover the pilgrimage journey to India and back, in which Monkey, now taken by Tripitaka as a disciple, accompanied the master and overcame eighty-one calamities in all to complete the mission successfully. Chinese readers may not be familiar with all the details of each of the eighty-one calamities the pilgrims had to overcome, but most school children would have heard of the all-powerful "Monkey King" "wreaking havoc in heaven."

Monkey, or Sun Wukong, was born out of an ancient rock created by the coupling of Heaven and Earth. This is a very significant reference to the genesis of Monkey as an offspring of Heaven and Earth, a very Taoist reference. Thanks to his courage, he was heralded as a leader of a group of monkeys at the Flower and Fruit Mountain and proclaimed himself as "The Handsome Monkey King." If he were content in being a king of monkeys enjoying bountiful fruits and wayward freedom, there would not be any story (and the Buddhist pilgrimage afterward). But he was not, as he wanted to pursue powers and immortality — another Taoist obsession. And he obtained these from a reclusive Taoist master. His powers were now truly magnificent. Monkey now had "seventy-two transformations," which means he can become all kinds of animals or pluck his hair to multiply himself into hundreds and thousands of his own mirror images. He could do his "Cloud Somersault" — a single leap goes high up in the sky and over a vast distance. He was also now gifted with "a pair of fiery golden eyes," which enables him to see far and deep through the disguises of all kinds of demons and spirits. Above all, he has his magical weapon: the "Golden Rod," which weighs 17,550 pounds — originally an undersea palace pillar from the Dragon King of the East Sea — and can enlarge and shrink at will, from a giant stick for battles to a tiny needle Monkey carries on his ear. However, despite his master's advice to keep humility, Monkey couldn't help showing off his powers. He comes back to his Flower and Fruit Mountain to lead his wild monkeys. Now with all his powers, he wanted more. He wanted an official position in Heaven — a very Confucian move. In Chinese cosmology, we find that the world of Heaven is very much a down-to-earth thing, with an emperor and a hierarchical governing structure. What is also interesting is that, in addition to the imperial structure, there are two parallel worlds consisting of Taoist and Buddhist gods and spirits, which are portrayed as the Jade Emperor's respected friends with great powers. In order to contain the wild and all-powerful Monkey, the Jade Emperor assigned him the "official" position of "an imperial horsekeeper." When Monkey found out it was a lowest kind of job not even on the official rank and file, he revolted against the "insult" by wreaking havoc in Heaven, and went back to his Flower and Fruit Mountain, declaring himself "the Great Sage Equalling Heaven." With a host of generals and warriors at his disposal, the Jade Emperor could not contain Monkey, and he had to seek the help of his ally the Taoist God Laozi, who was able to capture Monkey and locked him up in a fire stove and burned him for forty-nine days — to no avail. Monkey escaped in the end with increased powers — the purgatory fire only afforded him "a pair of fiery golden eyes." Finally, the Jade Emperor had to seek the help from the Buddha, who played a game of contest with Monkey to see who is more powerful. The Buddha asked Monkey what kind of powers he had, and Monkey replied, well, he could do "Cloud Somersault" — one jump could take him to tens and thousands of miles up in the sky. The Buddha said, fine, if you could jump off my palm, you win. Monkey could not take such insulting provocation. He took one jump off to the sky and after several more jumps he was deep and far in the cloud. He suddenly saw five pillars standing in thin air and figured it must be the end of the universe. He urinated at the end of the pillar to make a mark in case the Buddha would not believe where he had reached. It turns out that the five pillars were the five fingers of the Buddha. Then the Buddha turned over his palm and crushed Monkey under a magical mountain for 500 years, until the Tang Monk came and took him along as his disciple to accompany him on the pilgrimage.

Chinese readers tend to be quite sympathetic with Monkey in his fight against the Jade Emperor in Heaven, for they see many reflections of themselves in the character of Monkey. Who doesn't wish for immortality? Who doesn't want to be a high-ranking official? They probably all wish they could have those magical powers Monkey had and enjoy the freedom of a "Handsome Monkey King." They probably all wish they could have those powers to challenge all kinds of authorities in their lives as Monkey did in wreaking havoc in the Heavenly Kingdom. In a sense, Monkey was portrayed as a heroic figure, awesomely courageous, wonderfully fantastic, and funny and lively, quite a contrast to the stiff and authoritarian figure of the Jade Emperor. On the other hand, there are obvious defects in Monkey's character. They can be described as, well, "monkeyish." He is raw and wild, and his ego is magnified precisely due to his magical powers. The taming of Monkey necessitates an intervention from the Buddha. If the character of Monkey can be seen as representation of the Chinese character in general, the introduction of Buddhism is meant to serve a civilizing function to rectify the monkeyish aspects of Chinese character. Monkey needed to be brought on the right track, to take on a pilgrimage journey by overcoming eighty-one calamities in order to achieve Buddhahood.

Monkey's character is significantly improved over the long journey to fetch Buddhist scriptures. At first glance, the outcome of the journey was very much preordained in that the journey itself was arranged by the Buddha and the team of the pilgrimage was put together by *Guanyin*. And throughout the long arduous journey, whenever the team met up with monsters and spirits they could not handle, *Guanyin* would appear and offer crucial support. But of course, the significance of the journey lies in the journey itself. Monkey and the team must go through the treacherous journey and tackle the eighty-one obstacles one by one. It is precisely through such travail that we see a significant transformation of Monkey's character: he becomes much less egoistic and self-centered, much more disciplined and helpful to others, always putting the safety of his master on top of his priorities, and learning to act as a team leader and team member in leading and collaborating with two other disciples Pig and Sha Monk. With much self-sacrifice and constant battles against all kinds of monsters and evil spirits along the journey, it can be said that Monkey's eventual attainment of Buddhahood was well-deserved, and Buddhist pilgrimage brings us a much better character of Monkey.

One thing, however, did not change with Monkey — his rebellious character. The novel narrates a pilgrimage journey to fetch Buddhist scriptures, and in the process, the group of pilgrims all achieved Buddhahood when Buddhist scriptures were brought to China. That big picture, however, is simultaneously underlined with a consistent criticism, even mockery, of Buddhism throughout the fictional narrative. In the novel, the Tang Monk is supposed to be the symbol of Buddhist mercy and compassion, yet he is depicted in every sense as the anti-hero during the journey. Not only does he have a cowardly and feeble character, but his sense of compassion is simply misleading with poor judgment. He is always easily deceived by monsters and spirits disguised as normal human beings begging for sympathy. And he blames Monkey for protecting him from falling into the traps of those monsters in human skin. When the Tang Monk punishes Monkey for killing those monsters in the name of mercy and compassion, it is hard for readers to appreciate Tang Monk's kind-heartedness instead of Monkey's wit and bravery. Indeed, the Tang Monk as the Buddhist master is cast as a mere joke. That seems to be more than an understatement upon the sanctity of Buddhism. Moreover, just as the imperial world of Heaven mirrors the hierarchical empire on earth with its arrogance, pomposity, incompetency, and corruption, the Buddhist realm is depicted just as far from being a perfect world. The journey itself is preordained, as we know, but the obstacles on the way that Monkey had to overcome, namely, those monsters and spirits who are keen on eating the Tang Monk alive and whom Monkey had to battle against, are more often than not originally from the Buddhist realm which, as the narrative suggests, is in want of self-tightening and discipline. By the end of the journey when the group reached the land of the Buddha, readers are again reminded that bribery even exists in the Buddha land, as corrupt monks stand in the way for the pilgrims to have access to the real scriptures.

The most striking narrative comment on Buddhism seems to be about the "golden fillet" on Monkey's head. At the beginning of Monkey's induction as a disciple to follow the Tang Monk, a "golden fillet" was placed on Monkey's head. Whenever Monkey went back to his wild nature and disobeyed the Tang Monk, the latter would recite curses and the "golden fillet" would tighten up and inflict unbearable pain on Monkey who can't help but to submit. More often than not, though, the Tang Monk's curses were not rightfully applied. Monkey never consented to this restraint. Even at the very end of the story when Monkey had achieved Buddhahood, he still held grudges against it:

> "Master," Monkey said to Tripitaka, "I'm now a Buddha, the same as you. It's not fair that I should still wear this golden fillet, so that if you choose to recite your spell, you could still plague me. Make haste and say the "Loosening of the Fillet" spell, so that I may get it off and smash it to bits, in case other so-called Bodhisattvas may use it to play tricks and inflict pains on others."[6]

Undoubtedly, the introduction of Buddhism has had a long-term impact upon Chinese culture, but it seems very hard for Monkey to take any religion very seriously.

---

[6] Arthur Waley, *Monkey* p. 304. Tanslation modified.

Chapter 4

A Poetic Culture:
An Aesthetics of Life

Chinese culture is a poetic culture. Though the Chinese don't seem to take religion very seriously, they adore poets, both in their long traditional period and in modern times. As late as the 1980s when China began to open up again after the Cultural Revolution, the hero and icon for the youth was definitely the poet. Nowadays, the poet no longer enjoys such prestige and the Chinese youth today probably crave to become the next IT tycoon or something. But one can't be certain that the poet would never come back to be the hero again. After all, poetic impulse is very much integrated into the cultural vein. Even when economy holds sway in Chinese life today, children are still very much encouraged to recite famous poems of Tang and Song. It would really be a sin for any "educated" Chinese if they fail to familiarize themselves with some famous poems — if not "three hundred poems of Tang and Song" (as the title of the most popular primer collection of Chinese poems goes), perhaps at least a few dozens.

Chinese culture is a poetic culture based on two grounds, generally speaking. First, the Chinese culture enjoyed its first blossom when the Zhou Dynasty broke down into the Spring and Autumn and then the Warring States period, and there emerged "a hundred schools of thought" with such sage thinkers as Laozi and Confucius. Once the broad, general cultural framework had been set by these sage thinkers, the prime focus of later generations (lasting for 2,000 years) of the educated elite was mainly toward literature. And "literature" in Chinese tradition primarily refers to poetry (with prose as a close second), which is very different from the Western tradition — both in terms of the pre-eminence of literary genres and its cultural role. In other words, poetry is the treasure box of Chinese culture (and world culture, for that matter) as it is the accumulation and crystallization of the Chinese intellectual enterprise for over two millennia. Second, this treasure box affords Chinese culture with a heightened and enlightened aesthetic sensitivity, and a sophistication characteristic of the heart and mind of not only the educated elite, but also the Chinese people as a whole. It can be said that, to the Chinese, poetry is their way of life. In this chapter, I introduce some of the most common themes in Chinese poetic tradition with particular emphasis on the aesthetics of life bent on compassion and freedom.

POETIC EXPRESSION OF HEART AND MIND

> Poetry is the manifestation of one's wishes. "Wishes" are that which lie within one's heart and mind, and when they are expressed in words, it is called poetry. When human "emotion" occurs, it will find its expression in words. When words won't suffice to express it, one will sigh; when sighing won't suffice, one will sing; when singing won't suffice, one can't help dancing with one's hands and feet.

This is one of the earliest and most cited definitions of poetry in Chinese documents. It is taken from "Preface to *The Book of Poetry*," usually attributed to Confucius' disciple Zixia (507–400 BC). One of the most important reasons why poetry enjoyed such a prestigious position in Chinese culture is the fact that *The Book of Poetry* was deemed by Confucius as one of the six Confucian Classics. *The Book of Poetry*, generally believed to be compiled by Confucius himself, consists of some 300 earliest extant poems (thus *The Book of Poetry* is also referred to as *Three Hundred Poems* or simply as *Poetry*) in Chinese cultural history, dating many centuries before Confucius' time. Apparently, Confucius held great esteem for poetry; in his words: "to summarize the merits of *The Book of Poetry* in a nutshell, there is no single evil thought in it" (Analects 2). *The Analects* also records the following remarks by Confucius:

> Hey, young man, why don't you learn some *Poetry*? *Poetry* can help you express (what's inside you), to observe (the world), to fit

in (with the world), to utter your complaints (of the world); and can help you to learn to be a good son at home, and a good man in society; furthermore, it will enable you to learn the correct names of many birds, beasts, herbs and trees. (Analects 17)

Modern commentators make a great deal about the conflict between the so-called poetry-expressing-*zhi* (wishes) and poetry-following-*qing* (feeling, emotion, compassion) traditions in Chinese poetry; the former is said to be bent on moral and didactic functions of poetry, while the latter on individualist and lyrical functions.[1] In this manner, Chinese poetry (and Chinese literature as a whole) is neatly divided into two strands of "realistic" and "romantic" literature; that would be very much a modern bias, not very productive in our understanding of Chinese poetry. For merely a quick glance at the above two quotes by Confucius and his disciple clearly shows that they, by no means, confine poetry to the realm of morality. The notions of *zhi* (wishes) and *qing* (emotion) are used somewhat interchangeably — it is something that comes from within. Indeed, they are something that defines a human as a human, and poetry is expression, in language, of that fundamental quality of being a human, which is also supplemented by music, songs and dances. Human emotions are all-encompassing in relation to a myriad of aspects in life, chief among them, as the Confucians would argue, being moral affections. The problem with the modern division is that it refuses to see that human emotions would have anything to do with morals or values. In any case, Chinese poetry has always been *lyrical* in that it is an expression of one's heart and mind over a myriad of things in human life. When we look back upon this tradition, however, we can see Chinese poetry has focused on a cluster of themes, including love, homesickness, parting, socio-political critique, and particularly on freedom and "nature," which will be the focus of our discussion in this chapter.

关关雎鸠	"Guan, guan," cry the ospreys
在河之洲	On the islet in the river.
窈窕淑女	Graceful is this fair maiden,

---

[1] For a detailed discussion of this issue, see James J. Y. Liu *The Art of Chinese Poetry*.

君子好逑	A fine bride for a gentleman.
参差荇菜	Thick and thin grows the water mallow,
左右流之	Left and right one gets it in the flow.
窈窕淑女	Graceful is this fair maiden,
寤寐求之	Awake or asleep, I am seeking her.
求之不得	Seeking though I was, I could not possess her,
寤寐思服	Awake or asleep I was longing for her.
悠哉悠哉	Alas, longing and forlorn
辗转反侧	I tossed and turned in bed.
参差荇菜	Thick and thin grow the water mallow,
左右采之	Left and right one plucks it.
窈窕淑女	Graceful is the fair maiden,
琴瑟友之	With zither and zithern I will befriend her.
参差荇菜	Thick and thin grows the water mallow,
左右芼之	Left and right one gathers it.
窈窕淑女	Graceful is this fair maiden,
钟鼓乐之	With bells and drums I will gladden her.[2]

This is the very first poem in *The Book of Poetry*, and perhaps the most celebrated one. It is interesting to note that this poem has been traditionally read almost exclusively as a moral allegory, with "the fair maiden" in the poem somehow identified as an ideal mate, allegorically speaking, sought after by King Wen (1152–1056 BC), the founder of the Zhou Dynasty. The problem with this line of reading is its exclusivity. There is nothing wrong, and is indeed quite imaginative, to read the poem allegorically as extolling the virtue of King Wen. But if we understand Confucius correctly when he concludes that "there is no single evil thought in the entire *Book of Poetry*," he couldn't possibly mean to say that reading it as a simple love song, as we do now, would carry any connotation of "indecency." Quite the opposite. This poem has contributed a great deal to the poetic tradition of Chinese culture precisely as an expression of "love" — the most common and universal emotion (*qing*) between boys and girls. While stylistically significant, as

---

[2] Jie Cui and Zong-qi Cai eds. *How to Read Chinese Poetry* p. 1–2.

it invokes several formal strategies such as affective image (to use the crying birds to bring forth the feeling of love, here in this case in the first stanza) and incremental repetition, the poem presents an ideal image of a suitable bride in four characters: *yau tiao shu nu* — which has become a common ordinary term in contemporary Chinese usage and remains, for many Chinese men, the ideal bride of their dream. What exactly those four characters mean, though, would be open to interpretations. To translate it as "a graceful fair maiden" as quoted above is a very nice try. Gu Hongming, on the other hand, regards it as representing "the Chinese feminine ideal." As he explains, the Chinese words *yao tiao* mean literally secluded, meek, and shy (*yao*), and attractive and debonair (*tiao*), while *shu nu* means a pure, chaste girl: "Thus here in the oldest love song in China, you have the three essential qualities in the Chinese feminine ideal, viz. love of seclusion, bashfulness or *pudeur*, ineffable grace and charm expressed by the word debonair and last of all, purity or chastity. In short, the real or true Chinese woman is chaste; she is bashful, has *pudeur*; and she is attractive and debonair. This then is the Chinese feminine ideal — the 'Chinese woman.'"[3]

There are literally hundreds and thousands of love poems in the Chinese poetic tradition, many of the lines, if not the whole poem, have become so well known that they are not just part of the contemporary Chinese language but also sunk deep in the Chinese cultural consciousness. Let us read a couple of more.

相见时难别亦难	It is hard to meet, and parting is just as hard.
东风无力百花残	The east wind is listless, hundreds of flowers withered.
春蚕到死丝方尽	Not until its death does a spring silkworm stop spinning its threads;
蜡炬成灰泪始干	Only when a candle's wick is burned to ashes Do its tears dry up.
晓镜但愁云鬓改	Looking at the mirror at dawn, she would fear a change in her cloud-like temples;

---

[3] Gu Hongming (Ku Hung-ming), *The Spirit of the Chinese People* p. 100.

夜吟应觉月光寒	Chanting a poem at night, he would feel The moonbeams' coldness.
蓬山此去无多路	Mount Peng is not that far from here
青鸟殷勤为探看	Blue birds will be our messengers here-to-there.[4]

This is one of the "Untitled" poems by Li Shangyin (c. 813–858), a celebrated late Tang Dynasty poet. It is generally acknowledged that during the Tang Dynasty, Chinese poetry had reached full blossom both stylistically and aesthetically. Li Bai (701–762) and Du Fu (712–770) are considered two pillars for later generations to emulate. In the Qing Dynasty, a scholar compiled *Three Hundred Poems of Tang Dynasty* (*The Book of Poetry* is also called *Three Hundred Poems,* while containing, in fact, 305 poems in total), which has been so popular that it has become the standard primer for reading Chinese poetry. Even today, it can be said that, if children were not brought up reading the primer, they were probably not brought up in a *cultured* family. Within this collection, 22 poems by Li Shangyin are chosen, ranking him the fourth after Du Fu (38 poems), Wang Wei (29 poems), and Li Bai (27 poems). Li Shangyin's poems are noted for their metaphorical power and sophistication. The above "Untitled" poem is one of the best-known love poems in Chinese poetry, particularly the second couplet involving the images of the candle and the silkworm. If you want to express your feeling of love, wouldn't it be a thousand times better to say "Not until its death does a spring silkworm stop spinning its threads/Only when a candle's wick is burned to ashes do its tears dry up" (or better: in Chinese in a seven-character couplet) than to say "I love you, I love you, I love you so much!"?

In the long tradition of Chinese poetic culture, most of the poets were male, for sure. But there were quite a few women poets as well. Particularly during the Ming and Qing dynasties, there emerged thousands of women poets with published volumes of poems. This has to be considered a remarkable achievement in world literature. One of the most celebrated women poets — in fact, regardless of gender — is Li Qingzhao (1084–1155)

---

[4] Jie Cui and Zong-qi Cai eds. *How to Read Chinese Poetry*, p. 6–8. Translation slightly modified (6–8).

of the Song Dynasty. Li was born to a high-ranking scholar-official family, and her father was also a very talented poet, well appreciated by Su Dongpo (more on Su later). Even though women in traditional China were not allowed to sit for the Civil Examination and become scholar-officials, many gentry families would send their daughters together with their sons for private schooling (all education was private in the Dynastic Era). Li was also married to a talented scholar-official Zhao Mingcheng (1081–1129), particularly known as an expert in ancient Chinese epigraphy. The couple enjoyed a happy literary and cultural life with shared interests in poetry, art collections, and epigraphy. One of the famous anecdotes about their life goes like this. Once Zhao was called on official duty to leave home for a while, and Li sent him a touching poem expressing her feeling of love and longing for their meeting again. Upon receiving it, Zhao was really moved, but out of spirit of sport, he did not reply and did not go home either. Rather, he shut himself in his room and composed dozens of poems. A couple of months later, he presented his poems, with Li's poem inserted randomly among them, to one of his best friends for comments, who responded that only three lines were really excellent — and they were from Li's poem. In the Song Dynasty, a form of poetry called *ci* developed into full blossom, which was particularly suited for expressing personal emotions such as love and desire. The *ci* poems were written to fit into certain musical song tunes and Li Qingzhao was unquestionably recognized as the master of the form. The following is one of the most well-known *ci* poems by Li, composed "To the Tune of 'A Twig of Plum Blossom'," expressing the universal feeling of "lovesickness":

红藕香残玉簟秋	The fragrance of the red lotus lingers and the jade-like bamboo mat spreads the air of autumn.
轻解罗裳	Gently, I take off my silk skirt.
独上兰舟	Alone, I board a magnolia boat.
云中谁寄锦书来	Through the clouds who's sent a love letter?
雁字回时	The wild geese're returning, arrayed like a character when
月满西楼	the moonlight fills the western pavilion.
花自飘零水自流	All by themselves, the flowers fade and fall, and the water flows on.
一种相思	One type of lovesickness;

两处闲愁	two places of idled sadness.
此情无计可消除	This lovesickness, there is no way to eliminate it:
才下眉头	Just get it down the brows,
却上心头	It comes back again to my heart.[5]

Chinese poetry is essentially *lyrical* in the sense that poetry is an expression of what the Chinese call "*qing,*" or human emotions (feeling, compassion, etc.). "Love" is certainly one of the most ancient and ever-lasting themes that evoke human emotions. But there are several other types of affections that are recurring themes in Chinese poetry, particularly those directed at family or home, especially as a result of parting. This is of course perfectly understandable, given the supremacy of family and home in Chinese culture. The following is a most well-known poem about "homesickness" by Li Bai (701–762), usually considered one of the greatest poets of the Tang Dynasty:

静夜思	**Quiet Night Thoughts**
床前明月光	Before my bed, the bright moonlight;
疑是地上霜	I mistake it for frost on the ground.
举头望明月	Raising my head, I stare at the bright moon;
低头思故乡	Lowering my head, I think of my home far away.[6]

This poem is written in very simple language, with striking images about the moon as well as its soothing musicality (a sonorous "ang"-ending rhyme in Chinese). It has delighted Chinese readers over the centuries so much so that, if one has to name one poem among all Chinese poetry as the most frequently recited, this would be it. It is usually the very first poem Chinese children are taught to recite while growing up. Incidentally, Chinese children grow up with a poetic association with the moon as something capable of evoking human emotions (Chinese poetry is full of odes to the moon rather than to the sun). In any case, one can say that in Chinese culture, if one hasn't heard of Li Shangyin's "Untitled" love poem, where steadfast love is compared to a spring silkworm spinning its threads

---

[5] Jie Cui and Zong-qi Cai eds. *How to Read Chinese Poetry*, p. 18–19.
[6] Ibid., p. 110, translation slightly modified.

to the end, he may not be considered a "cultured person"; but if he hasn't heard of Li Bai's "Quiet Night Thoughts," he's simply not Chinese.

If Li Bai is considered the greatest poet of all times, Su Dongpo would be the greatest man of letters of all times, or the most *cultured* scholar in Chinese history. In addition to an illustrious and troubled official career, bent on fighting for the interests of the people, as we discussed in Chapter 2, Su excelled in almost all fields of arts and sciences of his day. He was gifted in pharmacology and gastronomy (a famous Chinese pork dish is named after him and still very popular today), and a superb calligrapher and painter. In literature, he was regarded as one of the "eight greatest prose writers" (together with his father and younger brother); and in poetry, he excelled in all the poetic genres *fu*, *shi*, and *ci* — particularly in *ci* poetry for he brought it to new heights. Here I will introduce two poems by Su, one is a *shi* poem addressed to his brother and the other a *ci* poem to his deceased wife.

辛丑十一月十九日既与子由别于郑州西门之外马上赋诗一篇寄之	**Xin-chou Eleventh Month, Nineteenth Day (1061): having parted from Zi-you outside the West Gate, I wrote this poem on horseback and sent it to him.**
不饮胡为醉兀兀	I haven't been drinking — why this wobbly drunken feeling?
此心已逐归鞍发	My heart races after you as you turn your horses toward home.
归人犹自念庭帏	The homebound thinking of course of a parent there,
今我何以慰寂寞	but how am I to ease my loneliness?
登高回首坡垄隔	Climbing a rise, I look back — you've gone beyond the slope;
但见乌帽出复没	All I see is a black hat bobbing up, then disappearing.
苦寒念尔衣裳薄	Bitter cold, and I recall what thin clothes you're wearing,

独骑瘦马踏残月	riding alone on a skinny horse, treading the last of the moonlight.
路人行歌居人乐	People go down the road singing, people in houses are merry;
童仆怪我苦凄恻	my groom can't understand why I'm so terribly gloomy.
亦知人生要有别	I do know life must have its partings;
但恐岁月去飘忽	Just afraid the months and years will whirl away too fast!
寒灯相对记畴昔	Facing each other by the cold lamp — I remember it as yesterday;
夜雨何时听萧瑟	When will we listen to the soft rustle of night rain again?
君知此意不可忘	You'll surely keep our agreement:
慎勿苦爱高官职	Not to get too wrapped up in dreams of high office![7]

    The titles of Chinese poems range from "no title" (as in Li Shangyin's poem above) to a very lengthy title as this one, offering a full context for composing the poem. If one does not know Zi-you is Su's younger brother — himself a very talented poet and prose writer as well — one might very well think this is a poem addressed to his lover (at least my students think so every time I quiz them). Such affection as recalling "what thin clothes you're wearing" and the times when "we listen to the soft rustle of night rain together" sounds very much like sweetheart words exchanged between lovers today. But "brotherly love," or "affection between gentry friends" are very common themes in Chinese poetry, particularly occasioned by their parting. This poem was written when Su Dongpo was twenty-six-years old and demonstrates a level of sophistication in his understanding of life — highlighting not only the bond between the brothers but also an enlightened detachment toward life (and I

---

[7] Watson, Burton trans. *Selected Poems of Su Tung-p'o* p. 21.

will come back to this point shortly). If the affection shown in the above poem was genuine and intimate, that shown in the following *ci* poem addressed to his deceased wife was strikingly moving and melancholic:

To the Tune "River City"

十年生死两茫茫	Ten years — dead and living dim and draw apart
不思量	I don't try to remember
自难忘	but forgetting is hard.
千里孤坟	Lonely grave a thousand miles off,
无处话凄凉	cold thoughts — where can I talk them out?
纵使相逢应不识	Even if we met you wouldn't know me,
尘满面	dust on my face,
鬓如霜	hair like frost.
夜来幽梦忽还乡	In a dream last night suddenly I was home.
小轩窗	By the window of the little room,
正梳妆	you were combing your hair and making up.
相顾无言	You turned and looked, not speaking,
惟有泪千行	only lines of tears coursing down--
料得年年肠断处	year after year will it break my heart?
明月夜	The moonlit grave,
短松冈	its stubby pines.[8]

This poem was addressed to Su's first wife Wang Fu (1039–1065) who married him at the age of sixteen — one year before Su went to the capital to take the Examination, and died thirteen years later. Two years after her death, Su married Wang Runzi (1048–1093), cousin of his first wife, who accompanied him for the next fifteen years of Su's tumultuous and exilic life until she died at the age of forty-six. Su's third wife was Wang Zhaoyun (1062–1095), who was a "sing-song girl" in Hangzhou and Su brought her home as a handmaiden when she was ten, and she became his companion ever since. There is much literature about Su's young "concubine," praising her beauty and sweet voice and intelligence — Su himself composed many poems about her. But Su loved his second wife

---

[8] Ibid., *Selected Poems of Su Tung-p'o*, p. 65.

so much that he was eventually buried with her according to his wish. And his first wife will be immortalized through this *ci* poem quoted above, composed ten years after her death. To say that Su Dongpo is the most cultured scholar, the most well-rounded personality in Chinese culture, means, first of all, his loving humanity, as so powerfully demonstrated in his poetic remembrance of his wife, which has certainly become one of the most celebrated poems in the Chinese tradition.

The above two poems by Su Dongpo were inspired by a temporary parting with his brother and an eternal parting with his wife, respectively. The following poem by Du Fu (712–770) dramatizes another type of parting, the forced parting between parents and sons, for the imperial war enterprises:

兵车行	**The Ballad of the Army Waggons**
车辚辚	The din of waggons!
马萧萧	Whinnying horses!
行人弓箭各在腰	Each marcher at his waist has bow and quiver;
耶娘妻子走相送	Old people, children, wives, running alongside,
尘埃不见咸阳桥	Who cannot see, for dust, bridge over river:
牵衣顿足拦道哭	They clutch clothes, stamp their feet, bar the way weeping,
哭声直上千云霄	Weeping their voices rise to darkening Heaven;
道旁过者问行人	And when the passersby question marchers,
行人但云点行频	The marchers but reply, 'Levies come often:
或从十五北防河	They take us at fifteen for up the river,
便至四十西营田	To garrison the West, they'll take at forty,
去时里正与裹头	Your Headman has at first to tie your turban,
归来头白还戍边	Grey-headed you come back home, then back to duty—
边庭流血成海水	The blood that's flowed out there would make a sea, Sir!

武皇开边意未已	Our Lord, his lust for land knows no degree, Sir!
君不闻	But have you not heard
汉家山东二百州	Of House of Han, its East two hundred regions
千村万落生荆杞	Where villages and farms are growing brambles?
纵有健妇把锄犁	That though a sturdy wife may take the plough, Sir,
禾生陇亩无东西	You can't see where the fields begin and end, Sir?
况复秦兵耐苦战	That Highlanders fare worst, they're hardy fighters
被驱不异犬与鸡	And so they are driven first, like dogs and chickens?
长者虽有问	Although you, Sir, ask such kind questions,
役夫敢申恨	Dare the conscripts tell their wretchedness?
且如今年冬	How, for instance, only last winter
未休关西卒	The Highland troops were still in the line
县官急索租	When their Prefect sent urgent demands,
租税从何出	Demands for tax, I ask you, from where?
信知生男恶	Son now we know, no good having sons,
反是生女好	Always better to have a daughter:
生女犹得嫁比邻	For daughters will be wed to our good neighbours
生男埋没随百草	When sons are lying dead on Steppes unburied!
君不见	But have you not seen
青海头	On the Black Lake's shore
古来白骨无人收	The white bones there of old no one has gathered,
新鬼烦冤旧鬼哭	Where new ghosts cry aloud, old ghosts are bitter,
天阴雨湿声啾啾	Rain drenching from dark clouds their ghostly chatter?"[9]

---

[9] Arthur Cooper trans. *Li Po and Tu Fu*, p. 167-168.

Figure 8: Du Fu

Whether Li Bai or Du Fu is the greatest poet (of Tang Dynasty, or of all times) is a debate that has been ongoing for many centuries in Chinese literary culture. It is generally agreed that Li Bai shines through with his poetic talent in expressing human emotions in a free and unbound fashion, whereas Du Fu's poems arouse one's deep sympathy and compassion by focusing on socio-political themes. In that sense, Du is more Confucian, that is, in the tradition of a Confucian critic. The above poem could serve as a classic anti-war protest *par excellence*, across ages and across national and cultural boundaries. The white bones left abandoned on the Steppes, the cries of old and new ghosts under damp and rainy weather — these are powerful naturalistic images condemning the inhumanity of wars ancient or modern, anywhere in the world.

DETACHMENT AND FREEDOM

In its long lyrical tradition, Chinese poetry has developed a distinct philosophical attitude toward life that lays the aesthetic foundation for Chinese culture. It is a philosophy of life characterized by detachment and freedom. The modern Chinese critic Lin Yutang once put it this way: "after surveying the field of Chinese literature and philosophy, I come to the conclusion that the highest ideal of Chinese culture has always been a man with a sense of *detachment (takuan)* toward life based on a sense of wise disenchantment. From this detachment comes *high-mindedness (k'uanghuai)*, a high-mindedness which enables one to go through life with tolerant irony and escape the temptations of fame and wealth and achievement, and eventually makes him take what comes."[10]

---
[10] Lin Yutang, *The Importance of Living* p. 1–2.

Figure 9: Tao Yuanming

In Chinese poetic tradition, a poet whose poems exemplified precisely such spirit was Tao Yuanming (or Tao Qian, 365–427) of the Six Dynasties period. It is in Tao's poems where we find, in Lin's words again, "human wisdom first reaching full maturity in a spirit of tolerant irony."[11] But appreciation of Tao Yuanming and his poems actually took a long time to materialize in the Chinese tradition. In his own times, Tao was not particularly appreciated at all, as well-known critics either totally ignored him or ranked him as a middle-tier poet. During the Tang and Song dynasties, however, as Chinese poetry reached its unprecedented height not only in terms of technical sophistication but also in regard to aesthetic taste, Tao's stature grew. While Du Fu of the Tang Dynasty was an admirer, Su Dongpo exalted Tao — he wrote more than one hundred poems "echoing" Tao Yuanming as if he were a reincarnation of Tao. To Su Dongpo, the beauty of Tao's poems lies precisely in the simplicity of its language, which is nevertheless rich and profound in meaning — not even Du Fu's poems surpassed that combination. And to Su Dongpo, it was the poet Tao, namely, his character — as revealed through his poems — that provides exemplary incentives for inspiration.

While many of Tao's poems can be read as realistic depictions of his life, he actually wrote a short prose of autobiography — even though he was referred to in the third person:

> I don't know where this gentleman was born and I am not sure of his name, but beside his house were five willow trees, from

---
[11] Ibid. p. 115.

which he took his nickname. He was of a placid disposition and rarely spoke. He had no envy of fame or fortune. He was fond of reading, without puzzling greatly over difficult passages. When he came across something to his liking he would be so delighted he would forget his meals. By nature he liked wine, but being poor could not always come by it. Knowing the circumstances, his friends and relatives would invite him over when they had wine. He could not drink without emptying his cup, and always ended up drunk, after which he would retire, unconcerned about what might come. He lived alone in a bare little hut which gave no adequate shelter against rain and sun. His short coat was torn and patched, his cooking pots were frequently empty, but he was unperturbed. He used to write poems for his own amusement, and in them can be seen something of what he thought. He had no concern for worldly success, and so he ended his days.[12]

So Tao was also amicably referred to as "Mr. Five Willows" in Chinese literary history. This biography, short as it is, captures the key elements of Tao's life as well as his philosophy of life. The fact that he loves wine and is often drunk is real and frequently seen in his poems. But Tao's wine and drunkenness are also poetic camouflages for his spirit of tolerant irony. The key statements in the biography are that he "had no onvy of fame or fortune" and "no concern for worldly success." This is, of course, easier said than done. But he did it, and was happy for it. As we know, Tao once held a governmental official job that supported his family well enough. And if he held on to the position, and performed well, he could have developed a career out of it with the prospect of "fame and fortune." A poet with a strong personality, however, finds it difficult to be sociable and likable, particularly to his superiors, in order to pursue an upward career path. So Tao announced that he "would not *kowtow* and bow to his superiors for the sake of five bushels of rice (referring to his official salary)," and quit the job and returned to his farmland, and spent the rest of his life affirming his decision. That was a bold decision with serious consequences. For that, you'd have to endure poverty with his short coat "torn and patched" and his cooking

---

[12] James Robert Hightower trans. *The Poetry of T'ao Ch'ien* p. 4.

pots "frequently empty," as a farmer's work can barely support his family. Tao is perhaps one of the few poets who actually had to beg for food, as he wrote down in one of his poems:

乞食	**Begging for Food**
饥来驱我去	Hunger came and drove me out
不知竟何之	To go I had no notion where.
行行至斯里	I walked until I reached this town,
叩门拙言辞	Knocked at a door and fumbled for words.
主人解余意	The owner guessed what I was after
遗赠岂虚来	And gave it, but not just the gift alone.
谈谐终日夕	We talked together all day long,
觞至辄倾杯	And drained our cups as the bottle passed.
情欣新知欢	Happy in our new acquaintance
言咏遂赋诗	We sang old songs and wrote new poems.
感子漂母意	You are as kind as the washerwoman,
愧我非韩才	But to my shame I lack Han's talent.
衔戢知何谢	I have no way to show my thanks
冥报以相贻	And must repay you from the grave.[13]

It is against the backdrop of "fumbling for words" to beg for food that we must appreciate the celebrated "Return" or "Return to the Farm" — the central theme of Tao Yuanming's philosophy of life, as he celebrated in the following two poems, one is a *ci* poem while the other a five-character *shi* poem, both to the same effect:

归去来兮	Ah, homeward bound I go!
田园将芜胡不归	Why not go home, seeing that my field and garden with weeds are overgrown?

---

[13] Ibid., p. 62. "I lack Han's talent" refers to the story of Han Xin (231–196 BC), an able general who helped to found the Han Dynasty. When Han was poor and despondent in his youth, a washerwoman took pity on him and fed him for several weeks. Han offered to repay her when he became "rich and famous," but was refused by the washerwoman as she declared that she helped him not for reward.

既自以心为形役	Myself have made my soul serf to my body:
奚惆怅而独悲	Why have vain regrets and mourn alone?
悟已往之不谏	Fret not over bygones
知来者之可追	And the forward journey I take.
实迷途其未远	Only a short distance have I gone astray,
觉今是而昨非	And I know today I am right, and yesterday a mistake.
舟遥遥以轻飏	Lightly floats and drifts the boat,
风飘飘而吹衣	And gently flows and flaps my gown.
问征夫以前路	I inquire the road of a wayfarer,
恨晨光之熹微	And sulk at the dimness of the dawn.
乃瞻衡宇	Then when I catch sight of my old roofs,
载欣载奔	Filled with joy I run.
僮仆欢迎	The servant boy comes to welcome me,
稚子候门	My little son greets me at the door.
三径就荒	Gone to seed are my garden paths,
松菊犹存	But pines and chrysanthemums are still here.
携幼入室	I lead the young boy in by the hand,
有酒盈樽	And on the table there stands a cup full of wine!
引壶觞以自酌	Holding the pot and cup I give myself a drink,
眄庭柯以怡颜	Happy to see in the courtyard the hanging bough.
倚南窗以寄傲	I lean upon the southern window with an immense satisfaction,
审容膝之易安	And note that the little place is cosy enough to walk around.
园日涉以成趣	The garden grows more familiar and interesting with the daily walks.
门虽设而常关	What if no one knocks at the always closed door!
策扶老以流憩	Carrying a cane I wander at peace,
时矫首而遐观	And now and then look aloft to gaze at the blue above.

云无心以出岫	There the clouds idle away from their mountain recesses aimlessly,
鸟倦飞而知还	And birds, when tired of their wandering flights, will think of home.
景翳翳以将入	Darkly then fall the shadows and, ready to come home,
抚孤松而盘桓	I yet fondle the lonely pines and loiter around.
归去来兮	Ah, homeward bound I go!
请息交以绝游	Let me from now on learn to live alone!
世与我而相违	The world and I are not made for one another,
复驾言兮焉求	Why drive round like one looking for what he has not found?
悦亲戚之情话	Content shall I be with conversations with my own kin,
乐琴书以消忧	And there will be music and books to while away the hours.
农人告余以春及	The farmers will come and tell me that spring is here,
将有事于西畴	And there will be work to do at the western farm.
或命巾车	Some order covered wagons,
或棹孤舟	Some row in small boats.
既窈窕以寻壑	Sometimes we explore quiet, unknown ponds,
亦崎岖而经丘	And sometimes we climb over steep, rugged mounds.
木欣欣以向荣	There the trees, happy of heart, grow marvellously green,
泉涓涓而始流	And spring water gushes forth with a gurgling sound.
善万物之得时	I admire how things grow and prosper according to their seasons,
感吾生之行休	And feel that thus, too, shall my life go its round.

己矣乎	Enough!
寓形宇内复几时	How long yet shall I this mortal shape keep?
曷不委心任去留	Why not take life as it comes,
胡为乎遑遑欲何之	Why hustle and bustle like one on an errand bound?
富贵非吾愿	Wealth and power are not my ambitions,
帝乡不可期	And unattainable is the abode of the gods!
怀良辰以孤往	I would go forth alone on a bright morning,
或植杖而耘耔	Or perhaps, planting my cane, begin to pluck the weeds and till the ground.
登东皋以舒啸	Or I would compose a poem beside a clear stream,
临清流而赋诗	Or perhaps go up Tungkao and make a long-drawn call on the top of the hill.
聊乘化以归尽	So would I be content to live and die,
乐夫天命复奚疑	And without questionings of the heart, gladly accept Heaven's will.[14]

归园田居其一	**Return to the Farm**
少无适俗韵	From early days I have been at odds with the world,
性本爱丘山	My instinctive love is hills and mountains.
误落尘网中	By mischance I fell into the dusty net
一去三十年	And was thirteen years away from home.
羁鸟恋旧林	The migrant bird longs for its native grove,
池鱼思故渊	The fish in the pond recalls the former depths.
开荒南野际	Now I have cleared some land to the south of town,
守拙归园田	Simplicity intact, I have returned to farm.
方宅十余亩	The land I own amounts to a couple of acres
草屋八九间	The thatched-roof house has four or five rooms.

---

[14] Lin Yutang, *The Importance of Living* p. 118–120 Translation modified.

榆柳荫后檐	Elms and willows shade the eaves in back,
桃李罗堂前	Peach and plum stretch out before the hall.
暧暧远人村	Distant villages are lost in haze,
依依墟里烟	Above the houses smoke hangs in the air.
狗吠深巷中	A dog is barking somewhere in a hidden lane,
鸡鸣桑树颠	A cock crows from the top of a mulberry tree.
户庭无尘杂	My home remains unsoiled by worldly dust
虚室有余闲	Within bare rooms I have my peace of mind.
久在樊笼里	For long I was a prisoner in a cage
复得返自然	And now I have my freedom back again.[15]

Apparently, what Tao celebrates here is, simply, freedom. Tao does not elaborate much about what kind of "cage" he has been a "prisoner" of, except to say he is escaping from the "dusty net." This may, in a narrow sense, refer to his official life, but more broadly, it really refers to social life in general. In that sense, it is an indictment of the Confucian emphasis on governmental and societal engagement. What Tao Yuanming advocates is a Taoist retreat from the "dusty net." What is more interesting and significant, however, is what and where Tao Yuanming retreats to. Tao mentions that his "instinctive love is hills and mountains," but overwhelmingly, he returns to his "fields" — to a farmer's life: a couple of acres of land, the thatched-roof house, dogs barking and cocks crowing, mulberry trees, and, perhaps more importantly, to his family home: his sons welcoming him at the door and his wife having already prepared a cup of wine and placed it on the table. These things are of course most common in an ordinary farmers' life. Here, under Tao's poetic exaltation, they retain an entirely new and higher metaphorical meaning, as a safe haven for retreat from the "dusty net." And Tao Yuanming celebrates it with joy and content, with an enlightened broadmindedness that embraces the reward of freedom out of such detachment to live a simple life, even if it means, occasionally or perhaps more often than not, he would have to tolerate a life of poverty. This is Tao's spirit of "tolerant irony." In a fundamental sense, Tao's philosophy of life is also Confucian, even though it was an indictment and reaction to Confucian values of engagement, in that Tao's retreat is ultimately this-worldly — it lies, not necessarily even in "the

---

[15] James Robert Hightower trans. *The Poetry of T'ao Ch'ien* p. 50.

hills and mountains," but right here in the ordinary village, in a farmer's home. In the Warring States period, there emerged the first major poet in China's literary history, Qu Yuan (343–278 BC). Dissatisfied with the world he lived in and depressed about the metaphysical meaning of life, Qu Yuan composed "nine questionings to Heaven," and finding no answer, he committed suicide by drowning himself in the river. Today, the Chinese people celebrate the Dragon Boat Festival in memoriam of the poet. But after Tao Yuanming, no Chinese poets committed suicide until the modern time. Because Tao had pointed a way out — to embrace a simple farmer's life with an enlightened sense of "tolerant irony." Of course, Tao Yuanming is not just an ordinary farmer, but rather a poet-farmer. The image that goes down in Chinese literature is a poet-farmer "picking chrysanthemums by the eastern hedge/ looking over the distant southern hills," enjoying a simple and peaceful life, though as if lost in thought, as Tao describes it most eloquently in the following short poem:

饮酒其五	Drinking Wine (No. 5)
结庐在人境	I built a hut beside a travelled road
而无车马喧	Yet hear no noise of passing carts and horses.
问君何能尔	You would like to know how it is done?
心远地自偏	With the mind detached, one's place becomes remote.
采菊东篱下	Picking chrysanthemums by the eastern hedge
悠然见南山	I catch sight of the distant southern hills:
山气日夕佳	The mountain air is lovely as the sun sets
飞鸟相与还	And the flocks of flying birds return together.
此中有真意	In these things is a fundamental truth
欲辨已忘言	I would like to tell, but lack the words.[16]

Tao Yuanming maintains that he can achieve freedom (hearing no noise of passing carts and horses) while living in this world yet sufficiently detached from it (building a hut beside a travelled road, or literally, building a hut in the human world). As Buddhism exerted more and more influence on Chinese culture, however, there emerged a more radical kind of aesthetics, which argues that to achieve freedom one pretty much has to

---

[16] Ibid., p. 130.

leave this "human world" and "lose himself" "in the hills and mountains" to seek for instantaneous enlightenment. This is called "Chan" Buddhism, which was later spread to Japan and became very popular, and since called "Zen" Buddhism in English via Japanese translation. The best Chan poet was undoubtedly Wang Wei (699–759) of the Tang Dynasty, who was a renowned poet and painter, and a devout Buddhist. One of his well-known Chan poems is as follows:

竹里馆	**The Lodge in the Bamboo Grove**
独坐幽篁里	Alone I sit deep in the bamboo grove,
弹琴复长啸	Plucking the lute and whistling along.
深林人不知	In the deep woods: no one knows,
明月来相照	The bright moon comes to shine upon me.[17]

As one can see from the above example, Chan poems are usually short, composed in pentasyllabic quatrains (Japanese poetry has developed a three-line format called *haiku*). This is because they are supposed to capture "Chan" — an instantaneous religious enlightenment, to which words are really redundant and must be understood as a vehicle to be discarded as soon as enlightenment is attained. The poem portrays a religious atmosphere to facilitate our understanding of enlightenment, and this usually results in a rather impressionistic landscape painting. Wang Wei's Chan poems are serenely imagistic resembling a Chinese landscape painting, or what the Chinese call a scholarly painting, and the two are in fact inseparable — two sides of the same coin. As Su Dongpo put it, there is a painting in Wang Wei's poems, and a poem in his paintings. But there is hardly a man in it. Human figures in such paintings are usually so miniscule to be noticeable at all. As in the poem above, the point is certainly not about the lute player, but rather the atmosphere in which he is engrossed deep in the bamboo grove and the whistling sound that echoes around, and suddenly the bright moon shedding light all over.

While Wang Wei is well known both in China and the world, another monk poet of the Tang Dynasty by the name of Hanshan (literally, Cold Mountain)

---

[17] Jie Cui and Zong-qi Cai eds, *How to Read Chinese Poetry* p. 55.

was somewhat known and somewhat obscure in Chinese literary history, but achieved international fame in modern times. In revolting against the materialist values of our modern world and to seek for individual freedom, the anti-establishment youth in the 1960s found an ally in Eastern Chan Buddhism, and the noted American poet Gary Snyder resurrected Hanshan through his translation of "Cold Mountain poems," as in the following:

可笑寒山道	The path to Han-shan's place is laughable,
而无车马踪	A path, but no sign of cart or horse.
取溪难记曲	Converging gorges — hard to trace their twists
叠嶂不知重	Jumbled cliffs — unbelievably rugged.
泣露千般草	A thousand grasses bend with dew,
吟风一样松	A hill of pines hums in the wind.
此时迷径处	And now I've lost the shortcut home,
形问影何从	Body asking shadow, how do you keep up?[18]

Interestingly, this poem echoes Tao Yuanming's "Drinking Wine" cited above in a number of ways. Like Tao's poems, Hanshan's poems also employ very simple (perhaps deceptively so) language. The questioning between "body and shadow" is also a recurring metaphor in Tao's poems. The poetic diction of "carts and horses" are exactly the same. But we see a clear difference of aesthetic taste: Tao Yuanming's idea of detachment is "to build a hut in this human world while hearing no noise of carts and horses," Hanshan's path (to enlightenment) sees "no signs of cart or horse." Tao's world is a lonely world of a recluse poet, even a harsh world of poverty, but nevertheless still a warm one where you find cocks crowing and dogs barking in his "fields and gardens." Hanshan's is a quiet and serene world of a monk poet, a world of "Cold Mountains."

In the end, I believe the Chinese much prefer a warmer world of detachment for individual and spiritual freedom, a world of simple life with simple joys, such as depicted in the following poem translated by the twentieth-century Chinese philosopher and cross-cultural critic Lin Yutang. This poem does not have an authorship attributing to a great

---

[18] Gary Snyder, *No Nature* p. 23.

poet, rather it was a popular poem circulating among the educated literary class by the late imperial period. It was translated as "Be Merry Poems," or literally, "Happy Recluse Poems":

水竹之居	I love my bamboo hut, by water included
吾爱吾庐	Where rockery o'er stone steps protruded
石磷磷乱砌阶除	A quiet, peaceful study, small but fine:
轩窗随意	Which is so cozy,
小巧规模	So delightful,
却也清幽	So secluded.
也潇洒	
也宽舒	
阆苑瀛洲	No marble halls, no vermillion towers
金谷红楼	Are quite so good as my secluded bowers
算不如茅舍清幽	The lawn embroidered so with buttercups
野花绣地	Greets me in rain —
莫也风流	Or in shine —
也宜春	Or in showers.
也宜夏	
也宜秋	
短短横墙	A short, low wall, with windows hid by trees;
矮矮疏窗	A tiny, little pond myself to please;
忔憎儿小小池塘	And there upon its shady banks:
高低叠障	The fresh air —
绿水旁边	A little moon —
也有些风	A little breeze!
有些月	
有些凉	
懒散无拘	And how about a quiet life leading?
此等何如	From balcony watch the fish feeding,
倚阑干临水观鱼	And earn from moon and flowers a leisure life:
风花雪月	Have friendly chats —
赢得功夫	Some incense —
好炷些香	And some reading?
说些话	
读些书	

日用家常	For household use, some furniture decrepit.
竹几藤床	Tis enough! The hills and water so exquisite!
靠眼前水色山光	When guests arrive, if there's no wine:
客来无酒	Put on the kettle —
清话何妨	Brew the tea —
但细烹茶	And sip it!
热烘盏	
浅烧汤	
净扫尘埃	O sweep thy yard, but spare the mossy spots!
惜尔苍苔	Let petals bedeck thy steps with purple dots.
任门前红叶铺阶	As in a painting! What' more wonderful:
也堪图画	Some pine trees —
还有奇哉	And bamboos —
有数株松	And apricots!
数竿竹	
数枝梅	
酒熟堪酾	When friend arrives that thou hast so admired,
客至须留	As by some idle nothing in common inspired,
更无荣辱无忧	Ask him to stay and throw away all cares:
退闲一步	And drink when happy —
着甚东西	Sing when drunk —
但倦时眠	Sleep when tired.
渴时饮	
醉时讴	
花木栽培	Let bloom in order pear and peach and cherry!
取次教开	The morrow lies in the gods, lap — why worry?
明朝事天自安排	Who knows but what and when our fortune is?
知他富贵几时来	And so be wise —
且优游	Be content —
且随分	Be merry![19]
且开怀	

---

[19] Lin Yutang, "Yi leyin shi bashou".

Chapter 5

The Rise of Modern Chinese Nationalism

When we talk about "Chinese culture" today, although we are well into the twenty-first century, it still quite often invokes the images of Confucius or calligraphy, the Great Wall or the terracotta warriors, Tai-chi or martial arts movies. These are certainly a part of the Chinese culture even today, and they remain as a part of the legacies of tradition. But if one's idea of "Chinese culture" still remains in the time-frozen zone of "ancient Cathay," as if "culture" and "China" are incongruent entities, it will certainly be detrimental to our understanding of Chinese culture. To understand Chinese culture is to understand Chinese culture as it is today. A Chinese today, in terms of his (and her!) *modus vivendi*, lifestyles, ideas and demeanors, is very different from someone who lived a hundred-fifty or a hundred years ago. Chinese culture has gone through a gigantic modern transformation, which is still witnessing ongoing change. Chinese culture today is a mixture of tradition and modernity, and for that matter, the effects of its modernity, even though only for a very short time period compared to its millennia-old tradition, outshine those of tradition. While culture may take ages to consolidate and take shape, it is also true that it can change dramatically in a short period of time, as evidenced by the modern Chinese experience.

Chinese culture as we know it today is a result of civilizational clashes between China and the West in the past 180 years. The clashes occurred when China and the West met in the form of the opium trade and through the role of Western missionaries who acted in effect as "cultural messengers." These events had devastating consequences for the opening up of Chinese modernity, one of which was the rise of a new consciousness — Chinese nationalism, a major feature of Chinese culture today.

OPIUM AND MISSIONARIES

The Chinese were not the inventors or architects of modernity that has been encompassing and engrossing the whole world. Nevertheless, the Chinese were forced into transforming their culture into modernity as a matter of survival because by the mid-nineteenth century, Western imperialism was already knocking at the door of China. In fact, the "Far East" was the very last frontier to be conquered by global imperialist enterprises that had initiated from a few European powers. It was most unfortunate that the encounter between the two civilizations took the form of opium trade. It is even more unfortunate that even today, when some of the dehumanizing trauma of the colonial experience, such as the slave trade, have been recognized and universally condemned, little attention has been paid to the opium trade in the West. As it symbolizes the beginning of Chinese modernity and plants the seeds for the rise of modern Chinese nationalism, the story needs to be told and understood.

It would be misleading to think that the mid-nineteenth-century encounter between China and the West was the very first time the two civilizations ever met. Just to name a few well-known interactions: the ancient Silk Road facilitated trade, most importantly silk, from China to Rome; groups of Jews came to settle in Kaifeng during the Song Dynasty; the travels of Marco Polo was one of the major incentives to ignite the European global exploration; and Jesuit missionaries came during the Ming Dynasty leaving an important legacy (more on this later). None of this, however, had a major impact upon the Chinese culture and its way of life. By the late imperial period, or during the Ming and Qing dynasties, China had made significant developments in commerce while becoming more authoritarian and autocratic in politics. After the fall of the Ming Dynasty, the Manchu Dynasty, as non-Chinese conquerors, were eager to demonstrate they were more Chinese than the Chinese themselves by upholding Confucian values in a rigid manner. Under the Confucian scheme, trade and commerce could not, and had never been, a priority for the government. There were already well-established four-tier social strata with scholar-officials at the top, followed by farmers and craftsmen, and merchants at the bottom. While commerce and trade were constrained and not encouraged within China, it should not be of any wonder that any form of foreign trade would be strictly regulated.

Despite its ideological constraint, trade and commerce flourished in the Ming and Qing dynasties even to the extent that the stigma of merchants being at the bottom of social strata was in name only — a wealthy merchant family would, for instance, make sure their eldest son would take the Civil Examination and become a scholar-official, while his younger brothers would become traders. The rise of the commerce and merchant class in late imperial China was in fact partly due to the first wave of global trade, the so-called Silver Age, opened up by the Portuguese and the Spanish. By the early nineteenth century, the British Empire ruled the waves and, through its East India Company, controlled the Eurasian trade. From the eighteenth century to the early part of the nineteenth century, British trade with China encompassed all imports from China resulting in large amounts of silver going to China as payment for such commodities as tea and porcelain to meet popular demand at home. Then the British East India Company devised an ingenious way to revert the trade deficit. They started to grow the narcotic drug opium in Indian colonies and then smuggled them into China via local Chinese merchants.

After decades of stealthy trade, its impact began to alarm the Qing court and the Emperor. Not only was the drug draining silver out of China, it was creating huge social problems with millions of addicts including those serving in the Qing army. In 1839, the Daoguang Emperor sent the scholar-official Lin Zexu (1785–1850) to Guangdong as Special Commissioner to ban the opium trade. Lin demanded the surrender of all opium supplies and destroyed them publicly at Humen in Guangdong. Knowing that the opium trade

Figure 10: Lin Zexu

was actually carried out with the knowledge and assent of the sovereign of England, which was hard to believe on the Chinese part, Lin wrote a letter to Queen Victoria, hoping the problem could be solved from its source:

> The Way of Heaven is fairness to all; it does not suffer us to harm others in order to benefit ourselves. Men are alike in this all the world over: that they cherish life and hate what endangers life. Your country lies twenty thousand leagues away; but for all that the Way of Heaven holds good for you as for us, and your instincts are not different from ours; for nowhere are there men so blind as not to distinguish between what brings life and what brings death, between what brings profit and what does harm. Our Heavenly Court treats all within the Four Seas as one great family; the goodness of our great Emperor is like Heaven that covers all things. There is no region so wild or so remote that he does not cherish and tend it. Ever since the port of Canton was first opened, trade has flourished. For some hundred and twenty or thirty years the natives of the place have enjoyed peaceful and profitable relations with the ships that come from abroad. Rhubarb, tea, silk are all valuable products of ours, without which foreigners could not live. The Heavenly Court, extending its benevolence to all alike, allows these things to be sold and carried away across the sea, not grudging them even to remote domains, its bounty matching the bounty of Heaven and Earth.
>
> But there is a class of evil foreigner that makes opium and brings it for sale, tempting fools to destroy themselves, merely in order to reap profit. Formerly the number of opium smokers was small; but now the vice has spread far and wide and the poison penetrated deeper and deeper......It appears that this poisonous article is manufactured by certain devilish persons in places subject to your rule. It is not, of course, either made or sold at your bidding, nor do all the countries you rule produce it, but only certain of them. I am told that in your own country opium smoking is forbidden under severe penalties. This means that you are aware of how harmful it is. But better than to forbid the smoking of it would be to forbid the sale of it and, better

still, to forbid the production of it, which is the only way of cleansing the contamination at its source. So long as you do not take it yourselves, but continue to make it and tempt the people of China to buy it, you will be showing yourselves careful of your own lives, but careless of the lives of other people, indifferent in your greed to gain to the harm you do to others; such conduct is repugnant to human feeling and at variance with the Way of Heaven. Our Heavenly Court's resounding might, redoubtable to its own subjects and foreigners alike, could at any moment control their fate; but in its compassion and generosity it makes a practice of giving due warning before it strikes. Your Majesty has not before been thus officially notified, and you may plead ignorance of the severity of our laws. But I now give my assurance that we mean to cut off this harmful drug for ever. What it is here forbidden to consume, your dependencies must be forbidden to manufacture, and what has already been manufactured Your Majesty must immediately search out and throw it to the bottom of the sea, and never again allow such a poison to exist in Heaven or on earth. When that is done, not only will the Chinese rid of this evil, but your people too will be safe. For so long as your subjects make opium, who knows but they will not sooner or later take to smoking it; so that an embargo on the making of it may very well be a safeguard for them, too. Both nations will enjoy the blessing of a peaceful existence, yours on its side having made clear its sincerity by respectful obedience to our commands. You will be showing that you understand the principles of Heaven, and calamities will be not sent down on you from above; you will be acting in accordance with decent feeling, which may also well influence the course of nature in your favour......[1]

Historians today make a big deal of the hypothesis that the letter had probably never reached Queen Victoria, as if it would have mattered (or even if it did, anybody would be competent to translate it). Even today, this letter invites scorn from Jonathan Spence, an eminent authority on modern Chinese history, when he comments that Lin "seemed to have believed that the citizens

---

[1] Arthur Waley, *The Opium War Through Chinese Eyes* pp. 28–31.

of Canton and the foreign traders there had simple, childlike natures that would respond to firm guidance and statements of moral principles set out in simple, clear terms."[2] In contrast to such latter-day coldblooded sophistry, however, there were actually many "simple and childlike" Victorians who sided with Lin and regarded it a disgrace for Great Britain to wage a war with China over the opium trade. William Gladstone, who later became Prime Minister four times in his life, was a "simple and childlike" statesman who opposed the war and regarded it as "a war more unjust in its origin, a war more calculated in its progress to cover this country with permanent disgrace" and as such, he was "in dread of the judgments of God upon England for our national iniquity towards China." Lin Zexu and Gladstone were too innocent to believe that British imperial interests, as represented by then Foreign Secretary Palmerston and opium trader William Jardine, would take into account "the principles of Heaven" or "the judgements of God." And it should also be noted that the Opium War was waged in accordance with democratic institutional mechanisms, as the matter was debated in the Parliament and it was Palmerston and Jardine who won the vote.

Lin Zexu was also innocent to believe that "Our Heavenly Court's resounding might" could control China's fate. To protect and promote "international trade," Britain sent its Royal Navy consisting of 4,000 troops to China's coast and China's coastal fortresses proved to be powerless against modern gunboats. Not only did the Royal Navy invade Guangdong but went up the coast all the way north to Tianjin, threatening the capital, and was poised to attack Nanjing when the Qing government had to surrender and sign the Treaty of Nanjing. According to the treaty, China was to cede the island of Hong Kong as a British colony, pay a war indemnity of 21 million silver dollars, open up five treaty ports — Canton, Xiamen, Fuzhou, Ningbo, and Shanghai — where British merchants and missionaries can reside, among other things. This was the beginning of a series of humiliating and unequal (Chinese call "gedi peikuan" — ceding territory and paying indemnities) treaties that China had to sign with various powers in the coming "hundred years of humiliation." After the British, the Americans, the French, and the Russians pursued their own treaties with China with various other supplements, and chief among them was the principle of extraterritoriality,

---

[2] Jonathan Spence, *The Search for Modern China* pp. 152–153.

according to which foreign nationals will be subject to their own national laws instead of the Chinese court. And the British did not have to worry that other nations would have an upper hand with more favorable terms as they would enjoy the "most favored nation status." In other words, all the benefits negotiated by other nations will be shared by the British. Except for compensating opium traders for their losses, however, the treaty did not resolve the issue of the opium trade. That would have to be settled in the Second Opium War (1856–1860) between China and the allied forces of Britain and France with collaborative assistance from the Americans and the Russians. The consequent Treaty of Tianjin demanded China to cede Kowloon to the British, pay 8 million silver dollars of war indemnity in addition to legalization of the opium trade, opening up of more treaty ports and granting Western missionaries the right to evangelize and own property throughout China. Two incidents of the Second Opium War have been memorialized into the modern Chinese national consciousness. During the First Opium War, the Qing army already had a taste of what a gunboat was capable of, but they did not realize the urgency of the crisis. More than a decade later, when the Qing court had to defend the capital against the invading British and French allied forces, they sent the elite Mongol cavalry who launched heroic, but suicidal, frontal charges against the gunfire of the British and French army — a vivid testimony of the clashes between a largely agricultural civilization and an industrialized one. When the allied forces got hold of the capital, they looted the city, grabbed many invaluable artworks from the imperial Summer Palace (Yuanmingyuan), and then burned it — its ruins now stand in Beijing as symbols for humiliation and artifacts of patriotism.

It was most unfortunate that opium acted as the impetus for the meeting of the East and the West. It was no less unfortunate that the first significant cross-cultural messengers were missionaries. One of the aftermaths of opium wars was the flood of Western missionaries in China as warranted by the treaties. It should be noted that this was not the first time Western missionaries came to China. Matteo Ricci (1552–1610) arrived in Macao in 1582 and from there he traveled to Beijing and was received by Emperor Wanli of the Ming Dynasty. The Jesuit mission in China was characterized by the accommodation strategy in which Ricci dressed himself as a Confucian scholar, mingled with and converted several prominent Confucian scholars by arguing that Christian beliefs were not alien to Chinese beliefs, but rather natural extensions and completion of them. When the Ming Dynasty was overthrown, the Jesuit missionaries remained and were welcomed to Emperor Kangxi's court. It was during Yongzheng's reign that China's door was closed to missionaries, for fear that Christian ideas, once spread to the masses, would induce unrest and turmoil. A couple of hundred years later though, along with the opium trade came a different type of missionary group, mostly Protestant, who showed little regard for Chinese culture and little interest in converting the ruling literati class. Instead, they targeted the marginal of the Chinese society — often in remote countrysides, mountainous areas, and the poorest regions — for converts. The missionaries were, however, opposed to the opium trade. Instead, they built churches, schools, and hospitals, and relied on material benefits to attract the Chinese converts, such that there were many so-called "rice Christians."

The introduction of the Christian mission into China triggered two major rebellions that devastated China and contributed a great deal to the rise of modern Chinese nationalism and communism. The Second Opium War was fought in the middle of the Taiping Rebellion that lasted from 1850 to 1864; it ravaged half of China (mostly in the South) and almost overthrew the Qing Dynasty. The rebellion started out in Guangxi, a mountainous province with many minority residents in the South, which was also devastated by the opium trade and frequently visited by Western missionaries. It was led by Hong Xiuquan (1814–1864) who was a Hakka minority and had failed the Civil Examination several times. Frustrated and destitute, Hong became seriously ill and had "mystical visions" lying in bed. Afterward, he pondered over what those dreams meant, and suddenly remembered a pamphlet from a Protestant missionary. The dreams were telling him, Hong proclaimed, that he was God-sent, as the younger brother of Jesus Christ, to lead a rebellion to get rid of "devils" — the Manchu government and Confucian teachings! He then went to Guangzhou to learn the Bible from an American Baptist missionary. He started preaching his own brand of Christianity and soon gathered followers. Mainly composed of Hakka people and Southern minorities, the uprising was very successful and swept across the southern part of China, and in just three years the rebel forces occupied Nanjing and established its own government called *Taiping Tianguo*, the Heavenly Kingdom of Peace, in the name of Christianity.

This "Heavenly Kingdom of Peace" was a brutal regime unprecedented in Chinese history, however. There were many popular uprisings overthrowing existing dynasties in Chinese history, in fact, the only means for dynastic changes as mentioned before. But this one had a cloak of a foreign religion, a foreign religion associated with the gunboat. It is customary to claim that Hong Xiuquan's Christianity is of his own making, and therefore not "authentic." That argument apparently ignores the fact there have been so many different sects in Christianity itself, and it would be foolhardy to believe any religion can be "authentic" when it meets and gets absorbed into a different culture. The Taiping Rebellion was eventually suppressed by local armies organized by the Confucian literati class (more on this in Chapter 7), but it was a last-ditch victory for the Confucians as they proved not to be up to the bigger challenge of transforming Chinese culture into modernity.

After the Taiping Rebellion, China went through the so-called "Self-strengthening Movement" led by literati-scholars like Zeng Guofan, Li Hongzhang, and Zhang Zhidong (1837–1909). After three decades of reform efforts, however, China was humiliated in another disastrous war, this time against the Japanese in the First Sino-Japanese War (1894–1895), which greatly shattered the confidence of the ruling literati class. This was followed by the tumultuous Hundred Days' Reform in 1898 endorsed by the young Emperor Guangxu to turn China into a constitutional monarchy, only to be curtailed, and the young Emperor was put under house arrest by Empress Dowager Cixi. In the meantime, Cixi had to deal with another popular uprising, the so-called Boxer's Rebellion (1898–1900), this time to support the Qing government against Western imperialism, particularly against Western missionaries.

The Boxers was a grassroot Chinese martial-arts organization, originated in Shandong province, who practiced martial arts, or *kung fu*, and claimed that such practice could make their body bullet-proof. The hostilities against missionary activities had been a long time in the making and were seeded in the treaties of the Opium Wars. Not only did the opium continue to be a social and economic problem well into the twentieth century, but the stipulation that the foreigners enjoyed extraterritoriality and missionaries could evangelize anywhere in the country under the protection of extraterritoriality, also caused much resentment among the local communities. As Gu Hongming commented in "*DEFENSIO POPULI AD POPULOS*, or The Modern Missionaries Considered in Relation to the Recent Riots," the Christian mission was supposed to help with "the moral elevation of the people," but instead it was "an open secret that it is only the worst, the weak, the ignorant, the needy, and the vicious among the Chinese" who had been converted, like those in the Taiping Rebellion, "which ought properly be called by the future historians of China, the Rebellion of the Chinese Outcasts of the Christian Missions in China."[3]

Hostilities and confrontations occurred at the grassroot level. Among Lutheran missionaries were some group of robbers who pillaged the city during the day and came back to the German legation quarters (which was outside Chinese jurisdiction) at night. There were also rumors that inside those churches, these "foreign devils" gauged out the eyes of the Chinese. So the Boxers started killing missionaries, in the name of "Supporting the Qing Government and Driving out the Foreigners." And Empress Dowager Cixi fell for it, declared war with the Eight Allied Powers — Britain, France, Russia, the United States, Germany, Italy, Austria-Hungary, and Japan. Encouraged by imperial support, the Boxers came to Beijing and besieged the Legation Quarters. The Eight Allied Powers then sent 20,000 troops and crushed the rebellion — their bullets did shoot through the bodies of those who had practiced years of martial arts. The allied victory was followed by looting and random killing. Empress Dowager Cixi had to flee the capital, and then was forced to send representatives to talk peace - at a great cost: an indemnity of 450 million taels of silver, more than the Qing government's tax revenue, to be paid over the next thirty-nine years, which literally made the Qing government bankrupt. In addition, foreign troops were to be stationed in Beijing.

China entered the twentieth century as a "hyper-colony," that is, under the threat of not one master but a cohort of masters. Or, according to a famous French cartoon, China was helplessly being carved up by the Powers.

---

[3] Gu Hongming (Ku Hung-Ming), *Papers from a Viceroy's Yamen*, pp. 37–38.

ARISE! YE WHO REFUSE TO BE BOND SLAVES!

Here is the distinctive feature of Chinese nationalism: the rise of modern Chinese nationalism began when the Chinese realized that they were a part of the new world of nations and were being colonized by powerful nations. The modern Chinese consciousness arises from this historical process of self-discovery in face of the encroachment of different powers, first Western powers in the nineteenth century and after the First Sino-Japanese War, particularly the Japanese.

It took humiliating defeats in a series of wars with the Western powers for the Chinese gentry class to begin to realize what kind of "world" they were now living in. During the so-called Self-strengthening Movement, the predominant concern was the gunboat power and how China could learn to acquire that power. In the treatise "On the Manufacture of Foreign Weapons" by Feng Guifen (1809–1874), generally considered a foremost theorist for the Self-strengthening Movement, we read the following lines:

> According to a general geography compiled by an Englishman, the territory of China is eight times that of Russia, ten times that of the United States, one hundred times that of France, and two hundred times that of Great Britain......Yet we are shamefully humiliated by the four nations, not because our climate, soil, or resources are inferior to theirs, but because our people are inferior......We should use the instruments of the barbarians, but not adopt the ways of the barbarians. We should use them so that we can repel them......Only thus can we restore our original strength, redeem ourselves from former humiliations, and maintain the integrity of our vast territory so as to remain the greatest country on earth.[4]

Here we see a new Chinese consciousness characterized by the new geographical knowledge of China in the world. It recognizes the power of weapons but is not ready yet to concede its own "civilized ways" to the "ways of the barbarians." From the beginning, this new consciousness was accompanied by a sense of humiliation, and aspired to be "the

---

[4] Feng Guifeng, *Jiaobinlu kangyi*, pp. 197–200.

greatest country on earth" — in such aspiration, though, it already tacitly acknowledged that China is now one nation among many, and one of the least powerful for that matter despite its largesse.

Ever since the Self-strengthening Movement, China embarked on the road to achieve "wealth and power" for the state — a quintessential nationalist goal. Merely intent on manufacturing weapons won't get you there, however, and China's humiliation reached its climax when it lost to Japan in the First Sino-Japanese War (1894–1895). The war signaled the rise of Japan as a world power. Just as China was trying to modernize herself during the Self-strengthening Movement, during which, for instance, it built the largest navy in East Asia, Japan was also racing on the path to modernization after the Meiji Restoration (1868). During the war, however, the Beiyang Navy, the crown symbol of the Reform movement, was destroyed by the Japanese counterpart. And China had to sign a "peace treaty" by ceding Taiwan as Japanese colony plus a huge war indemnity. Japan was traditionally a tributary state and was considered a "little brother" for patronage, though sometimes troublesome. This defeat completely shattered the Chinese confidence once and for all. The spectre of Revolution was on the horizon.

In the aftermath of the war, a deep sense of crisis gripped the nation: "The Crisis of China today has no parallel either in the Spring and Autumn period or in all the dynasties from the Qin and Han down through the Yuan and Ming," as the famous literati-scholar Zhang Zhidong put it. Zhang's was one of a plethora of voices that came forth after the war demanding for change and was considered on the conservative side, as it wanted to uphold "Chinese learning as the foundation" during such transformation. Nevertheless, it is interesting to observe that Zhang's argument for the "foundation for Chinese learning" was based on a nationalist sense of self: "If a Chinese student does not know Chinese learning, it's like a person without a surname, a horse without a bridle, a boat without a helm. The more Western learning he possesses, the more hateful of China he will become. Even if he becomes a capable man of vast learning, how can he be of any use to the state?"[5] Instead of appealing to the Queen of England about the immorality of the opium trade, Zhang appealed to Confucian

---

[5] Zhang Zhidong, *Quan xue pian*, p. 91.

inner-self-cultivation and called on the youth to internalize the sense of humiliation — know thy shame:

> "Confucius says: 'Know thy shame, thou shall have courage.' Mencius says: 'If you are not ashamed of being inferior to others, how can you achieve what others have achieved?' Opium is a poisonous drug despised and prohibited by all other countries in the world, but in our China, the entire country is addicted to it as if to seek self-destruction... To revive Confucianism, we must begin with the act of giving up opium by educating the people with a sense of shame."[6]

After the fiascos of the Hundred Days' Reform and the Boxer's Rebellion, Empress Dowager Cixi had to institute a series of reforms, including, for instance, abolishing the thousand-year-old Civil Examination system in 1905. But it all turned out to be too late, as the tides of revolution were sweeping the country. The days of the Qing Dynasty itself were numbered. It finally crumbled in the Revolution of 1911 and the first "republic" in Asia — Republic of China (ROC) was founded on January 1, 1912 with Dr. Sun Yat-sen (1866–1925) as the first President, even though Dr. Sun was in exile overseas when the Revolution took place. After China's defeat in the First Sino-Japanese War, the Nationalist Revolution gradually became the mainstream force, thanks to the relentless efforts of its

Figure 11: Sun Yat-sen

---

[6] Ibid, p. 106.

leader Dr. Sun Yat-sen, who founded the Nationalist Party, or KMT, and put forward his theory of *Sanmin zhuyi* — the Three Principles of the People, namely, nationalism (*minzu*), democracy (*minquan*), and welfare (*minsheng*). For much of the 20th century, China was engulfed in a competition between nationalism and communism ideologically, and between the Nationalists (Kuomintang, KMT) and the Communists (Chinese Communist Party, CCP) politically with a very ironical result: while the KMT lost the mainland and retreated to Taiwan, nationalism had now overtaken communism as the accepted official discourse by the CCP regime today. It is no wonder that Dr. Sun Yat-sen is considered the Father of modern China by both KMT and CCP.

Dr. Sun's "Three Principles of the People" served as the foundation for a rallying call for Nationalist revolutions, which not only overthrew the Qing Dynasty but also led China to eventual victory in the War of Resistance against Japan. Many of Dr. Sun's themes have sunk deep in modern Chinese consciousness. Like Zhang Zhidong, Dr. Sun tried to instigate a deep sense of urgency and crisis that China was faced with. And he went one step further by giving a new name to this crisis:

> Our people keep thinking that China is only a "semi-colony" — a term by which they seek to comfort themselves. Yet in reality......It is the colony of every nation with which it has concluded treaties; each of them is China's master. Therefore China is not just the colony of one country; it is the colony of many countries. We are not just the slaves of one country, but the slaves of many countries...... Therefore, to call China a "semi-colony" is quite incorrect. If I may coin a phrase, we should be called a "hyper-colony."[7]

In the face of such existential crisis, China could rely on nothing but a new sense of nationalism to save herself:

> Today we are the poorest and weakest nation in the world, and occupy the lowest position in international affairs. Other men are

---
[7] Sun Yat-sen, *Sources of Chinese Tradition*, pp. 107–108.

> the carving knife and serving dish; we are the fish and the meat. Our position at this time is most perilous. If we do not earnestly espouse nationalism and weld together our four hundred million people into a strong nation, there is danger of China's being lost and our people being destroyed.[8]

And more importantly, Dr. Sun offered a most powerful explanation as to why China suffered from such a crisis and why nationalism was the only way out:

> For the most part the four hundred million people of China can be spoken of as completely Han Chinese. With common customs and habits, we are completely of one race. But in the world today what position do we occupy? Compared to the other peoples of the world we have the greatest population and our civilization is four thousand years old; we should therefore be advancing in the front rank with the nations of Europe and America. But the Chinese people have only family and clan solidarity; they do not have national spirit. Therefore even though we have four hundred million people gathered together in one China, in reality they are just a heap of loose sand.[9]

The Chinese referred to as "a heap of loose sand" became the most powerful metaphor for arousing Chinese nationalism, as it strikes at an essential pulse of Chinese culture. Chinese culture, as we have discussed before, had relied on the polity of family-state in which people's identities are based on family and clan lineages. This is, for instance, most evident in the social and organizational structures of overseas Chinese communities in the late nineteenth and early twentieth centuries. This is also part of the reason why the Chinese lost in the series of wars with Western powers because it was not the "Chinese" who were fighting against foreign powers, but rather the Manchu royal family and their army. In fact, during

---
[8] Ibid, p. 107.
[9] Ibid, pp. 106–107.

the Opium Wars, for instance, many Chinese were helping the British and the French. Not only were there Chinese merchants serving as middlemen for the opium trade, but Chinese workers were hired to carry and load cannons on the gunboats. The "numbness" of the Chinese was best captured in an autobiographical story by Lu Xun (1881–1936), the most celebrated modern Chinese writer. Lu Xun went to study in Japan in his youth and he chose medicine as his subject. In some of his classes when the lecture ended early, as he recounts:

> The instructor would show slides of scenery or current events. The Russo-Japanese War (1904–1905) was being fought at the time and, understandably, a good number of slides were devoted to the military situation. And so it was that I often had to become part of the fun as my classmates clapped and cheered. At the time, I hadn't seen any of my fellow Chinese in a long time, but one day some of them showed up in a slide. One, with his hands tied behind them, was in the middle of the picture; the others were gathered around him. Physically, they were as strong and healthy as anyone could ask, but their expressions revealed all too clearly that *spiritually* they were calloused and numb. According to the caption, the Chinese whose hands were bound had been spying on the Japanese military for the Russians. He was about to be decapitated as a "public example." The other Chinese gathered around him had come to enjoy the spectacle.[10]

Lu Xun's main point was the last sentence: that crowds of Chinese had "come to enjoy the spectacle" as if it was none of their business — "it" means the fact that a major war between two foreign powers were being fought on Chinese territory (the Northeast of China, or Manchuria), and the fact that a Chinese compatriot allegedly sided with one of them and was about to be beheaded in a spectacle. Lu Xun then concluded bitterly that it would be utterly pointless to become a modern physician to help build strong Chinese bodies — it was their mind that needed enlightening, and he decided to become a writer to shake up the Chinese mind.

---

[10] Lu Xun, *Diary of a Madman and Other Stories*, p. 23.

Lu Xun became a leading writer of the Literary Revolution, which was considered part of the New Culture Movement that very much shaped up modern Chinese culture as we know it today. While the New Culture Movement was cosmopolitan in nature in its open embrace of Western cultural ideas, as we will discuss in more detail in Chapter 6, it also had its nationalist impulses. While Lu Xun's autobiographical story was taken as a quintessential nationalist metaphor, he was most well-known as the fiercest iconoclast condemning traditional Confucianism during the New Culture Movement. That was hardly appreciated by the Nationalists. According to Dr. Sun's "Three Principles of the People," traditional Chinese culture still had a major role to play, as he put it:

> Besides arousing a sense of national solidarity uniting all our people, we must recover and restore our characteristic, traditional morality. Only thus can we hope to attain again the distinctive position of our people.
>
> This characteristic morality the Chinese people today have still not forgotten. First comes loyalty and filial piety, then humanity and love, faithfulness and duty, harmony and peace...... Now, under foreign oppression, we have been invaded by a new culture, the force of which is felt all across the nation. Men wholly intoxicated by this new culture have thus begun to attack the traditional morality, saying that with the adoption of the new culture, we no longer have need of the old morality......This kind of reasoning is certainly mistaken.[11]

While Dr. Sun's "Three Principles of the People" exerted tremendous influence in the formation of modern Chinese identity, politically he was very much a failure. The founding of the ROC did not put China quickly on the path to "wealth and power," rather it suffered from its birth pains. While Dr. Sun was initially heralded to serve as the provisional President of the republic, internal power struggles followed and the military strongman Yuan Shikai (1859–1916) emerged as the President of the republic. Then

---

[11] Sun Yat-sen, *Sources of Chinese Tradition*, p. 109.

Dr. Sun called for a "Second Revolution," but his KMT forces were crushed by Yuan who headed the first modern army having been built up in the last years of the Qing government. But Yuan's rule turned out to be short-lived as well. He did try to institute modernizing measures for reform but felt instinctively against sharing power with a parliament. In the end, Yuan announced in 1916 that he was restoring monarchy with himself as the new Emperor. But that turned out to be a gross misjudgment as the Chinese public were in no frame of mind to go back to monarchy. Yuan ended up being deserted by friends and foes alike and died shortly afterward out of depression and illness. China entered the so-called Warlord Period with various generals previously under Yuan jostling for power in the Beiyang government.

A major reason that Yuan's government lost any credibility was the fact that Yuan signed a secret (later leaked to the public) agreement with the Japanese accepting their notorious "Twenty-One Demands." These demands basically meant that Japan should enjoy all the treaty benefits that the Qing government had signed with Western powers. During the 1910s, the external threat of being carved up by Western powers was somewhat lessened as they were busy engaging themselves in the bloody First World War. But a new monster was on the horizon — it became increasingly apparent that Japan attempted to swallow China alone. When the "Twenty-One Demands" were made public, it ignited nationwide anti-Japanese protests and boycotts of Japanese goods. From then on, Chinese nationalism became increasingly associated with, and eventually synonymous with, popular resistance against Japanese aggressions.

During the First World War, China joined the Allied side by sending hundreds and thousands of Chinese laborers to dig war ditches on the condition that all German spheres of influence would be returned to China. When the Allies won the war, Chinese representatives were sent to Versailles, demanding to make good on their promise and also to cancel the "Twenty-One Demands" by Japan as well as other privileges such as extraterritoriality conceded under other treaties with the Western powers. Not only did the British and the French ignore the Chinese requests, they handed over the province of Shandong, the previous German sphere of influence, to Japan. The news ignited popular disgust and indignation. On May 4, 1919, university students in Beijing gathered in Tiananmen Square and protested against imperialism and the government's ineptness. After demonstrations, they raided an official's residence and set it on fire. This is the famous May Fourth Movement, which swirled into a nationwide patriotic movement joined in by all ranks of life including students, workers, and merchants alike. Under popular pressure, the Chinese government officials refused to sign the Versailles Treaty even though Japan took hold of Shandong as their sphere of interest.

The May Fourth Movement was a landmark event. It signaled the rise of a new wave of nationalism that would eventually change China. At the forefront of the May Fourth Movement (and the New Culture Movement at a larger scale) was a new generation of Western-educated youth, who had gone abroad (either Europe/America or Japan) to study after the Civil Examination was abolished in 1905. Not only did they introduce all kinds of new ideas, which crystallized in the May Fourth demands for "Mr. Democracy" and "Mr. Science," but they also brought back a heightened sense of nationalism along with their personal experience abroad. One of the new ideas that was brought to China was "Communism" after the October Revolution in Russia, and the Chinese Communist Party (CCP) was founded in 1921. This new socio-political situation gave Dr. Sun Yat-sen new incentives to regroup the KMT — along the Soviet line of a Nationalist party in strategic partnership with the nascent CCP. When Dr. Sun died of illness in 1925, the momentum of another Nationalist revolution in coalition with the CCP was already unstoppable. When it did take place in 1927, the joint forces of KMT and CCP, very much a young student-army trained by Soviet advisors, swept across the country overwhelming the warlord forces along the way. Before the Northern Expedition was completed with full victory, however, the KMT and the CCP split up when the KMT carried out a bloody purge against CCP members. Nevertheless, China was once again under a unified central government led by Generalissimo Chiang Kai-shek (1887–1975).

The so-called Nanjing Decade (1927–1937) was a decade for modernization drive in nation-building in spite of both internal strife and external threat. Internally, Chiang was able to crush warlord rebellions and maintain a fragile balance within different factions of the KMT, but he could not exterminate the Communists who rebelled and survived the purge and set up their own Soviet state. Externally, while the Revolution made significant progress in its anti-imperialist agenda such as revoking (or at least in the process of revoking) extraterritoriality, the Nanjing government was faced with an increasingly aggressive Japan. Merely a couple of years after the Nanjing government was established and ready to embark on the modernization project, Japan took action precisely to prevent that from happening. On September 18, 1931, Japan invaded the Northeastern provinces of China, and propped up the already dethroned last Emperor Puyi for a puppet regime called Manchuria. That enraged the Chinese public and set fire to Chinese nationalism. When the national army retreated, various volunteer resistance forces erupted and continued their activities throughout the war. This was really the beginning of the Second World War if we shift from a Eurocentric perspective, according to which it did not start until Hitler invaded Poland in 1939.

The Nanjing government adopted an appeasement policy toward the Japanese aggression, hoping the League of Nations would be "fair" in its diplomacy. But the Chinese knew Japan would never stop its aggression until China became its vassal state providing the much needed manpower and resources for its imperialist ambition. The Chinese, on the other hand, had a different idea. They wanted to be nobody's vassal state but stand on their own in the world. This time, it was not only a few elites but the general public who insisted on that idea, thanks to the enlightening effects of nationalism. In spite of patriotic frenzy, however, the government knew China was not ready to fight against Japan militarily. It needed time to turn an agricultural China into an industrial one. So China's industrialization and modernization drives became a race in time against the step-by-step encroachment of Japanese forces, from Northeast to Central East regions of China.

In the meantime, Chinese patriotic fervor was inflamed with every inch of Japanese advance in China, accelerated by the government's censor not to make any protest against the Japanese moves in fear of escalating the confrontation. For Chiang had another reason not to engage an all-out war with Japan: to be able to fight against foreign invasion, first of all it would require internal unity, which meant he had to first suppress the Communist insurgence at home. Incidentally, one of the excuses for the Japanese to "enter China" was to help China exterminate the Communists. The Chinese public were unconvinced. The Nationalist Army tried four encirclement campaigns against Communist forces and failed. But the fifth campaign was successful, thanks to the adoption of German military advisors' tactics. By October 1934, the Communists were driven out of their Soviet base in Jiangxi and had to embark on the year-long Long March, which saw its forces greatly diminishing from 100,000 troops to about 8,000. But they survived and retreated to a base in North Shaanxi. Along its way, the Communists seized upon the patriotic sentiment and called for a united Chinese resistance against foreign invasion. But Chiang was determined to solve the Communist question once and for all. He flew to Xi'an and urged his general Zhang Xueliang (1901–2001) to launch a final offensive against the Communist forces. Zhang's troops were stationed there after their retreat from the Northeast. Ever since the Japanese invasion, they had been bearing public indignation and outcry for "not firing a single shot against the Japanese." This time, Zhang kidnapped Chiang, urging him to fight against the Japanese instead — this is the so-called Xi'an Incident. But the military coup immediately backfired among the Chinese public. The Chinese media unilaterally condemned Zhang's action and called for the immediate release of Chiang, as the public understood that nobody other than Chiang could lead China in the War of Resistance against Japan. Most importantly, Stalin agreed. It was in the strategic interest of Soviet Union for China to have a capable leader to resist Japan. So a truce was brokered between the CCP and the KMT. Chiang was consequently released and could not but change his strategy — accepting the CCP in a united front to fight against the Japanese.

After the Xi'an Incident, it was clear that both sides were preparing for the inevitable war. Militarily, China still could not fight the war, as its industry was simply not equipped with the war, and there was no navy or air force, even though German advisors had been training the Chinese army. But the Japanese would not wait. On July 7, 1937, skirmishes between Japanese and Chinese forces took place near the Marco Polo

Bridge outside Beijing. Japanese encroachment in North China had never stopped after they invaded the Northeast provinces, and usually the Chinese tolerated and retreated for "peace." But this time, China had no room for further appeasement, as nationalist furore was at its tipping point. Any further suppression of patriotic fervor to resist would backfire against the government itself. Chiang Kai-shek could not continue the policy of appeasement for buying time after the Marco Polo Bridge incident anymore. Total war broke out. The best China could rely on was morale, a truly nationwide support for the war from all walks of life. The KMT and the CCP were in a united front again, and the Chinese people were ready to fight, and ready for sacrifices — without weaponry in a war, it would mean to use your naked bodies to shield the enemy's gunfire. It was through such purgatory that a new nation would be born. The war was to be a test for Chinese nationalism.

At the first stage of the war, although the Japanese army met stiff resistance, notably in the battle of Shanghai, the battle of Taierzhuang, and the battle of Wuhan, they were able to occupy large coastal areas and major cities in East China. In the meantime, the Chinese government relocated to Chongqing as the war-time capital, in the interior, to prepare for a protracted war, which was the grand strategy for the resistance. It was a historical exodus involving the migration of millions of people together with large-scale industrial infrastructure. Universities were also relocated and wartime campuses were set up in the interior regions. When the war became a stalemate, it turned into a war of attrition. For China to win a protracted war, it was only possible when the whole nation was mobilized into the war effort; in other words, it had to become a people's war, a total war. That meant utmost sacrifices on the part of the people. The bombing of Chongqing, for instance, remained an untold story in WWII. From 1938 to 1943, when China had no air force, the Japanese Imperial Army Air Force carried out a sustained terror bombing on the provisional capital with hundreds of raids and thousands of tons of bombs dropped on the city, mostly in residential areas, resulting in hundreds and thousands of civilian casualties. It was a "terror bombing" because it was indiscriminately targeted to terrify the government and the people alike, and to crush the Chinese spirit of resistance. But the people responded with a *Gung-ho* spirit and the wartime capital stayed on.

China was on the winning side during the First World War, but that victory brought in the Japanese aggression. After the Second World War, China successfully drove out the Japanese. Yet, not much credit has been given to the terrific sacrifices and contributions of the Chinese to the World War. Ever since the Opium War, China's War of Resistance against Japan was the first and only one that China fought and won as a nation. But still, it did not become "one of the greatest nations on earth" in the eyes of the West. That is part of the reason why Chinese nationalism is still alive and kicking strongly even today.

Unlike in post-war Europe, where the German nation had gone through a process of soul-searching and come to terms of its past in reconciliation with its European neighbors, where the Holocaust is universally and indisputably acknowledged and condemned, the reconciliation in East Asia is far from over. The seeds had been sown during the war itself. The Allied forces never trusted the Chinese Nationalist Army and the war ended abruptly with two atomic bombs. On the other hand, there had been a de facto civil war going on between the Nationalist Army and the CCP-led "Eighth Route Army" at the later stage of the war. As the latter went on to win the ensuing Civil War and establish the People's Republic of China in 1949, Japan was realigned in a new political order as an ally of the West. Both the CCP and Japan were free to offer distorted "histories." Under the CCP regime, the Chinese people were told it was the Eighth Route Army — and until quite recently, the Eighth Route Army alone — who were fighting Japanese invaders. The Japanese, on the other hand, did not even admit they "invaded" China. School children learn from history textbooks that Japanese army "entered" China and the bombing of Chongqing or the "Rape of Nanjing" never existed.

I myself grew up under the CCP propaganda about the Eighth Route Army fighting fantastically against the Japanese, but always wondered why it was only the "Eighth Route Army" and what the other routes of army were doing. After I came to America, I thought I could finally find out some objective account about that part of the history. It turned out, however, the American media were much more interested in condemning the inhumanity of the two atomic bombs and the internment of Japanese Americans during the war. Then I came across Jonathan Spence's monumental book on modern Chinese history *The Search for Modern China*, which is widely used as a textbook for college courses on modern China. In this over-800-page book, I found one short paragraph on the "Rape of Nanjing." Professor Spence acknowledges that the "Rape of Nanjing" (though he did not use the term here) "must rank among the worst in the history of modern warfare," and then writes:

> There is no obvious explanation for this grim event nor perhaps can one be found. The Japanese soldiers, who had expected easy victory, instead had been fighting hard for months and had taken infinitely higher casualties than anticipated. They were bored, angry, frustrated, tired. The Chinese women were undefended, their menfolk powerless or absent. The war, still undeclared, had no clear-cut goal or purpose. Perhaps all Chinese regardless of sex or age seemed marked out as victims.[12]

By contrast, I also discovered how Lin Yutang — a Chinese writer based in America during the war, writing in English — offered his account on the "Rape of Nanjing." As Lin pointed out, the Chinese determination to resist was fastened precisely by the inhuman behavior of Japanese soldiers as they advanced to the capital of Nanjing:

> Not until now, since God created man, had human eyes seen laughing soldiers throw a baby into the air and catch it expertly on the point of a sharp bayonet as it fell and call it sport; nor until now had blindfolded prisoners been stood up beside a trench and used as targets for bayonet practice, for systematic education in homicide. Two soldiers pursuing the retreating Chinese army from Soochow to Nanking, had a bet with each other as to who was going to kill the first hundred persons, and their individual records were followed day by day with enthusiasm by their comrades. The noble code of the *Samurai* might explain it to

---

[12] Jonathan Spence, *The Search for Modern China*, p. 448.

the people of that feudal society, but not to the people of other nations. These things are not possible with normal men. They were not possible even in the feudalism of medieval Europe. They were not possible with the African savages. They were not possible when men were half-cousins of gorillas, swinging from tree to tree in primitive jungles. They were not possible with the gorillas themselves. Gorillas fight and kill only for their females. There is no record in anthropology that men killed men for the delight of it even in the most primitive stages of civilization.

No, the terror was that of men, of what men of one race could do to fellow men of another race. Gorillas can not round up gorilla prisoners, put them in a matshed, pour kerosene on it and set it on fire, and laugh. Gorillas copulate in daylight in the open, but they do not enjoy looking at other he-gorillas in the act of copulation and wait in glee for their turn, and they do not put bayonets through the genital organs of the she-gorillas after they are through. Their delight is not so refined as to force the mate of the she-gorilla to stand by while they rape and abuse his wife.[13]

The legacy of China's War of Resistance against Japan is most symbolically demonstrated today in the fact that "The March of the Volunteers" has become the national anthem of the PRC. Composed by Nie Er (1912–1935) to a text by Tian Han (1898–1968) as a response to the Japanese aggression in Northeast China, "The March of the Volunteers" first came into being in 1932. Thanks to the promotion of YMCA clubs in China, mass singing became a spectacular wartime scene. "The March of the Volunteers" was one of the most popular war songs sung en masse by volunteers in the rear and soldiers at the front (certainly not limited to the Eighth Route Army):

| 起来！不愿做奴隶的人们！ | Arise! ye who refuse to be bond slaves! |
| 把我们的血肉， | With our very flesh and blood |

---

[13] Lin Yutang, *A Leaf in the Storm*, p. 215.

筑成我们新的长城！	Let us build our new Great Wall
中华民族到了最危险的时候，	China's masses have met the day of danger,
每个人被迫着发出最后的吼声。	Indignation fills the heart of all of our countrymen.
起来！起来！起来！	Arise! Arise! Arise!
我们万众一心，	Many hearts with one mind,
冒着敌人的炮火，	Brave the enemy's gunfire.
前进！	March on!
冒着敌人的炮火，前进！	Brave the enemy's gunfire,
前进！前进！进！	March on! March on! On![14]

I must confess that every time I listen to this song, I have goose bumps — I feel hot-blooded, hyper-emotional, almost wanting to hit somebody. I hope one day the Chinese will drop this wartime song as its national anthem and replace it with a mellowed and harmonious tune in the tradition of Confucian and Taoist aesthetics. But then, how would you imagine peace in Europe, and the very EU project, if the Holocaust were believed to have never happened, or if an expert on European history would tell you that the Nazi soldiers' killing of the Jews were perhaps because "they were bored, angry, frustrated, tired"?

---

[14] The English translation was by Lin Yutang, "Singing Patriots of China," p. 70.

Chapter 6

Embracing the World:
Cosmopolitan Visions

When we say that Chinese culture today has a strong sense of nationalism, it does not mean that it is self-absorbing and self-defensive, obsessed with its own tradition and "fundamentals." On the contrary, Chinese modernity has been very much an open and cosmopolitan process about engaging and even embracing the "Other" — the very notion of nationalism was indeed a foreign adaptation. It is not so much that the Chinese did not have self-awareness before Western gunboats opened up the Chinese shores, but that the notion of being Chinese had been a cultural and civilizational one. The Chinese thought, whether Confucian, Taoist, or Buddhist for that matter, is by nature universal and cosmopolitan. At the heart of the Chinese worldview is the notion of "*tianxia*" — "All under Heaven," so to speak. The Chinese did differentiate between "Chinese" and "barbarians," but that was based on universal morals rather than racial or ethnic divides. In other words, "Chinese" and "barbarians" were interchangeable depending on whether or not you follow a set of moral standards that would define you as "human" or "humane" rather than a crude beast. Confucius was explicit in his view that he would rather stay among the "barbarians" if the Chinese had lost all their "rites" and "music."

When the Chinese realized that what they had thought as "all under heaven" was actually only part of the globe, and that the "Other" was not so much as "barbarians" as "superior" to Chinese in many ways, it was inherently difficult, culturally speaking, for the Chinese to call for protection or reservation of "Chinese culture" on the ground that they are Chinese — because that is not the Chinese way. Instead, the predominant cultural attitude has been one of assimilation, adaptation, and integration despite the rise of nationalism in face of Western colonial encroachment. In short, the cosmopolitan attitude held sway. There have been different takes and competing voices in regard to the means and styles of engaging the "Other" (Western culture) as well as of reflecting on the "Self" (traditional Chinese culture). And these voices can also be examined in two phases: the late Qing period and the Republican period. This chapter will examine several distinctive, but interrelated, cosmopolitan modes of thought by leading intellectuals in two phases of Chinese modernity. As it turns out, however, none of these won out. It was another kind of radical cosmopolitanism, or "revolutionary cosmopolitanism" that turned out to be hegemonic for much of the twentieth-century China, which will be the subject of discussion in Chapter 7.

EVOLUTION AND GREAT UNION

In Chinese cultural history, as we have seen, translation of foreign religion and ideas, that is, Buddhism, had been a defining feature for a thousand years since the Tang Dynasty. When the Western gunboats opened up China's coastal "treaty ports," two distinct kinds of Westerners came onto shore: (opium) traders and missionaries. The traders were, of course, interested in making money, but the missionaries brought cultural exchanges. Missionaries were the pioneers in bringing Western culture and knowledge into China and many missionaries also became noted Sinologists, such as James Legge, who translated Chinese classics into English. The Bible, for instance, was translated into many Chinese dialects. But the missionaries' activities went far beyond religious conversion. They were also instrumental in setting up newspapers and journals in China where all kinds of cultural knowledge about the West were introduced and translated. They not only served as the initial window to the world to many Chinese (certainly not merely the Chinese converts) but also set the example of print culture in modern China. It is not an overstatement that Western missionaries played a major role in opening up a whole new vista of knowledge to the learned Chinese intelligentsia.

Besides opium, the gunboat was another iconic symbol that the Chinese were most impressed about. To Chinese scholar-officials of the nineteenth century, the first thing the Chinese had to do was to learn how to make these awesome weapons, as demonstrated, for instance, in the title of the celebrated article "On the Manufacture of Foreign Weapons" by Feng Guifen, a foremost theorist for the Self-strengthening Movement. But they also quickly realized the importance of translation and translators and the necessity of translating modern knowledge. As Feng put it in another article titled "On Learning Western Knowledge," China faced an acute problem of lack of qualified translators, as "our officers from the governors down are completely ignorant of foreign countries… The Chinese officers have to rely upon stupid and preposterous interpreters (*tongshi*) as their eyes and ears… If we wish to use Western knowledge, we should establish official translation bureaus in Canton and Shanghai… Westerners should be appointed to teach them the spoken and written languages of the various nations."[1] After the Second Opium War, the Qing court set up Zongli yamen (Office of Foreign Affairs) in 1861, and Tongwen Guan, or School of Combined Learning, under the Office of Foreign Affairs the following year under the advice of Prince Gong and Robert Hart, Inspector-General of China's Imperial Maritime Custom Service. Tongwen Guan was principally a foreign languages school and marked the beginning of an important modern institutional mechanism for translating and introducing Western knowledge and culture into China. Over more than a hundred years now, translation has drastically changed Chinese culture for good in terms of its language and the very mindset of the Chinese. Throughout the modern period to the present, "foreign languages" as a major has enjoyed a much higher prestige in Chinese universities and society at large than in the West.

---

[1] Feng Guifen, *Jiaobinlu kangyi*, p. 210.

Figure 12: Yan Fu

It is generally acknowledged that the "Father of Translation" in modern China was Yan Fu (1854–1921). This is not because he was the first Chinese translator, or the most prolific or the most popular — that title should perhaps go to Lin Shu (1852–1924) who, not knowing a word of English, translated with the help of an aid all kinds of Western novels into classical Chinese — but because the impact of what he translated changed the Chinese mindset most significantly. He translated the idea of evolution — the ideas of progress and competition into China from the following list of texts written predominantly by Victorian thinkers:

- *Evolution and Ethics* by Thomas Henry Huxley (1896–1898)
- *The Wealth of Nations* by Adam Smith (1901)
- *The Study of Sociology* by Herbert Spencer (1903)
- *On Liberty* by John Stuart Mill (1903)
- *A System of Logic* by John Stuart Mill (1903)
- *A History of Politics* by Edward Jenks (1903)
- *The Spirit of the Laws* by Montesquieu (1904–1909)
- *Primer of Logic* by William Stanley Jevons (1909)

The idea of evolution proved to be so popular and overwhelming in modern China that one may argue that Chinese culture today is very much British and Victorian. Indeed, you may very well find a Chinese today who is more steadfastly inclined to the ideas of evolution, progress, and competition than a Briton who may think of herself as having "progressed" from these ideas.

Just like the Crusade in the Middle Ages, wars could have the unintended consequences of facilitating cultural exchanges. After two opium wars, Chinese scholar-officials were shocked to realize the challenge they were facing, and efforts were made to "learn from your enemy." One of the measures was to set up Fuzhou Arsenal and the associated Fuzhou Naval College in 1867. Two French naval officers were recruited as teachers and Yan Fu was among the first cohort of students who were trained in navigation and marine engineering. This was by no means an honourable career choice for Yan at the time when taking the Civil Examination was still the norm for an official career. In hindsight, however, this move set Yan at the forefront of the modern trend of Western learning. Indeed, after ten years of Western-style learning and on-board training, Yan was again among the very first group of Chinese students sent by the Chinese government to study at the Royal Naval College at Greenwich in Britain in 1877. During his two years of study there, Yan proved to be the most conscientious and observant student both inside and outside classrooms. It was often noted that the young man struck an unusual friendship with the senior government official Guo Songtao, the first Chinese ambassador to Britain at the time. Congenial and open-minded, Guo was an exceptional scholar-official who observed that the British parliamentary system was closer (than the current Chinese system) to the Confucian ideal in representing the will of the people. The senior diplomat and the young student protégé would enjoy heart-to-heart conversations inspired by their new experience and knowledge in England. But Guo's career was abruptly cut short and he was sent home precisely because of his unorthodox ideas. While Yan moved up his career ladder steadily after his return, his ambition and insight were hardly recognized and appreciated while he served as a naval official in the government.

Not until fifteen years later, when China suffered a humiliating defeat at the First Sino-Japanese War of 1895, did Yan Fu take center stage of the Chinese intellectual scene. During the War, the entire Beiyang Fleet, the most powerful navy in Asia at that time and crown symbol of the Self-strengthening Reform Movement of the Qing government, was crushed by the Japanese. Yan Fu had been serving in the navy and many of his classmates and friends died. But China's defeat was not merely military. It was a fundamental psychological blow to the Chinese elite. The Chinese had always viewed Japan as a cultural attaché within the Chinese cultural sphere. Now they had embarked on the westernization program after Meiji

Restoration and successfully demanded that the Chinese kneel down and kowtow for peace. What was the secret? What had Japan learned from the West? That was the overwhelming question. A host of voices erupted at the time offering explanations and calling for change, such as those from Zhang Zhidong, Kang Youwei, and Liang Qichao. Yan Fu was certainly one of the prominent voices and perhaps the most influential one.

Yan claimed that the secret lies in Victorian England or, in the ideas of evolution, of progress and competition, as propounded by such Victorian thinkers as Huxley, Spencer, Mill, and Smith. And it lies in a different kind of socio-political system where freedom and democracy are fundamental values and rules of the game.

The secret to the success of the British society, as Yan pointed out, was that it was governed by the principle of "Freedom as Foundation and Democracy as Instrument" (*yi ziyou wei ben, yi minzhu wei yong*). In other words, the people are deemed as "free" and they enjoy freedom. As such, they are said to have some unalienable rights and participate in their own governance through a democratic institution, namely, a parliamentary democracy. The idea that the people are born free and therefore are equal was quite contrary to the Chinese family-state model of governance under the Legalist-Confucianist principle of hierarchical subordination where the people are deemed as "subjects" to be governed. It is no surprise that Yan resorted to the Mencian ideal of "putting the people first" and accuses the dynastic imperial families of "stealing" the State from the people. "The people should be the real masters of the world," as Yan claims, "and yet the Emperors have always tried to make them weak and foolish, to make them fool-hardy, inept and incompetent, so as to preserve for eternity the State they have stolen."[2] China, then, must change to survive, to avoid being humiliated by Japan. "For China to achieve wealth and power, one cannot but practice the politics of benefiting the people. That must begin with enabling the people to make interests, and that in turn begins with affording the

---

[2] Yan Fu, "Pi Han" p. 36.

people with their self-capability and freedom, and that in turn begins with the self-governance of the people."[3]

Most importantly Yan Fu provides a new philosophy of the world, or a new cosmology, to justify the change through translating the Victorian ideas of evolution and progress to China. Yan Fu was best known for translating Thomas Huxley's *Evolution and Ethics* into *Tian yan lun*, which can be back-translated as "On the Way of Heaven." On the first look, Yan's translation is far from being "faithful" to the original text even though he has been regarded as the "father of translation" by propounding that the key principles of translation should consist of "faithfulness, fluency, and beauty" in the "Preface" to the text. The text was rendered into classical Chinese in which Yan utilizes the existing classical Chinese vocabulary while injecting into them new "exotic" meaning. Among the key ideas of social Darwinism, "natural selection" is called *wu jing tian ze* and "survival of the fittest" is called *shizhe shengcun*. These two most powerful ideas exerted a huge influence upon a whole generation of Chinese intellectuals. The translated text was by no means word-for-word or even sentence-by-sentence rendering of the original, but very much selected and reorganized by the translator. Moreover, apart from the "translated text," Yan added his own "commentaries" quite liberally onto the translated text, offering his own views and understanding of the general context of social Darwinist ideas, particularly those of Herbert Spencer. One wonders why he chose Huxley's *Evolution and Ethics* to introduce social Darwinist ideas, for, as the title suggests, Huxley regards "evolution" and "ethics" as two distinct realms, the former representing the natural world and the latter the human world. Huxley was by no means advocating "the rule of the jungle" and "natural selection" as our ethical principles. Yet, Yan did grasp the essential message from Huxley, namely, that the theory of evolution has provided us a new understanding of the universe based on which a new "ethics" of human society ought to be promoted: a rather positive, promising, and energetic human agency. Huxley would have been very pleased if he had learned that, in his preface to Yan's *Tian yan lun*, a noted Qing scholar ranked Huxley's text through Yan's translation as equal to and distinct from the Chinese classics that emerged in the Spring and Autumn period,

---

[3] Yan Fu, "Yuan Qiang" p. 14.

because that was precisely Huxley's point. In *Evolution and Ethics*, Huxley has taken a lot of effort to elaborate his thesis that a modern ethics must be born out of our new scientific understanding of the universe, namely, the theory of evolution, in comparison with our old ethics, both West (Greek) and East (Indian). Both in the East and West, our traditional philosophies and religions were based on an understanding of the universe in which human existence was seen as a process of suffering and pain. Given what we now know through our scientific knowledge of the universe, the process and principles of evolution, Huxley claims that those ancient times were mere infancies of human civilization, and we should now "cast aside the notion that the escape from pain and sorrow is the proper object of life. We have long since emerged from the heroic childhood of our race…the attempts to escape from evil, whether Indian or Greek, have ended in flight from the battle-field… We are grown men, and must play the man

…strong in will
To strive, to seek, to find, and not to yield,

cherishing the good that falls in our way, and bearing the evil, in and around us, with stout hearts set on diminishing it. So far, we all may strive in one faith towards one hope:

… It may be that the gulfs will wash us down,
It may be we shall touch the Happy Isles,
…but something ere the end,
Some work of noble note may yet be done."[4]

It is quite fitting that Huxley ends his lectures with poetic lines of Alfred Tennyson, generally acknowledged as the voice of the upbeat Victorian Age. Huxley didn't know that the same lines that reflected British imperial confidence would also inspire millions of Chinese via Yan's translation. Through Yan's *Tian yan lun*, Chinese readers were enlightened to learn that the law of the universe was a matter of struggle for existence. Just as individuals would struggle for existence, "to strive, to seek, to find, and not to yield," nations also compete for wealth and power, and in this lies the

---

[4] Thomas H. Huxley, *Evolution and Ethics*, p. 37.

secret to the power of Western nations and the weakness of China. Nations that cannot compete will be subjugated, colonized, and eliminated. That is how nations function and relate and react to one another in the world.

Written in classical Chinese and borrowing terminologies from Chinese antiquity, Yan's *Tian yan lun* presented a credible alternative world outlook drastically different from traditional Chinese views, sending a shock wave to the Chinese intellectual world. Indeed, it became a canonical text for the modern era into which China had to inevitably progress. Its influence upon contemporary and younger generations of intellectuals was well documented. Not only did it impress Yan's contemporary intellectuals of different factions, but also exerted huge impact upon both nationalist and cosmopolitan intellectuals of the younger generation. It inspired Nationalist revolutionaries such as Sun Yat-sen, Chen Tianhua, Zou Rong, and Hu Hanmin who credited Yan's book as follows: "Once Yan Fu's books appeared, the idea of 'struggle for existence' was widely received and changed the tempo of the Chinese people."[5] Among leaders of the cosmopolitan New Cultural Movement, Lu Xun's infatuation with Yan's book in his youth was well known, as he "would read *Tian yan lun* whenever he could find any free time, while eating pancakes, peanuts and chili."[6] None other than Hu Shi, however, best captured the impact of Yan upon him and his whole generation: "When China was defeated in successive wars and suffered great shame after the Sino-Japanese War of 1895 and the Boxer Rebellion in 1900, such dictum of 'survival of the fittest' and 'struggle for existence' were really like a hard pounding on one's head, a major stimuli for a large number of people. In a few years, these ideas were like wildfire, burning inside so many hot-blooded youth."[7]

Kang Youwei (1858–1927), a contemporary of Yan Fu, was perhaps better known as an intellectual leader of the One Hundred Days' Reform Movement, a failed attempt to turn China into a constitutional monarch. What is much less known, however, is Kang's cosmopolitan vision, as laid out in his *Datong shu* (Great Union, or Cosmopolitanism), written in 1902

---
[5] Hu Hanmin, quoted in *Yan Fu dazhuan*, p. 163.
[6] Lu Xun, *Lu Xun quanji*, vol. 2, p. 295–296.
[7] Hu Shi, *Hu Shi wenji*, p. 70.

Figure 13: Kang Youwei

but not published until 1935. This book is unique in that it outlines a comprehensive utopian blueprint for a cosmopolitan world. But Kang did not regard it as an unrealistic utopian fantasy; rather he laid many specific proposals and concrete mechanisms for its realization. Kang's cosmopolitan discourse can be seen as an attempt to reconfigure Chinese and Western knowledge into a new universalism at the threshold of Chinese modernity. Critically combining Confucian and Buddhist ideals with the theory of evolution and progress, Kang envisioned a modern cosmopolitan world that would be desirable and tenable. In this One World, the ultimate goal for human existence is the attainment of pleasure and happiness. However, Kang's assessment of the current situation of the world was rather bleak. Kang devotes the entire first chapter illustrating the various kinds of "suffering" humans have to endure in this world, including the suffering of life itself, the suffering of human emotion, the suffering of human government, the suffering of natural disasters, and so on. And he attributes the root cause of all human suffering to what he calls the "nine boundaries," namely, the boundaries of nation, class, race, gender, family, property, disorder, species, and pain. To achieve the ultimate cosmopolitan goal of pleasure and happiness, Kang claims that all that is needed is to dissolve the nine boundaries, and the rest of the nine chapters of the book elaborate his approaches to break these nine boundaries, with each chapter focusing on each boundary.

What is most noteworthy in Kang's boundary-dissolving roadmap to the One World is that he targets the very idea and existence of "guo" (nation-state) as the primary boundary and source of suffering to the cosmopolitan world. Kang observes that, for a human life to achieve mature adulthood, it takes numerous hardships, including nine-month pregnancy, risks at labor, and battles against various kinds of diseases and accidents in childbearing. Yet, once wars arise between states and men are called to serve their states, hundreds and thousands of lives disappear in a moment. Human beings are collective animals, and group identities lead to the formation of states, and states necessarily lead to wars out of their own interests.

To Kang Youwei, "guo" was not merely a modern invention, but had a long history of inglorious existence as the source of bloody wars and human suffering in both China and the world. To prove his point, Kang went through a lengthy historical account of the traumas brought about by competing states. In Chinese history, ever since the tribal ancient times down to the present, bloody wars had characterized the rise and fall of successive dynastic states. Particularly notorious, for instance, was the so-called Warring States period when different states competed for power and supremacy while ordinary people became victims of prolonged instability and cruel warfare. Indeed, whenever dynastic states fell apart, China would go through dark periods of human suffering caused by peasant uprisings and competing warlords. That is why the Confucian ideal has always called for the Great Unification, and only when China was under unification could people enjoy relative peace and prosperity. And in Western history, the situation was even worse in terms of bloody warfare among the states. Instead of admiring the rise of the Nation and Nationalist Imperialism, Kang sees Western history as an endless cycle of human suffering brought about by large- and small-scale warfare among competing states, from Egyptians, to Greeks, to Romans, to Persians, to Germanic peoples, to Russians. "Since the Roman Empire in Europe, there occurred more than eight hundred large-scale warfare, not counting the small-scale ones, and the consequent disaster and misery inflicted upon the people are simply unspeakable."[8]

Kang then goes on to lay out concrete measures and steps to dissolve the states with a three-stage approach, appropriated from the Confucian three-stage theory of history. In the first stage, a kind of League of Nations will be set up to coordinate the different interests of the states and to ultimately diminish the power and self-interests of independent states.

---

[8] Kang Youwei, *Kang Youwei datonglun erzhong*, p. 118.

To achieve that, one must start with the disarmament of nations, as military prowess is the root cause for war atrocities. Kang understands that nations would certainly try to protect their own military interests, but that is precisely the reason to curb and gradually decrease the very notion of nation-states. Kang believes disarmament is the inevitable trend of world history and it should be the primary task for the League of Nations. In Kang's scheme, the League of Nations in the first stage is only a kind of public parliament, not a public government, and people's lives are still bound and organized within respective nations. Gradually, it will move to the second stage where a public government will be set up and nations would cede portions of their territories to the governance of the public government. Kang lays out a meticulous list of functions of such a public government, in which the establishment of a worldwide transportation network plays a major role, while the exercise of civil rights from bottom up serves as the foundation and guarantee for the public government as a constitutional democracy. The public government in the second stage is like the federal union of the United States, and as the nations gradually become less useful, the Great Union, or *datong*, will be achieved and the world will be a peaceful place to live.

While Kang singles out "guo," or the state, as the primary boundary to dissolve in order to achieve the cosmopolitan world, he identifies race as a more difficult obstacle than the state to overcome on the way to the One World of peace and pleasure. Given the new geopolitical knowledge of the world, Kang acknowledges that the world would still be differentiated and divided by five races, the white race in Europe, the yellow race in Asia, the black race in Africa, and the brown race in the Pacific and South Asian islands, even when the states are evolved into the unified public government. In the cosmopolitan One World, however, there will be only one race and one people, and Kang's proposed strategies to achieve racial union and harmony reflect a great deal of the influence of the evolutionary theory.

What Kang offers is a long-term eugenic project of racial integration through racial mixing and intermarriage so as to eliminate racial differences and inequality. But there is an obvious racial hierarchical assumption underlying Kang's eugenic project of racial mixing. Kang tacitly acknowledges the white racial dominance in the world as a result of the evolutionary logic of the "survival of the fittest." In this logic of "the superior wins and the inferior loses," the white race is able to permeate the globe, thereby subjugating the indigenous races, just as the Chinese have successfully migrated southward and westward driving the local tribal peoples to the mountains. "In this world, people of the silver populate the whole globe, yet people of the gold race are still the majority race in numbers, so it can be said that the yellow and the white races jointly control the entire world. The white race is more powerful therefore the superior winning race, yet the yellow race, endowed with natural wisdom, outnumbers the white race. Therefore, it is not a matter of racial extinction for the yellow race, but rather integration and transformation into one."[9] Kang's racial scheme constitutes part of his overall cosmopolitan discourse designed to obfuscate racial distinctions eventually. In his three-stage evolution toward the One World of peace and pleasure, the joint co-dominance of the yellow race and the white race is only the second-stage phenomenon, and their further interbreeding is supposed to lead to the final integration into one people of mixed-bloods, hence the extinction of racial distinctions altogether.

While it is true that Kang's racial thinking was deeply influenced by evolutionary theory and takes the white predominance for granted, Kang's cosmopolitan solution to racial inequality still subverts Western eugenics in that the former aims at racial mixing and integration into one, while the latter strives for purity to maintain white superiority. Moreover, Kang's evolutionary stand on the race issue is not an essentialist one either. While Kang accepts the predominance and the superiority of the white race as consequent of evolutionary process, he asserts that racial quality of the people is not fixed, and can be changed, or improved. While he regards the black and the brown as inferior races with their "unbearable bodily stench" and "bestial" facial appearances, he also points out an Englishman living in India for two or three generations

---

[9] Ibid, p. 167.

would "degenerate" into "yellowish blue."[10] "Therefore, in order for all races to homogenize into one, the first thing is to relocate people to their proper environment, the second is to intermarry among races, and the third is to change diet and enhance sports. Once these three measures are taken simultaneously, racial boundaries will disappear and the Great Union will be achieved."[11]

One of the most radical critiques in Kang's cosmopolitan discourse is his unprecedented feminist stance to eliminate the gender boundary. In Kang's eye, gender inequality is the cruelest and the most unfair one in human history. As all beings contain yin and yang, human beings comprise of males and females, and in all human faculties, the female is no less capable than the male; yet for thousands of years, in China and around the world, the female has been subjugated into a lesser kind who has endured unspeakable suffering. Kang lists a number of injustices done to women, both in the East and West: they cannot serve as public servants, cannot take civil examinations, cannot become Congresswomen, cannot become citizens with rights and responsibilities, cannot interfere in public affairs, cannot become scholars, cannot be independent, and cannot enjoy freedom, especially freedom in marriage, and as such, they are merely prisoners and slaves of men. For the complete independence of women, Kang proposes a radical solution in the cosmopolitan world: there should be no marriage and no husband and wife in the Great Union, but only partners who agree to share their lives based on a one-year renewable contract.[12]

Kang's cosmopolitan vision also includes leveling classes, dissolving the family institution, abandoning private property, unifying the measuring system for social order, equalizing the species, and ultimately arriving at the Great Union where pleasure is the sole pursuit for humankind. What is perhaps most noteworthy of Kang's cosmopolitan discourse lies in its manifest intentionality: the pursuit of pleasure. It is the nine boundaries that caused the human suffering in this world, and once the boundaries are all dissolved, the cosmopolitan world will be one complete place with

---

[10] Ibid, p. 168.
[11] Ibid, p. 174.
[12] Ibid, pp. 230–234.

all kinds of pleasures for human beings to enjoy. In the Great Union, one will have the pleasure of residency, as one will not have to build their own houses but live in big public housing and huge fancy hotels; one will have the pleasure of transportation, as there will be self-moving boats on water and self-moving vehicles on land; one will enjoy the pleasure of food, as food will be plentiful and robots will bring food to your private rooms; and one will also enjoy the pleasures of clothing, machinery equipment, perfume, bathing, spiritual cultivation, and ultimately the pleasure of the soul. It is quite interesting to note that, in the end, Kang defines evolution in terms of pleasure: "The thousands of measures and remedies of all sages are all instruments to help human beings to get rid of suffering and to find pleasure. That is the only Way. If it increases pleasure and decreases suffering, that is evolution. And it is the good Way. If it increases suffering while adding no pleasure to human life, that is degeneration. And its Way is no good… When the nine boundaries are all gone, human sufferings are eliminated, and what is left is only pleasure."[13]

CHINESE RENAISSANCE

Figure 14: Hu Shi

Unquestionably, intellectuals of the late Qing period like Yan Fu and Kang Youwei left a significant impact upon a later generation of cosmopolitan elites who sought their education abroad. One of the reform policies the Qing government was forced to adopt was to abolish the thousand-year-old Civil Examination system in 1905, after which a new generation of Chinese were to seek their education abroad to study Western knowledge. By the mid-1910s, they were ready to step onto the center stage of the Chinese intellectual world and initiate a

---

[13] Ibid, p. 361.

"Chinese Renaissance," also referred to as the New Culture Movement (1916–1919). It was really a cultural revolution that overturned the essential features of Chinese culture; from then on, Chinese culture would be irreversibly "modern." The New Culture Movement was a cosmopolitan movement, and its central features were to embrace the world by heralding "Mr. Democracy" and "Mr. Science" while engaging in an iconoclastic reevaluation and criticism of traditional Chinese culture. It started out as a "Literary Revolution" prompted by the debates surrounding the question of the modernity of the Chinese language. And these debates were carried out among Chinese students in America at the time, and the central figure was a young man called Hu Shi (1891–1962).

In the summer of 1915, a group of Chinese students gathered to spend the summer at Ithaca, New York. They included Hu Shi, Zhao Yuanren (Yuen Ren Chao, 1892–1982), Mei Guangdi (1890–1945), Ren Hongjun, Tang Yue, and Yang Quan. Some of them like Hu Shi were attending Cornell University there, while others like Mei Guangdi were just visiting. One of the topics among their summer conversations was the Chinese language. It was Hu Shi who put forward a provocative and revolutionary claim: the Chinese language is dead! What he meant was that the written classical Chinese, or *wenyan*, which had served as the standard universal medium of writing for the Chinese, was dead, or at least half-dead, as many of its features such as diction and allusions were removed from everyday life and had become obsolete. In other words, Chinese writing had become separated from Chinese speech. What Hu proposed was to replace the dead or half-dead *wenyan* with a vernacular style of writing called *baihua*, in other words, to write as you speak. This was a revolutionary proposal because the vernacular writing, though it had been in practice in popular literary genres such as fiction and drama, was considered vulgar and lowly to the chagrin of an educated literati scholar.

Among his fellow overseas students, Hu Shi was quite a loner as most of his friends opposed his view. His chief opponent was Mei Guangdi, a disciple of Irving Babbitt at Harvard University. Babbitt's New Humanism inherits the tradition of the cultural criticism of Matthew Arnold and, like Edmund Burke, detests French revolution and romanticism. To Babbitt and his Chinese disciples, the East and West would benefit each other by upholding the best in their traditions and a revolutionary break from its tradition would be like "throwing the baby out with the bath water." To replace *wenyan* with *baihua* would be throwing away the very best that embody the Chinese civilization. So the debate went on by exchange of letters among the elite group of overseas students for another year until Hu Shi took it back to China. A group of students who had returned from Japan had launched a new journal *The New Youth*, and when Hu's "A Modest Proposal for Literary Reform" was published therein, it was enthusiastically promoted by Chen Duxiu and other contributors to the journal, thereby igniting, not just a "literary reform," but a "Literary Revolution." The movement was a major success. Only after a few years, had the vernacular Chinese (*baihua*) replaced the classical Chinese (*wenyan*) as the medium of writing for all major newspapers, and was accepted as the standard medium for classroom teaching in schools. The thousand-year-old classical Chinese was pronounced "dead" and the new "modern Chinese language" was born. It was born out of three major sources: drawing from traditional vernacular Chinese writings as practiced in popular fictions and dramas, the "new literature" created in *baihua* by the new generation of writers and journalists following Hu Shi's call, as well as through large-scale translations. The New Culture Movement opened up new waves of translation, as all kinds of ideas and masterworks from the Western cultural tradition were introduced and translated into *baihua* Chinese, many via Japanese translations of Western languages. As the new vernacular Chinese became the standard, many of the translated terminologies from the previous late Qing period, such as those by Yan Fu, became obsolete and eventually replaced with new ones. Neologism and loanwords are a major feature of the modern Chinese language. In fact, they deeply characterize the modern Chinese. Hundreds of loanwords such as *geming* (revolution), *kexue* (science), *jingji* (economy), *gonghe* (republic), *jingcha* (police), including some transliterations like *shafa* (sofa), and *xiangbin* (champagne) have already become common usage today that we cease to consider them "loanwords" at all.

While Chinese disciples of Babbitt such as Mei Guangdi and Wu Mi later formed an influential cultural conservative group, "The Critical

Review," their efforts were largely overshadowed by the triumphant New Culture Movement. It started out as a "Literary Revolution," but it soon turned out to be an all-encompassing "cultural revolution" — revaluation of all existing values, a very Nietzschean notion. Indeed, "the Chinese language is dead" is somewhat comparable to Nietzsche's dictum "God Is Dead." When classical Chinese was replaced by the vernacular, the entire Chinese cultural values were turned upside down, and along with it, the massive introduction and translation of all kinds of Western ideas such as science, democracy, humanism, equality, women's rights — chief among them was the notion of a critical attitude.

Indeed, the very fact that it was Hu Shi who brought about the Literary Revolution demonstrates his cosmopolitan critical knack. Hu was born to a traditional literati-official family, whose father was a high-ranking literati-official but died when Hu was very young. He went through rigid traditional learning through private schooling, and had achieved a solid foundation in Chinese learning when he went abroad. Hu was one of the first cohorts of Chinese students sent to study in America on the Boxer Indemnity Fund established on the partial refund of the indemnity paid to the United States by the Qing government out of the Boxer Rebellion debacle. After the Civil Examination was abolished in 1905, the annual national exams to select candidates to study in America became a major attraction for the Chinese youth. Having passed with full mark on the subject of Chinese philology, Hu Shi was among the second cohort of seventy students successfully selected In 1910. Hu's classical training in Chinese philology cannot be underestimated, as it forms a solid foundation in his later role as a cross-cultural critic. Hu grew up at a time when the traditional system of Chinese learning was breaking down as symbolized by the abolishment of the Civil Examination in 1905. Nevertheless, majority of the nation's elite still managed to receive a complete traditional education through private schooling when they grew up. By the time they went to high school, they began to be exposed to "new learning," or "Western learning" such as English and science subjects. Hu Shi's adoption of his own name was perhaps the most symbolic of the times he was in. During his high school years, Hu decided to adopt for himself a new "scholarly name": *shizhi*, or simply *shi*, meaning "adapt" or "fit," apparently a parody on *shizhe shengcun*, or "survival of the fittest" as Yan Fu's translation of evolution theory was the vogue at the time. But it was their study abroad that afforded them a cosmopolitan outlook unprecedented in the history of Chinese learning, particularly in the case of Hu Shi.

For Hu Shi shone brilliantly as a Chinese student at Cornell University. That does not mean, however, Hu was a stereotypical hardworking Chinese student with good grades. In fact, he entered Cornell in 1910 as an agriculture major student, but later he realized he was ill-suited to the subject and changed to humanities instead. At Cornell, Hu truly engaged in American life and emerged not merely as a Chinese student leader but also as a cosmopolitan student leader critical of both China and America. He participated in a number of church activities in Ithaca and took a keen interest in American religious life such as the Quakers and Mormons. He indulged in election campaign activities during the 1912 general election. During his Cornell years, Hu became a gifted public speaker, delivering public speeches to the American public in the Ithaca area as well as around the country. The year 1912 saw the founding of the first republic in Asia, the Republic of China (ROC), which aroused much interest in America to know about the historical event. As Hu Shi recalls, there were many demands for lectures at the time, yet only one Chinese student in engineering — who graduated from St. John's University, an Episcopalian missionary college in Shanghai — was capable of delivering public lectures. He couldn't handle all the requests and asked Hu to take over some of them. Eventually, Hu became so popular that he was running around the country delivering public lectures to the extent that Cornell University thought his public engagement was hindering his academic studies.[14] In the meantime, Hu also served as President of the Cornell Cosmopolitan Club, a student organization consisting of members of all nationalities. In other words, while Hu became a public spokesman for Chinese affairs, he was speaking from a cosmopolitan perspective, as demonstrated clearly from his speeches and writings at the time.

---

[14] Hu Shih, *The Personal Reminiscences of Dr. Hu Shih*, p. 51.

When the ROC was founded on January 1, 1912, Hu Shi hailed for the coming of democracy in China. In "A Republic for China," he dispelled the popular belief in America that democracy was ill-fitted to China, informing them that "behind the monarchs and the aristocrats there has been dominating in China, a quiet, peaceful, oriental form of democracy." This is articulated, for instance, in *The Book of Documents*, the oldest of China's Classics, as "the Golden Rule for the rulers:

The people should be cherished.
And should not be downtrodden.
The people are the root of a nation:
If the root be firm the nation is safe."[15]

And Hu also cites Mencius, "the Montesquieu of the Orient," in advocating "the people" as the fundamental source for the sovereign. As Chih-ping Chou noted, Hu Shi was generally much more sympathetic to Chinese culture in his English-language writings, whereas he was well known for his sharp and iconoclastic critique of Chinese culture in his Chinese writings. This does not amount to the inconsistencies of his thought but rather reveals his different approaches to a different audience.[16] What matters, however, is to see that Hu's take on Chinese culture, whether in English or in Chinese, derived from his cosmopolitan outlook in which Chinese cultural issues are part of the problems of the modern world we all live in. Hu had already developed his cosmopolitan critical knack in his Cornell years.

Hu Shi's American years also saw the coming of the First World War, and he was attracted to the peace movement and Wilsonian principles for world peace. His essay "Is There a Substitute for Force in International Relations?," which won the prize for International Polity Club competition in 1916, demonstrates not only Hu's sophistication in terms of his grasp of liberal cosmopolitan philosophy of peace, but also his superb skills in English

---

[15] Hu Shi, *English Writings of Hu Shih*, p. 1.
[16] Chih-ping Chou, "Introduction".

composition as a college student. In his farewell lecture on retiring from the Presidency of the Cornell Cosmopolitan Club, Hu responded to two issues of concern from some members: (1) the Club should not be involved in the peace movement and (2) there are "too many Jews and negroes" in the club. As Hu argues, one of the essential duties of the Cosmopolitan Club was "to promote friendly and commercial relations, and a higher standard of order and justice between different nationalities…(and) for the establishment of international peace and good will." And as such, the Club should be "proud" that "it is the only student organization that takes into its membership 'men of all nationalities', irrespective of color, birth, creed, or pecuniary conditions."[17]

So it is essential to bear in mind Hu's cosmopolitan educational background to his call for arms for the Literary Revolution. In his own memoirs, Hu recalled it as if it were an accident of history. The fact that he was prompted to raise the discussion of the modernity of Chinese language was due to an eccentric behavior of one of the government guardians for this group of students. This official, another graduate of St. John's University, would insert a slip together with the monthly check of government allowance to students in the envelope, and on the slip were usually written a couple of slogans, and one of them read: abolish the Chinese character! Hu was so annoyed, as if he believed this St. John's graduate was not qualified to talk about Chinese language and culture.[18] Hu did not explain why he thought this official with a missionary education and enthusiasm was not qualified to tackle such an important issue as the Chinese language. What is unsaid, apparently, is that it takes a scholar like him, who is not only well-trained in Chinese learning but has also "seen the world," to be able to converse on the subject of the Chinese language reform. As Hu Shi's story informs us, the Chinese language had been under attack ever since China was forced to open up to Western influence, particularly through the advance of the missionary enterprise. Many intellectuals at the time advocated abolishing the Chinese characters altogether to adopt a phonetic script system just like

---
[17] Hu Shi, "Lest We Forget" pp. 3, 6–7.
[18] Hu Shi, *The Personal Reminiscences of Dr. Hu Shih* p. 119.

the Western languages, as they believed the written language was the very embodiment of the backward, feudalistic traditional culture that ought to be overthrown. In comparison, Hu Shi's proposal to replace classical Chinese with the vernacular Chinese, or *baihua*, was indeed a "modest proposal." It became a great success because it was practical and feasible while achieving the purpose of awakening the Chinese with a new sense of urgency to be compatible with modern civilization.

Therefore, the New Culture Movement ignited by Hu Shi's "modest proposal" for the vernacular Chinese as the new national language fundamentally changed Chinese culture as we know it today. Under its banner of "Mr. Democracy" and "Mr. Science" lies a "critical attitude" — a cosmopolitan critical attitude. Hu Shi emerged as the archetypal leader of modern Chinese intellectuals and advanced this new paradigm of Chinese culture in two interrelated dimensions: a critique of the traditional Confucian politico-cultural system so that it was deconstructed once and for all, never to be defended and recalled as "foundation" as such, while with the promise to build a "new civilization" through "Westernization" as much as possible.

It is not coincidental that Hu Shi made two references to St. John's University in Shanghai, as it was the most successful missionary college in Republican China. Missionary schools offered another channel for elite education for the Chinese youth after the Exam was abolished. St. John's graduates permeated all walks of life in the Republican period. It turns out that the most well-known liberal cosmopolitan intellectual other than Hu Shi was also a St. John's graduate: Lin Yutang (1895–1976).

Figure 15: Lin Yutang

Hu Shi was made a cosmopolitan intellectual during his college years in America. Lin Yutang also went to America and later Germany for his graduate studies, but his cosmopolitan education started at home through his mission school education in Xiamen and Shanghai. While Hu Shi shone brilliantly at Cornell, Lin Yutang excelled at St. John's. Lin was in every sense "the most distinguished student" in his college years. He participated in all kinds of extracurricular activities and made unparalleled achievements in his intellectual pursuits. He was President of the Class of 1916, and like Hu Shi, developed superior skills in delivering public speeches. He won awards for his literary writings and served as Editor for *The St. John's Echo*, a St. John's student journal and Editor-in-chief of *Johannean*, the St. John's College yearbook. He was voted by fellow students as "the Best English writer," "the Best English speaker," and "the Best English debater."[19]

As Lin emerged as an intellectual leader in the 1930s in Shanghai, one of the roles he assumed was President of the Liberal Cosmopolitan Club — "a club of men who are citizens of the world who can think, or are willing to make an effort to think, over and above the merely nationalistic lines."[20] In his inaugural speech entitled "What Liberalism Means," Lin defines "liberalism" in terms of an appreciation and tolerance of the Other. As Lin put it, liberalism is "an attitude of mind, a way of thinking," an open-minded attitude trying to reach out to the Other in contrast to the "savage-herd instinct" that only sees self-righteousness: "The new liberal attitude of trying to see some sense instead of nonsense in the foreigner's customs, laws and religion is such a belated development in history that…[t]here is simply no natural instinct to support it. It is only with right education, immense tolerance and an extreme effort of the mind that a man may finally bring himself to take a liberal attitude toward the habits of the foreigner."[21]

As we had noted before, the New Culture Movement as ignited by the Literary Revolution had two goals: to promote "Mr. Democracy" and to promote "Mr. Science." In order to herald Chinese culture into "a new civilization," the other side of the New Culturalist agenda is "re-evaluation of all values," which turned into a fierce attack upon Chinese cultural tradition — in all of its elements, even to the extent of proposing

---
[19] *The Johannean*.
[20] "Proposal for a Liberal Cosmopolitan Club in Shanghai".
[21] Lin Yutang, "What Liberalism Means."

to abolish the Chinese characters altogether. While Lin Yutang echoed and supported the New Culturalists' progressive agenda of modernizing Chinese culture, he differed from their iconoclastic approach. Instead, he laid out his own cosmopolitan vision that entails a reconstruction and resurrection of Chinese culture to be incorporated into a "new civilization" to be built from both Eastern and Western cultural resources. In other words, Lin's approach to Chinese traditional literature and culture was to modernize and transform it into a set of illuminating resources for modern human civilization, and it still had a major role to play in the formation of our common world civilization.

On both Chinese language and literature, Lin Yutang outlined a distinct path for modernization and carried them out in his literary practices. Lin started out his career as a linguist with modern training, and maintained a life-long obsession with the Chinese language reform that culminated in his invention of the first Chinese typewriter. Contrary to popular New Culturalist belief that Chinese characters must be replaced by a phonetic script system, Lin resolutely claims: "If China is not going to perish, there will be two scripts in the future: one is the Chinese characters and the other is [the] *pinyin* phonetic notation system."[22] Those who advocate the abolishment of Chinese characters altogether, in Lin's opinion, forget that language and letters have both "aesthetic" and "utilitarian" value. Chinese language reform must walk on both legs to be successful. The *pinyin* system is necessary only as a secondary supplement and should conform to international norms as much as possible, while Chinese characters will stay but must be "systematically modernized." That includes standardization of some characters and gradual simplification of the characters. Lin launched several literary journals in the 1930s on which a set of simplified characters were first employed for trial. His life-long obsession with the invention of a Chinese typewriter started with his original concern and research on a scientific system of indexing Chinese characters. The invention was successfully completed eventually when Lin stayed in America after the Second World War, but was disastrous to his personal finances due to its

---

[22] Lin Yutang, "Tan zhuyin zimu ji qita," p. 351.

failure of mass production. In his later years in Taiwan, he was particularly frustrated to see that the Chinese character reform made no progress in Taiwan while mainland China under the Communist rule was actually pushing it forward. "I had spent fifty years researching the issue and went bankrupt trying to solve it,"[23] Lin reminds his readers, and would support the initiative regardless which political party was carrying out the initiative.

Lin's contribution to the formation of "new literature" after the Literary Revolution was equally significant. Lin argued that Chinese culture had had too much "literature" — in the sense of "writerly" *belle lettres* devoid of originality and thought. We should set the ideal of literature much higher than that in modern times and regard literature as expression and criticism of life. The unique approach Lin adopted to rejuvenate Chinese literature was to introduce the idea of "humor" into Chinese culture. It was Lin Yutang who first coined the new word *youmo* to translate "humor" — which has become a word of common usage among the Chinese today. Lin's cross-cultural translation of humor was designed to modernize Chinese literature and culture, transforming traditional Chinese culture from the shackles of Neo-Confucian constraint and orthodoxy. By promoting a livelier and more familiar style of writing, he aimed to introduce a new world outlook. This was largely thanks to his bilingual and bi-cultural background. Lin was unique among modern Chinese writers as a bilingual writer of both English and Chinese works and in fact his first pieces of literary writings were in English. In 1930, Lin started a weekly column called "The Little Critic" in the English-language journal *The China Critic*. Written in English in the familiar essay style, these weekly "Little Critic" essays were later "translated" into Chinese and published in his Chinese-language journals. But it did not mean Lin was advocating "wholesale westernization" at all. On the contrary, he warned that vernacular Chinese writing should not become "a housewife's rattle" — talkative, long-winded, and pointless. Instead, we should take great care to cultivate the vernacular Chinese in terms of "lucidity, perspicuity, cogency of thought, truth, and appropriateness of expression" as commonly found in Western literature.[24] In the 1930s,

---

[23] Lin Yutang, "Lianhebao chuangyong changyongzi de gongxian".
[24] Lin Yutang, "Lun Hanzi suoyin zhi ji xiyang wenxue," p. 367.

Lin further developed his own *yuluti* style of writing, a semi-classical vernacular style, in contradistinction to both the crude "housewife's rattle" and the seemingly sophisticated "translated style" modeled upon Europeanized sentence structure and diction. To Lin Yutang, for Chinese culture to be reborn, it was certainly not the right approach to westernize and Europeanize the very Chinese language and its writing style.

In his seminal work *The Importance of Living*, Lin reinterprets Chinese cultural wisdom and articulates a "lyrical philosophy" based on an aesthetics of freedom and life. In developing a "lyrical philosophy" out of Chinese cultural tradition, Lin rediscovers and refashions Chinese cultural resources on a global stage and demonstrates the resourcefulness and vitality of traditional culture for China's modernity. To Lin, the highest ideal of Chinese culture is embodied in "a man with a sense of *detachment* (*takuan*) toward life based on a sense of wise disenchantment." And he reconstructs this man who can embody the highest ideal in his biography of Su Dongpo:

> One might say that Su Tungpo was an incorrigible optimist, a great humanitarian, a friend of the people, a prose master, an original painter, a great calligrapher, an experimenter in wine making, an engineer, a hater of puritanism, a yogi, a Buddhist believer, a Confucian statesman, a secretary to the emperor, a confirmed winebibber, a humane judge, a dissenter in politics, a prowler in the moonlight, a poet, and a wag. And yet that might miss the sum total of what made up Su Tungpo. I can perhaps best sum it up by saying that the mention of Su Tungpo always elicits an affectionate and warm admiring smile in China. For more than other Chinese poets', Su Tungpo's personality had the richness and variety and humor of a many-sided genius, possessing a gigantic intellect and a guileless child's heart — a combination described by Jesus as the wisdom of the serpent and the gentleness of the dove.[25]

---

[25] Lin Yutang, *The Gay Genius: Life and Times of Su Tungpo* (vii–viii).

To invoke Su Dongpo as the ideal prototype for Chinese culture is certainly a far cry from New Culturalist iconoclastic take on Chinese cultural tradition. But Lin also understands the times he lived in were by no means conducive to such a cosmopolitan ideal. On other occasions, Lin invokes a more Taoist figure of a rugged individual as the best embodiment of such an ideal in modern times, and gives us a dire warning of the alternative. The "scamp," as Lin argues, is "probably the most glorious type of human being" to uphold human dignity:

> In this present age of threats to democracy and individual liberty, probably only the scamp and the spirit of the scamp alone will save us from becoming lost as serially numbered units in the masses of disciplined, obedient, regimented and uniformed coolies.[26]

---

[26] Lin Yutang, *The Importance of Living*, p. 12.

Chapter 7

Radical Revolutions to a Super-State

A super-state is what the Chinese are living under today, a Communist state empowered by global capitalism. This has tremendous implications on the Chinese culture. The Confucian tradition, for instance, went through the most spectacular destruction under the Communist super-state until quite recently when it was again recuperated into a mainstream ideological discourse. In that respect, one could argue that the Confucian teachings are in a sense skin-deep in Chinese culture today. What is perhaps more relevant is what constitutes and what has made the super-state possible. For that, we need to trace a darker, more destructive revolutionary side of Chinese culture. In many ways, "a powerful nation" was a shared dream of generations of modern Chinese intellectuals, but the final outcome of a Communist super-state was very much the consequence of the radicalization of the Chinese mind under the global influence of Communism—otherwise also called "revolutionary cosmopolitanism." This chapter discusses how the modern Chinese were overwhelmed in "becoming lost as serially numbered units in the masses of disciplined, obedient, regimented and uniformed coolies," and the intellectual struggle still facing Chinese today.

TAIPING COMMUNISM

The Communist revolution and its consequences were part of the Chinese modernity experience. Chinese modernity was beset with revolutions. It was a series of revolutions that culminated in the Communist revolution. When Chinese modernity was opened up in the Opium War of 1840, the first major revolution took place a decade later: the Taiping Rebellion of

1850–1864. The Communist revolution was in a sense a twentieth-century strengthened and a successful version of the nineteenth-century Taiping.

As we noted before, the so-called *Pax Sinica* in Chinese history was always initiated and followed by a most destructive dynasty-changing war(s), most commonly in the form of peasant uprisings. In historical hindsight, we can see these wars were usually the bloodiest in human history. Part of the reason for such repeats of human devastation lies in the tension between Confucian emphasis on order and stability (rigidly enforced in peace times) and the Confucian notion of the legitimacy of the rule under the Mandate of Heaven. For the Mandate of Heaven to be revoked and reinstituted, the Chinese have never figured out a peaceful mechanism other than by means of these wars and uprisings and revolutions. Both the Taiping and Communist revolutions were rooted in Chinese tradition, but both also took on distinctive "modern" characteristics in that they were cosmopolitan revolutions embracing and prompted by Western cultural advances.

Historians tend to analyze historical events on economic factors. There were certainly economic grounds for a peasant uprising in the middle of the nineteenth century as economic hardship was accelerated by the widespread opium trade. But the origin of the Taiping was explicitly cultural or cross-cultural—down to one man's encounter with Christian missionary work. Hong Xiuquan (1814–1864) was born to an ordinary farmer's family. Since he showed signs of intelligence and diligence as a child, the family saved and tried hard to ensure he could study and hopefully pursue a scholar-official career. Hong passed the local (and the lowest) level of Civil Examination, which qualified him to be a local school teacher but failed, not once, but four times in his further attempts. On his second attempt taking the exam in Guangzhou, the provincial capital of Guangdong, he met a Western missionary handing out pamphlets with

Figure 16: Hong Xiuquan

Chinese translations of excerpts of the Bible on the street. Hong took the pamphlets and kept them. At the failure of his third attempt, Hong had a mental breakdown. He had a dream and a vision—in which a celestial father instructed that he was the chosen one and was endowed with the duty, aided by his Elder Brother, of wiping out the demonic teachings in his country. Hong then remembered what he had read in the Bible pamphlet and believed the celestial father was God, the Elder Brother was Jesus Christ and he was the younger brother. From then on, he gave up pursuing the scholar-official career, and started teaching in local schools and preaching in local communities. Many of his first group of converts were his family relatives, cousins, and members of the village clan. In 1847, Hong Xiuquan and his cousin Hong Rengan went to Guangzhou to study the Bible with the American Southern Baptist missionary, Reverend Issachar Roberts. Based on Gutzlaff's Chinese translation of the Old and New Testaments, Hong later edited his own version of The Taiping Bible. Hong and his converts started to organize the Society of the God Worshippers and started to burn all Confucian and Buddhist statues and books.

The Taiping uprising broke out in late 1850 and the following year, Hong Xiuquan declared the founding of the Taiping Heavenly Kingdom with himself as the "Heavenly King." In 1853, the Taipings captured Nanjing and made it their capital. For more than a decade until Nanjing fell into the hands of the Chinese gentry army led by Zeng Guofan, much of southern China was war-torn and devastated. At about the same time when China was gripped under the Taipings, the United States also went through a civil war. It is often said that the American Civil War was the most ferocious and cruel war with mass mobilization and modern weaponry. Its ferocity and cruelty, however, would pale in comparison to the Taiping Rebellion. Unlike other wars with foreign invaders during the latter half of the nineteenth century, such as two Opium wars, the Sino-French War, and the First Sino-Japanese War, where casualties were limited to the fighting troops on both sides, the Taiping Rebellion and its suppression was a total war with mass mobilization and civilian targets. The death toll for the American Civil War was about 0.6 million, whereas it was 20–80 million for the Taiping Rebellion. And this was accompanied by genocides and massacres. When the Taipings occupied Nanjing, all of the Manchu residents were killed, including women and children as they were denounced as "demons." This was, of course, by no means the only occurrence of genocides and mass killings. When the Manchus conquered the city of Yangzhou (near Nanjing) in 1645, they spent ten days killing all the residents there they could find; and when Zeng Guofan's army retook Nanjing from the Taipings, they again went on massive pillage and killing of civilians under the Heavenly Kingdom. On these occasions, Confucian notions of benevolence and Buddhist ideas of mercy never seemed to apply.

What then was this bloody revolution for? Hong Xiuquan, the Heavenly King and brother of Jesus, became corrupt as soon as he established his palace in Nanjing. On the one hand, for almost a decade in the palace, Hong never attended the business of governing his Heavenly Kingdom. Instead, like some of the most notorious emperors, he indulged himself in his numerous concubines (officially he had 88 as compared to 18 for Emperor Xianfeng of the Qing at the time). But that does not mean he was not in control. The Heavenly court soon deteriorated into a bloody power struggle between the Heavenly King and the "East King" Yang Xiuqing (1821–1856), who was actually running the regime and later claimed himself to be God on earth in contrast to Hong's self-proclamation as the brother of Jesus. The conflict resulted in the death of not only Yang, but his entire family: his wives and concubines, and all of his children. Nevertheless, the Taiping revolution would not be possible to start off in the first place without a grandiose promise of utopian paradise. And Hong's vision was strictly Christian. If the ultimate objective of Western missionaries was to turn China into a land of Christianity, Hong partially succeeded in making that a reality in the Taiping-controlled territory. Throughout the "Heavenly Kingdom," Buddhist monasteries and Taoist temples were destroyed, and Confucian teachings and other folk religions were strictly banned; everybody must do "God Worshipping." The Taiping Bible was the only acceptable book for guiding civil examinations for scholars. Hong Xiuquan was indeed a purist as he amassed all the Confucian texts he could find and burned them piece by piece—quite reminiscent of the infamous act of the First Emperor of Qin who "burned Confucian books and buried Confucian scholars alive." The Taiping rule was also a very "clean" one: no opium, tobacco, alcohol, gambling, prostitution, and concubinage allowed. Offenders were met with death penalty. This Heavenly Kingdom was a classless society with absolute equality and communal sharing. No such thing as private property ownership existed, and all land was held and distributed by the State. The sexes were also declared to be equal, and more importantly, segregated. Men and women lived under separate quarters to avoid intimate contact. Women were equal to men, but they had to wear headscarves to cover up their faces. You can't say the Taipings were simply reactionary traditionalists, as they also promised modernization measures such as building railways and national postal services. In any case, in the name of the Christian gospel, the Taipings established a totalitarian and a highly militarized super-state.

The Taiping paradise bore striking similarities with the Communist state to come less than a century later. The Taiping Heavenly Kingdom proved to be premature and short-lived due to two factors, both internal and external. The Taiping's initial sweeping military success in southern China and their radical cultural-religious stance shocked the Confucian literati class. If the Taipings were to have their way, all Confucian teachings and way of life would be considered "demonic" and banned. It was therefore a life-and-death clear-cut fight: either the Confucians were "demonic," or the Taiping Christians were "demonic." While the Manchu "banner-men," who were once ferocious warriors, had become corrupt and feeble, local Chinese gentry class were able to muster enough strength to resist and eventually crush the Taiping rebellion. The Xiang Army led by Zeng Guofan (1811–1872) and the Huai Army led by Li Hongzhang (1823–1901) proved to be resilient and resourceful enough to overwhelm the Taipings in the end. But it was not these Chinese local armies alone that defeated the Taipings. Not only was the rise of the Taipings a direct result of missionary enterprise in China, its defeat was, to a large extent, also due to Western intervention. According to one historian, since the two sides were almost evenly balanced on the war front, the final outcome of the war was in fact "determined by the diplomatic and military interventions" from Western countries.[1] Despite the Taipings' connections with Western missionaries,

---

[1] Stephen R. Platt, *Autumn in the Heavenly Kingdom*, p. xxv.

Western governments were wary of these self-proclaimed Christian rebels and their overwhelming concern was to keep China stable to trade with. When the Taiping army attacked Shanghai, part of which had already been under British and European rule according to the treaties, European mercenaries formed their own army and successfully resisted the Taiping attacks. Under the command of Frederick Townsend Ward (1831–1862), an American sailor and soldier, and later succeeded by Charles George Gordon (1833–1885), a British Army officer, this army—consisting of Chinese soldiers but trained by Western officers—became known as the Ever Victorious Army and played a significant role, and probably tipped the balance, in the final outcome of the war.

As we mentioned before, the so-called "Chinese model of government" for a *pax sinica* was out of a convergence of Confucian and Legalist philosophies. It was based on the Legalist philosophy that the First Emperor of Qin unified China and set up a fearsome super-state credited with the infamous act of "burning books and burying Confucian scholars alive." After Han Confucianists compromised to accommodate and converge with Legalist principles, the Confucian order, characterized by a family-state and a moral government, prevailed ever since in spite of dynastic changes. However, the opening up of China after the Opium War brought serious challenges to that order: Chinese culture would change. There could be different scenarios for such change to take place by accommodating and appropriating the challenges of the Western civilization. There appeared a number of visions for a modern China and Chinese culture. Many longed for a "wealthy and powerful nation-state" but based on individual rights and freedom. What is usually neglected is that, in fact, it was the Taipings who first offered a cross-cultural vision: a totalitarian super-state based on their appropriation of Christian theocracy to replace the Confucian order. They were very successful at the beginning and wreaked havoc over half of the land. But it proved to be a bit premature. The Confucian literati-class, fearful that they might experience another First Emperor of Qin "burning books and burying Confucian scholars alive," put up a dogged fight in alliance with the Western-trained Ever Victorious Army. But when these two factors changed over the following decades after the Taipings, it is not too surprising that the Communist movement would swirl and overwhelm China.

The Communist movement was an international movement that swept through almost the whole world and conquered half of it in the twentieth century. Not only did Russia become a communist superpower, but it significantly changed the Western democracies from within as communist/socialist forces occupy main opposition forces in many Western countries. The Chinese Communist movement was part and parcel of the international movement. Without the international appeal of its ideology as well as strategic and military support from Soviet Russia and the Communist International, the Communist success in China would be unthinkable—an unparalleled advantage to the Taiping revolution. On the other hand, the aftermath of the Taiping turmoil was actually the erosion of Confucian power to exert much influence upon the kind of modernity process China would embark on—paving the way for an eventual triumph of the promise of an international utopia of a classless paradise, very much in the footsteps of their Taiping predecessors.

FROM RESTORATION TO REVOLUTION

When Zeng Guofan's Xiang Army eventually crushed the Taiping rebels, some of his generals were said to have encouraged him to go all the way to Beijing and topple the Qing court and establish his own dynasty. Militarily speaking, Zeng was in a unique position quite capable of achieving that, as the Manchus had become feeble and very "cultured" after enjoying several hundred years of peaceful and aristocratic life. But Zeng disbanded his army immediately after victory. He was a model Confucian and loyalty to the throne was a prime virtue of Confucianism. Instead, Zeng Guofan, and particularly Li Hongzhang, were entrusted with much power to launch a Confucian Revival—also called "Tongzhi Restoration," or Self-strengthening Movement, or "Yangwu" (foreign affairs) movement—to empower the Qing Dynasty. A number of modernization measures were adopted in the hope of overturning the tide of dynastic decline. A special "translation school" (Tongwen Guan) was set up to introduce knowledge and documents in Western languages.

The first group of young Chinese boys were selected and sent to study in American schools and colleges in the first Chinese Educational Mission. And they even built a navy—supposed to be the most powerful one in Asia at the time with its signature Beiyang Fleet. But it all came to nothing when China suffered from a humiliating defeat in the First Sino-Japanese War of 1895 and the entire Beiyang Fleet was destroyed by the Japanese navy.

While the Confucian literati class were able to pull enough strength to quell the Taiping Rebellion, it turned out that they were ineffective to "revive" or "restore" China onto the path of modernity as the Meiji Restoration did for Japan. It was partly because of the huge devastation the decade-long Taiping Rebellion caused nationwide, and partly because of the cultural inertia the ruling literati class suffered from in dealing with the new challenge. They were simply unequipped to understand the scale of the challenge, which might necessitate a more fundamental change to the status quo. The "Self-strengthening" reformers headed by Li Hongzhang and Zhang Zhidong (1837–1909) proved to be the last generation of Confucian scholar-officials characterized by their loyalty not only to the throne but also to the quintessential of Chinese cultural orthodoxy. Their strategy toward the Western challenge can be summarized by Zhang Zhidong's famous dictum: "Chinese learning as foundation and Western learning as application" (*zhongxue wei ti xixue wei yong*), in other words, trying to absorb new technological knowledge from the West, such as new weaponry, but keeping the Chinese way of being, politically and culturally. There were inevitable tensions in such a split paradigm. The first Chinese Educational Mission was aborted partly because the young Chines boys were found to be becoming "less Chinese" as they grew up studying in American schools. China's defeat in the First Sino-Japanese War sent a shock wave among the Chinese educated class. From then on, the call for "Revolution" would hold sway, as China's survival in the new world was believed to be a problem not only in the technological and military fronts, but more importantly in the political and cultural realms, which eventually led to an all-out assault against the very "Confucian foundation."

The first revolution that came about to threaten the "Confucian foundation" was the short-lived One Hundred Day's Reform in 1898 led by Kang Youwei and Liang Qichao who advocated constitutional monarchy. The reformers advised the young Emperor Guangxu to promulgate a series of imperial edicts targeted at major political, cultural, and educational changes to bring about a constitutional monarchy. But the Qing court was not ready to release power. Empress Dowager Cixi put the young Emperor under house arrest and purged the radical reformers, most of whom had to flee to Japan. In retrospect, the failure for China to turn into a constitutional monarchy had huge significance for the kind of modernity China would embark on. In terms of actual power for governing, the change from an imperial state to a constitutional monarchy would indeed constitute a revolution. But it would still retain the crown, which would have huge symbolic value to maintain cultural stability and an orderly transition to modernity just as the British monarchy (and the postwar Japanese) has demonstrated. But cultural continuity and stability were not modern Chinese cultural features. Instead, ruptures and breakdowns prevailed. It was a "continual revolution," a more and more radical revolution one after another.

While the reformers pushed into exile continued to advocate constitutional monarchy with their loyalty to the Emperor, they were soon challenged by a new group of revolutionaries: the Nationalist Republicans under the leadership of Dr. Sun Yat-sen under the banner of "driving out the Manchus and restoring China as Chinese." To the Nationalist revolutionaries, with the goal of setting up a republic, which they eventually succeeded in in 1912, ethnicity could be weaponized (by referring to the Manchus with derogatory slang of "*dalu*" in the first place), and Chinese cultural tradition needed to be preserved somehow, most importantly as "cultural heritage," for the sake of national pride. Their competitor, the Communist revolutionaries, however, would embrace none of these. They were cosmopolitan universalists promising a utopian vision of emancipation for all races and peoples via class struggle—Chinese cultural tradition, in this respect, represented nothing but feudal dregs to be discarded with. Much of the twentieth-century China would see a bitter struggle, ideological as well as military, between these two revolutionary camps. The key to the Communist success lay in the radicalization of the Chinese mind and emergence of a new generation of modern Chinese intellectual class educated abroad.

One of the major policies put forward by the Reformers of 1898 was to abolish the thousand-year long Civil Examination system so as to make way for a modern kind of education on liberal arts and sciences. Several years after Empress Dowager Cixi put the young Emperor under house arrest and killed the Reform, the Qing government put forward its own "New Policies" in 1905, meant to rescue the sinking dynasty, and one of them was abolishment of the Examination system. This had far-reaching consequences for Chinese modernity. For the past millennium, the Examination system had produced a ruling class of scholar-officials, which was the cornerstone of "Confucian foundation." To be a scholar means you are trained in Confucian classics and are able to write elegant prose usually of a moral nature. During the the Qing Dynasty, there were fewer official posts for an increasing number of scholars, and the system was already in a crisis. As Western gunboats came to China, intellectual leaders focused on learning new scientific and technical knowledge from the West, such as making bombs. After 1905, the Chinese youth started to gain their educational and cultural capital by studying abroad, mostly via two routes: Euro-America or Japan. Those studying in Japan outnumbered those in Euro-America, as it was closer and cheaper, to go and study in Japan. And many of them went to military academies or to major their studies in science or engineering. New professions, such as the soldier, the scientist, and the revolutionary, were expected to rival the once unchallenged superior position of scholar-writers in modern China.

But still, many of them focused their studies on arts and letters. And from this generation of students abroad, there emerged an idea: it took a cultural revolution to save China, even though the last dynasty in China's history had collapsed and China had already become a republic. The Literary Revolution ignited a "Chinese Renaissance," or the New Culture Movement in the late 1910s, which shaped the modern Chinese cultural life. Literature was, therefore, of paramount significance and modern Chinese writers played the role of Enlighteners. On the one hand, the New Culture Movement was very much cosmopolitan in nature, translating all kinds of literary texts and philosophical ideas into China and embracing new cultural values from the West, but at the same time, it was a radical revolutionary movement aimed at westernizing Chinese culture as much as possible, if not "totally." In Nietzschean terms, it was to "re-evaluate all values." In other words, all the values the Chinese had been accustomed to, Confucian values, must now be re-evaluated and be overturned in light of the new cultural values from the West across an entire range of way of life, not just in terms of political system, but also in terms of women's position in society, foot-binding and concubinage, family values, education, ideas of individuals, rights and freedom, and so forth. Under the New Culturalists' attack, the "Confucian foundation" finally collapsed.

The new educated class of students who returned from abroad mainly consisted of two groups: those who went to study in Euro-America and those who went to Japan, or better and more accurately defined: those to the United Kingdom and the United States versus those to Japan and France, and the latter group was by and large the source of radicalism. The two most notable leaders from this camp were Chen Duxiu (1879–1942), who later became the founding General Secretary of the Chinese Communist Party (CCP), and Lu Xun (1881–1936), perhaps the most prominent modern Chinese writer who later became the iconic "banner" for the CCP ideology and revolutionary cause.

Chen Duxiu was first sent by the Qing government to study in a military preparatory school in Japan, but was influenced by socialist ideas and participated in student revolutionary activities to topple the Qing government. In 1915, he came back to Shanghai and launched the journal *Youth* (changed to *New Youth* a year later, which became the signatory platform for the New Culture Movement) to advocate a "thought revolution." It was in the hands of Chen Duxiu with his radical and uncompromising call to arms that Hu Shi's "modest proposal" for the vernacular *baihua* was heralded, igniting a far-reaching Literary Revolution. But Chen was a powerful and radical writer in his own right. In his celebrated article "To the Youth" in the inaugural issue of the journal, Chen outlined six values the "new youth" in China should aspire to: independence, instead of obedience; progressiveness, instead of conservatism; aggressiveness, instead of passivity; cosmopolitanism, instead of isolationism; being down-to-earth and practically oriented, instead of indulging in composing *belles-lettres* and being hypocritical; and searching for scientific truth, instead of believing in fictional and imaginary heresies. In short, as Chen put it, "If Chinese are ashamed of their being an uncivilized people, advance from their stage of barbarism and catch up with (modern civilized West), we must uphold science and human rights as two keys."[2] Furthermore, it was Chen Duxiu who summarized the key agenda of the New Culture Movement as "democracy and science," and personified these two terms as "Mr. De" (*de xiansheng*) and "Mr. Sai" (*sai xiansheng*) in Chinese[3]—turning them into two powerful modern Chinese words of contemporary usage.

"To uphold Mr. Democracy, we have to oppose Confucianism, Confucian rites and laws, chastity, old ethics and old politics; to uphold Mr. Science, we have to oppose old arts and religions; to uphold both Mr. Democracy and Mr. Science, we have to oppose traditional learning and old literature," cries Chen.[4] And he was not miserly of his pen in his scathing attacks upon Confucianism—old religions and arts and literature. The term "old" here retains a powerful ideological connotation. Armed with an evolutionary/Hegelian/socialist view of Historical Progress, all traditional Chinese culture was "feudal" and therefore must be dumped in the unstoppable history of progress. Confucianism is simply incompatible with modern life, as one of Chen's treatises suggests. Modern life is economic by nature and the basis of which is the autonomy of the individual. The Confucian teaching, on the other hand, forbids individual independence as its central ethics is familial: when your parents are still alive, you ought not to have your own economic independence. In Western democracies, family members can have their own beliefs and participate in different political parties, something unthinkable under

---
[2] Chen Duxiu, *Duxiu wencun*, p. 9.
[3] Ibid., pp. 242–243.
[4] Ibid.

the Confucian scheme. And women can also participate in all kinds of social life, even in political movement, whereas in China, Confucianism still preaches chastity, forbidding widows to remarry and practicing separation of women in social life. "Confucius was born in feudal times, so his morals were feudal morals and his teachings were based on the feudal *modus vivendi* of the feudal times."[5]

Figure 17: Lu Xun

In attacking the Confucian culture, however, none was more relentless and effective than Lu Xun, the iconoclastic writer. In modern Chinese intellectual history, perhaps nobody was a more fearless and thorough critic of traditional Chinese culture than Lu Xun. Lu Xun grew up in a declining Jiangnan gentry's family, and his whole temperament was Chinese to the core, but became more and more alienated from it because of his years in Japan. Due to a humiliating experience in the classroom, as he recounted later, he decided to give up his study to become a doctor and to become a writer instead, as he realized that the Chinese mind, instead of the body, was more in need of salvation. For ten years, after he came back from Japan, Lu Xun served quietly as a low-ranking bureaucrat in the government. When Hu Shi and Chen Duxiu were calling for a "Literary Revolution" in the *New Youth*, Lu Xun answered the call by writing the short story "Madman's Diary," which was hailed as the first modern short story written in the vernacular *baihua* and set the standard for modern Chinese fiction, and immediately established Lu Xun as the first master of the new literature in the vernacular language.

"Madman's Diary" consists of a series of random "diaries" written in vernacular *baihua* Chinese by a "madman" who is supposed to be the

---
[5] Ibid., p. 85.

narrator's childhood friend. The narrator appears in the "Preface," which is written in classical Chinese, explaining that the "madman" had actually "recovered" and was currently awaiting "a substantive official appointment." In fact, the narrator and the "madman" can all be seen as representing the authorial voice. The setting is a southern village (just like Lu Xun's hometown), and the story does not have much of a plot. Seemingly, the diaries contain random notes by the "madman" suffering from hallucinations of everybody in the village attempting to eat him up. In fact, as the readers will soon realize, the "madman" is indeed the only one who is awake—the enlightener who is caught up in the dark and seen by everybody else in the village as "mad" because his new ideas defy "common sense." In other words, the village people are all, knowingly or unknowingly, cannibals and they have been participating in the feast of cannibalism for centuries.

> You have to *really* go into something before you can understand it. I seemed to remember, though not too clearly, that from ancient times on people have often been eaten, and so I started leafing through a history book to look it up. There were no dates in this history, but scrawled this way and that across every page were the words BENEVOLENCE, RIGHTEOUSNESS, and MORALITY. Since I couldn't get to sleep anyway, I read that history very carefully for most of the night, and finally I began to make out what was written *between* the lines; the whole volume was filled with a single phrase: EAT PEOPLE![6]

To indict the entire Confucian culture as cannibalistic is a very severe charge, particularly when the Confucian emphasis has always been on humanity/humaneness (benevolence, righteousness, and morality). Progressive intellectuals in the West today, who are aware about the cannibalistic discourse in *Robinson Crusoe* may find it unbelievable that a most progressive modern Chinese writer stereotyped his own culture as cannibalistic. But that was exactly what Lu Xun was fighting for and was beloved for. With piercing sarcasm and relentless self-critique, Lu Xun's

---

[6] Lu Xun, *Diary of a Madman and Other Stories*, p. 32.

writings are known as enlightening the "national soul" of the Chinese. The "souls" of the Chinese as depicted in "A Madman's Diary," however, had been corrupt after thousands of years of cannibalistic practices. The village people lived in a closely-knit community, blind, and stubbornly opposed to any new ideas and changes outside. The Zhao family certainly represents the power and order of the community, but the enlightener's point is that everybody in the community, including the "madman's" own brother and sister, is complicit in maintaining a cannibalistic order. The "madman's" charge against the Confucian order was total and relentless. The village was an "iron house." You either break it or be suffocated in it. The "madman's" last diary entry goes:

> Maybe there are some children around who still haven't eaten human flesh.
>
> Save the children…[7]

However, the "madman" himself does not belong to these "children," as we are told in the Preface written in classical Chinese (which represents the "old" order) that the "madman" is now cured and awaiting an official appointment—ready to join the cannibals.

As Lu Xun's critique of the cannibalistic nature of Confucian morality suggests, to crack open the "iron house" of the suffocating inertia of Chinese cultural tradition, the only way is to break it. That was what modern Chinese youth were inspired to do—to break away from the tradition and search for the nascence of a "new civilization." After the collective assault of the New Culturalists such as Chen Duxiu and Lu Xun, the Confucian ground was hollowed out and Chinese culture was awaiting a radical transformation. While the New Culture Movement still offered many possibilities for the modern Chinese culture to take shape, world political events hastened its revolutionary radicalization. In the 1910s, democracies were going down the hell in the first major world war, in the middle of which the Russian Communists successfully launched the October Revolution of 1917. Communism by now was no longer a "spectre haunting Europe,"

---

[7] Ibid, p. 41.

but a real state-sponsored international force. It soon reached China. The CCP was established in 1921, headed by no other than the New Culture Movement leader Chen Duxiu. Furthermore, the 1920s saw China engrossed in another wave of Nationalist Revolution, this time, however, the Nationalists allied themselves with the nascent Communists under Dr. Sun Yat-sen's new policies. In other words, the Nationalist Revolution of 1927 was won very much based on the Communist ideology, or at least a convergence of Nationalist and Communist ideologies. When the two ideologies clashed in the middle of their allied military campaign against various warlord powers, and the Nationalists successfully carried out a bloody purge against the Communists in their united front, the end result was twofold: the Nationalist won militarily and established the Nanjing government but nevertheless did not win the ideological battle. The intellectual youth who occupied the backbone of its revolution were hardly convinced of the Nationalist argument. Quite the contrary, it paved the way for China's royal roads to Russia. As Lin Yutang, who was by no means in the Communist camp, testified in 1930:

> Anybody who visits the new book shops on Foochow Road [in Shanghai] will see that over 70 per cent of the new books on the market have to do with Russia, Karl Marx, and names ending in a—ov, or a—lev. A list of the literary works of Russian authors which have been translated in the last two years would put to shame any professor of modern Russian literature in Harvard or Columbia . . . For Russia has conquered Young China and claimed her as her own. People who imagine that the ideas and ideology of the students of today are those which precipitated the May 30th Affair in 1919, or those that made possible the Nationalist Revolution in 1927 are sadly mistaken. Young China has gone red in the last three years *after* the nationalist revolution.[8]

Crushed by the Nationalists during the bloody purge, the CCP launched several unsuccessful uprisings and then led the remaining armed forces to

---

[8] Lin Yutang, *The Little Critic*.

the mountains to engage in guerrilla warfare, and eventually they set up a Soviet Republic in Jiangxi. While on the defensive militarily in the 1930s, the CCP shifted its focus on ideological battles and was definitely taking an offensive there. Now that the KMT was condemned as "reactionary" as they had "betrayed the revolution," the CCP presented itself as the only progressive force carrying on the revolution—a class revolution. The CCP's strategy was to seize the moral high ground and achieve ideological dominance so as to win maximum popular support, particularly among the youth. While they suffered from a series of military setbacks and eventually were forced to abandon their Soviet base in Jiangxi to embark on the "long march," finally setting up a base in Yan'an, a remote town in northern Shanxi, the ideological battle was won quite successfully, as evidenced in the large exodus of intellectual youth from urban centers like Shanghai to Yan'an when the all-out War of Resistance against Japan broke out in 1937.

The ideological battle was fought mainly in the fields of literature and arts. In 1930, the CCP set up the League of Left-wing Writers (Left League) in Shanghai as its front organization with Lu Xun hailed as its nominal and spiritual Head. During the Great Revolution of 1927, Lu Xun was by no means a converted Marxist and in fact was attacked by young Chinese Marxists as outdated and belonging to the "old world." Lu Xun fought back but he also tried hard to catch up the trend of Young China—not only by reading up on Marxist theory, but by actually translating many Russian and East European literary works and Marxist theoretical treatises. The establishment of the Left League was to unify the Leftist writers to speak in one voice under the direct leadership of the CCP, and then to exert dominating impact on the Chinese mind. The first was to win over Lu Xun, so the young Marxist theorists' attacks upon Lu Xun were ordered to stop. When Lu Xun re-emerged as the leader of the Left League, he did not use his pen miserly—he became the most ferocious warrior using his pen as "daggers" thrown at the ideological enemies.

According to the Communist ideology, literature is but a propaganda tool for the Communist revolutionary cause worldwide. Anybody in the way of this revolutionary cause was deemed an "enemy." This did not simply refer to those who were opposed to the Communist ideology, but also to those who were neither for nor against it, because the mere existence of such neutrality, particularly when it also gained a great deal of popularity, was very much in the way of the CCP's effort to achieve hegemony in the ideological front. The Left League launched a series of "campaigns" to achieve uniformity and predominance. Lu Xun's "zawen" (miscellaneous essays) proved to be the most powerful "daggers" thrown at "enemies" of various kinds.

But the 1930s literary scene was by no means unified and uniform. The Literary Revolution not only marginalized some writers, such as the so-called Saturday School or "Butterfly" writers, but it also engendered different schools of writers. In fact, one of the major phenomena in modern Chinese literature and culture is the mushrooming of different literary "societies" and "schools." On the liberal front, there was the "Xinyue (Crescent Moon) Society" headed by Hu Shi, the poet Xu Zhimo, and the critic Liang Shiqiu, who were basically trained in England and America. They would certainly not follow the banner of the Left League. In fact, Xu Zhimo was noted for his outspoken criticism against Soviet Union and Communist ideologies, and practices as an editor of *Chenbao*. When Liang Shiqiu returned from his study at Harvard University, he became a staunch follower of Irving Babbitt's ideas advocating such principles of discipline and tradition in literature. As if publicly pronouncing his Leftist turn, Lu Xun engaged himself in a major polemics against Liang Shiqiu, announcing that all literature is class-based—a central tenet of the Communist ideology. But the polemics by no means focused on an intellectual debate on the nature and function of literature, whether class-based or not. Rather, in a camouflage style typical of Lu Xun's "random essays," they seemingly talk about irrelevant things, full of innuendoes, poses, and gestures (such as calling Liang "Professor" while in fact Lu Xun was a much better known writer and 22 years senior to Liang), and then in a sleight of hand, the "dagger" will hit the opponent's weak points—more often than not, in a form of character assassination. The height of Lu Xun's attack against Liang lies in his calling Liang "a fatigued running dog of the capitalist class," which supposedly demonstrated Lu Xun's power of his pen.

And there was the "Analects" school loosely led by Lin Yutang. While critically aware of the red tide inundating the intellectual world of the 1930s China, Lin Yutang certainly did not jump into the crowd. Instead, he launched several literary journals advocating humor and leisurely style of writing, which proved to be very popular among the intellectual youth—particularly college students, for instance. That posed a danger to the CCP effort for ideological hegemony, even though Lin Yutang had never attacked the Communist ideology and targeted the ruling Nationalist government for his liberal critique. The Left League decided to launch "campaigns" to discredit the craze for humor and leisurely writing as "ornamental" and bourgeois. It was Lu Xun who was leading the charge, mocking Lin's promotion of an aesthetics of individuality as reactionary, just as Gu Hongming's fetishes for women's bound feet and as hypocritical and traitorous as Zheng Xiaoxu's advocating the "Kingly Way" while serving as the premier for the puppet Manchukuo regime.[9] These attacks were not only meant to be "daggers," but poisonous daggers thrown in the dark, as these polemical essays were all published with a series of "pen names" that kept Lin guessing who the real attackers were—Lu Xun and Lin Yutang used to be very close friends! In his counterattacks, Lin pointed out the danger of treating literature as propaganda tool and insisted on keeping a "leisurely" space for literature away from politics. To Lin, the idea to treat literature as a propaganda tool for the Communist revolutionary cause smells something very "old," rather than "fashionable and progressive," as it resonated with the strict and orthodox Confucianist dictum that "literature ought to carry the Way."

As the fiercest warrior from the Left League, Lu Xun engaged in polemical fights with almost all other groups or schools of writers. There was also the so-called "Third Category" writers surrounding the journal *Les Contemporains* edited by Shi Zhicun, for instance, who were actually left leaning but not necessarily following Party orders. And there were also the "Beijing school" of writers headed by Zhou Zuoren, Lu Xun's younger brother with whom Lu Xun ceased to communicate with due to a family feud. It seems Lu Xun's fighting spirit would never wane, but sometimes he felt weary, complaining in private that he was being dragged onto the stage to please the party chief. Shortly before Lu

---

[9] Lu Xun, "Tiansheng manxing", pp. 432–433.

Xun's death, the tension between Lu Xun and his party chief Zhou Yang (1908–1989) went public as Lu Xun threw a number of "daggers" at Zhou. As Lu Xun was charging at the forefront in the ideological battles, the CCP policy suddenly changed in order to accommodate the political circumstances to make the most political gain. The CCP now decided to call for a "united front" against the encroaching Japanese invasion, so its tactics must change, which means some of the polemical fights must stop. Either the message was not conveyed clearly to Lu Xun or there were personality conflicts between the two—Lu Xun felt he was belittled and condemned his party chief publicly. Later after Zhou Yang was relocated to Yan'an, he reported the affair to the real party chief Mao Zedong, whose verdict was that Zhou made a tactical error in infuriating Lu Xun even though he was following the CCP policy, but Zhou soon rose in the CCP rank to become one of Mao's most trusted propaganda chiefs. As for Lu Xun, he died soon after the affair and was spared of any reports to Mao. Indeed, ever since his death in 1936, Lu Xun had been hailed as a "national soul" representing the conscience of modern Chinese people and was further deified under the CCP regime as an ideological banner for the Chinese Communist cause. But his close disciples such as Hu Feng (1902–1985) would suffer and be put into prison under the Communist state—which Lu Xun contributed resolutely to its birth and was fortunate enough not having to live under.

YAN'AN TALKS AND ITS SHADOWS

When we talk about the horror and madness of the Cultural Revolution today, we should not think that it was simply accidental that such madness took place in the decade spanning the years from 1966 to 1976, the period officially allocated to the Great Proletariat Cultural Revolution. Its origins were developed from Chinese modernity. By the 1930s, the means and tactics of waging a class war in the ideological front had already matured. The pen had become bloody indeed. The difference was that the Left League was by no means in power, and they sometimes could not impose unilateral control among their own ranks.

This aspect changed in the Yan'an "Rectification Campaign." When the all-out War of Resistance against Japan broke out in 1937, the Nationalists and the Communists were again in a united front. After initial resistance, the Nationalist government relocated to Chongqing as its wartime capital while the CCP consolidated its base in northern Shanxi province with Yan'an as their red capital. Along with the great exodus of millions of coastal populations to the inland provinces, a great number of intellectual youths from Shanghai and other major cities flocked to the red base Yan'an to pursue their romantic revolutionary ideals. On the one hand, this movement certainly greatly strengthened the CCP force, but it also created new problems as these urbanite intellectual youths were not exactly accustomed to the strict discipline of a Soviet party life. After a series of intense power struggle, Mao Zedong had emerged as the leader of the CCP, but his power was by no means consolidated yet. With the sudden influx of intellectual youth in Yan'an, Mao carried out the "Rectification Campaign" to unify the "thoughts" of the Party, which resulted, for the first time, in Mao's unchallenged supreme leadership within the CCP.

How do you unify one's thoughts? Actually, you start with "open democracy": writers and intellectuals were encouraged to speak out their thoughts openly, often by pasting big-character posters onto the walls in public. Urbanite youth flocked from Shanghai to Yan'an out of idealism, but once settled in a deprived remote town under strict military rule, many of them would find it difficult to adjust and hard to swallow. It would not be surprising they had many grievances in their "thoughts." One young writer named Wang Shiwei, for instance, complained that, instead of a shiny lighthouse for a dark China, the Yan'an he had experienced was in fact dark and depressive; instead of being an equal and ideal environment, daily food was rationed strictly in accordance with hierarchical status with high-ranking CCP officials enjoying privileges. Once the vermin were out in the open, it was time to crack down. Mao Zedong delivered a series of talks, later dubbed as "Yan'an Talks," on the nature of literature and arts and the role of writers and intellectuals under the CCP ideology. He was of the opinion that literature must serve the people's cause of revolution strictly under the ideological control of the CCP leadership; and therefore, the role of writers and intellectuals were to be "workers of the arts and letters," virtually a cog in the machine of the party system. To share the message across and to be understood correctly, the CCP adopted the effective technique of "criticism and self-criticism," which first originated in Soviet Russia. After Mao delivered his talks, study sessions were organized in which everybody must share their thoughts about the talks. Everybody must pass the test. You can't simply say you approve the Leader's talks in a general way. You need to go through "criticism and self-criticism," that is, you had to openly point out what you know about others who have uttered politically incorrect "dark thoughts," and criticize them; and more importantly, openly admit what you yourself have said or thought about that were not in line with the Leader's talks. In case you had any doubt about how your idealism must conform to the firm discipline of the Party, by this time when they were undergoing "criticism and self-criticism," Wang Shiwei had already been arrested, expelled from the Party, publicly denounced as a "counter-revolutionary." Instead of executing him (which was later done by the CCP secret service during the Civil War), Wang must first go through the process of re-education to reform his mind as a negative example for everybody else. By way of "criticism" against others, party loyalty was strengthened because you learn that you can't really trust anybody, even your friends, after you have joined the revolution. By way of "self-criticism," you needed to confess and open up your heart to the party, and thus, you and the party become inseparable.

That was how you unified thoughts. After the establishment of the People's Republic of China in 1949, the CCP launched a series of "campaigns" against writers and intellectuals to unify the thoughts. All the way through to the Great Proletariat Cultural Revolution, the techniques the CCP employed were the same as those in the Yan'an Rectification Campaign, but amazingly Chinese writers and intellectuals fell for it repeatedly and seemed to be rather surprised after each campaign. For instance, shortly after the CCP gained power, there was an ideological campaign against Liang Shuming (1893–1988), a philosopher who promoted agrarian reform and thought his ideas were in line with Mao's. On one occasion, Liang openly challenged Mao on his policies and Mao would have none of it and openly called his name, labeling him a "counter-revolutionary." And there was an ideological campaign against Hu Feng, the most famous disciple of Lu Xun. This was in fact the continuation of the conflict between Lu Xun and Zhou Yang within the Left League in the 1930s. Hu Feng considered himself the authentic follower of Lu Xun, and continued to disagree with Zhou Yang, which meant their dissent from the spirit and principles of Mao's Yan'an Talks. Now in power, Mao had no tactical concerns, and even if Lu Xun were alive, he would have adopted the same decision against his disciple Hu Feng: labeling him as a "counter-revolutionary," launching a nation-wide critical campaign to humiliate him, and put him in prison for twenty years. It was not Hu Feng alone. The campaign identified more than two thousand followers of Hu, named them as the "Hu Feng Counter-Revolutionary Group," and arrested almost a hundred hard-core members. An even bigger campaign against any intellectual dissent was launched in 1958 in the so-called "Anti-Rightist Campaign," of which Deng Xiaoping was put in direct charge. The means and techniques of the campaign were identical with those in the Yan'an Rectification Campaign, but when Mao Zedong called on the intellectuals to criticize the party and the government, many were indeed encouraged to air their views, only to be crushed a couple of weeks later and identified as a "Rightist" and sent to labor camps in remote and poor regions to be "re-educated."

When the Great Proletariat Cultural Revolution was launched in 1966, there was hardly any dissent voice left. And the "revolution" had hardly anything to do with "culture." After the Great Famine of the later 1950s and early 1960s, Mao's esteem was tarnished and his hand-picked successor Liu Shaoqi (1898–1969) (and Deng Xiaoping to a lesser extent) was gaining higher reputation. Mao then turned against those revolutionaries within the CCP, calling upon the Red Guards to guard him from those usurpers (who were called "capitalist revisionists") taking power away from the "great proletariat." It was a "revolution" in the sense that it was a power struggle within the CCP, as Mao again resorted to a Yan'an-style mass campaign to overturn its own governmental establishment. As a result, many previous guards of Mao's line now found themselves humiliated and sent to labor camps or put into prison, such as Zhou Yang and Deng Xiaoping. Liu Shaoqi was arrested, beaten up, and eventually tortured to death. If Mao's "continual revolution" to get rid of his potential political opponents had anything to do with "culture," it was that in a frenzied classification and identification of the people according to their classes, anybody with "culture," that is, those with some education, was identified as a potential enemy, ranked No. 9 (nicknamed "stinking No. 9") among a list of enemy categories. Many writers and intellectuals who had previously luckily escaped from persecution either by lying low or enthusiastically embracing the Communist ideology and hence given high-ranking official posts (such as Lao She), now found themselves "enemies of the state"— Lao She, for instance, committed suicide after being humiliated in open "struggle sessions" (a variation of the "criticism and self-criticism" method). Literature was not only a propaganda tool, but achieved unprecedented stereotypical uniformity. All literary and artistic creation must center on the theme of class struggle. In all movie theatres nationwide, you could get to watch "Eight Sample Movies." And a novel was always about how workers or peasants (the good guys) eventually exposed and overcame the plots of some class enemy (the bad guys), and believe it or not, these fictional bad guys often carried the surname of "Qian" (as its literal meaning is "money") — the same as mine, and I grew up reading such novels! Indeed, you can say this was a "cultural" revolution when surnames were politicized and played an important role in the class struggle.

After Mao died in 1976, the CCP had a coup and Mao's widow Jiang Qing and the so-called "Gang of Four" were arrested and put into prison. Gradually, those CCP elites who were side-lined and persecuted by Mao were reinstated and Deng Xiaoping re-emerged as the leader. China would embark on the Reform Era. There would be gigantic changes in the life of Chinese people, particularly economically but also culturally. Reform would not be possible without "opening-up." In fact, it started with "emancipation of one's mind." In that light, the 1980s almost witnessed a small Renaissance in terms of intellectual freedom and literary and artistic creation. It was somewhat going back to the New Culture Movement in the 1910s, when writers again assumed the role of "enlighteners," this time against the CCP party control of literature and thought. For instance, you have the "misty poets," a group of young poets who were composing poems few could understand. Ironically, the less understood, the more popular they became, as people were so tired of those formularized propaganda poems, or "Eight Sample Movies." Also, as a reversion to the prevalent attitude of condemning everything traditional as "feudal" and "poisonous" during the Cultural Revolution, there emerged a "Root-seeking" school or a trend to look back upon China's own tradition more sympathetically. Mo Yan's novel *Red Sorgum*, for instance, was adapted into a very popular movie directed by Zhang Yimou. The theme of the story goes back to the Japanese atrocities during the war, and somehow re-awakens the nationalist consciousness of the contemporary Chinese.

But Mao's shadow lingers on. In case one's mind gets really emancipated and opened up, Deng Xiaoping spelled out clearly the "Four Cardinal Principles" under the new Reform Era: the principle of upholding the socialist path, the principle of upholding the people's democratic dictatorship, the principle of upholding the leadership of the CCP, and the principle of upholding Marxism-Leninism and Mao Zedong Thought. In other words, despite its economic policy of loosening state control of economic affairs, allowing private enterprises, embracing global capital for investment, the CCP is not conceding any ground in terms of its ideological control. Writers and intellectuals continued to run the risk of being accused of "liberalization" as they were put under constant check by the government propaganda team and would gain ground or suffer setbacks along with the twists and turns of political climate in the 1980s. The mini-enlightenment of the 1980s ended with the "people's democratic dictatorship" over the student protest movement in 1989, as tanks were summoned to the Tiananmen Square to crush the peaceful student demonstrations.

One of the major reform measures in the new era was the re-opening of the College Examination system, which produced a new generation of college students and intellectual youth. One of the freedoms that was opened up to many was to study abroad or simply immigrate abroad. That meant a new possibility for intellectual dissent. After the crackdown in 1989, many writers and intellectuals found themselves living overseas in exile. As global capital entered China, Chinese culture also became diasporic and global. The different fate in terms of their reception for the two Chinese writers who have recently won the Nobel Prize in Literature highlights the dilemma of intellectual discourse in China today.

It has been a national frustration that Chinese writers had never been awarded the Nobel Prize for Literature, even though Hu Shi and Lin Yutang had been nominated before. In 2000, the Nobel Prize for Literature was awarded to Gao Xingjian for his Chinese-language novel *Soul Mountain* (*Lingshan*). Instead of rejoicing, the award posed a huge embarrassment for the Chinese government. Gao was born in 1940 in China, survived the Cultural Revolution and understood what the "Four Cardinal Principles" meant inside out. By the late 1980s, Gao emigrated to France and had become a French citizen when the award was given. The novel *Soul Mountain* was semi-autobiographical, detailing his travels in China with memoirs of his life growing up under the Communist China. The Nobel committee praised the book as "an oeuvre of universal validity, bitter insights and linguistic ingenuity." What the committee did not say was that, the novel, and particularly his second novel *One Man's Bible* (*Yigeren de Shengjing*), were probably the best literary accounts to date in Chinese on the nature of the Communist experience in China. As it contains scathing critique of the Communist regime, Gao and his works have been banned in mainland China. While he has been warmly received in overseas Chinese communities (including Taiwan and Hong Kong), the majority of the Chinese in mainland China do not even know the name of Gao Xingjian.

In 2012, Mo Yan was awarded the Nobel Prize for Literature. This time, it was endorsed by the Chinese government and hailed as, finally, "the first Chinese writer to win the honor." But it also immediately caused heated controversies as many Chinese writers and intellectuals (quite a few are living in exile) questioned his association with the party. Mo Yan grew up in a farmer's family, and later joined the People's Liberation Army where he started his writing career. He has been one of the most prolific and accomplished contemporary writers during the Reform Era. Influenced by "magical realism" of Latin American literature (Gabriel García Márquez), he was praised by the Nobel committee as a writer "who with hallucinatory realism merges folk tales, history and the contemporary." Mo Yan's writings do offer social commentaries and criticisms of contemporary Chinese life, but his brand of criticism is very different from that of Gao Xingjian. In any case, Mo Yan's style of criticism is acceptable to the Chinese government. And he does not challenge the "Four Cardinal Principles," at least symbolically, as, for instance, he collaborated with the Party's call for "political correct" behavior to publicly hand-copy Mao Zedong's "Yan'an Talks on Literature and Art" in commemoration of the 70th anniversary of the speeches in May 2012, shortly before the Nobel Prize was awarded.

In the mid-1990s, Li Zehou and Liu Zaifu, two well-known Chinese intellectuals, called for "Farewell to Revolution," believing that a healthy future for Chinese culture relies on bidding farewell to revolution, which characterized Chinese modernity and had brought traumatic effects upon Chinese culture today.[10] For Chinese culture to say farewell to revolution, however, it need to find a peaceful mechanism to settle conflicts and reach consensus. Upholding the "Four Cardinal Principles," just like upholding the Confucian-Legalist "Three Fundamental Obediences and Five Constant Virtues," are no guarantees for harmony and stability. If China is engulfed in another revolution in the twenty-first century, one should not be surprised. Except that this time, given China is already the world's second economic power, it will not only shake up China, but the world at large.

---

[10] Li Zehou and Liu Zaifu, *Gaobie geming*.

Chapter 8

The Rise of China and Its Cultural Challenge

When the Great Proletariat Cultural Revolution came to an end in 1976, China was on the verge of collapse. Behind the Iron Curtain were a people exhausted of political campaigns in the name of class struggle while barely making a living at all. I was at Year One in middle school and I remember I was wearing my father's used work clothes to school. Everything was rationed — peanuts were something I cherished only once a year during the Chinese New Year. That was the reality of the Communist utopia. Then, peasants began to defy the party doctrine by growing vegetables and raising chicken in their own backyard out of sheer necessity, ignoring the risk of being labeled as a "capitalist" with dire consequences. Thousands and thousands of people were risking their lives against the cold waters and military barricades to illegally cross the border to Hong Kong. This time, however, the potential mass unrest played a favorable impact upon the power struggle in the party elite in which the "reformers," many of whom had been persecuted during Mao's rule and had recently been readmitted to the party leadership, took the opportunity and resolutely turned away from Mao's orthodox principles. Deng Xiaoping, who emerged as the leader of the new party elite, would lead China into the Reform Era. Instead of blocking illegal migrants by force against the barbwire along the Shenzhen River, what the reformers did was to "open up" part of Shenzhen as a "special economic zone" and invited those capitalists in Hong Kong and abroad to set up their factories there, so that hungry Chinese workers could have jobs and feed themselves. That was how "*gaikai*" — "*gaige*" (reform) and "*kaifang*" (opening up) — started.

When you reflect upon Chinese modernity as a whole, the post-Mao Reform Era of the last four decades resembles to a large extent the post-Taiping Tongzhi Restoration, both coming out of revolutionary ravages and both enjoying a period of political stability and economic growth. The Self-strengthening Movement ultimately failed, ushering in more and more radicalization all the way to the madness of "continual revolution" of the Great Proletariat Cultural Revolution. After four decades of "gaikai," China has now become an economic superpower in the world. For those who understand the Chinese modernity process, in which the pursuit of a "wealthy and strong nation" against colonial encroachment of the powers won almost universal consensus among all strands of the intellectual class, they should appreciate that the Chinese probably deserve some pride in terms of its national standing in the world today. Yet, amidst the hype of the "rise of China," one ought to be clear-minded that Chinese modernity, and "*gaikai*," is still an ongoing process. "Gaikai" is only a half success and Chinese modernity has not found its breakthrough moment yet. This is mainly because, while China is now an economic giant, it is a cultural dwarf. China's cultural soft power in the world is negligible, if not in the negative territory. China's economic engine will continue to power on despite internal and external challenges ahead. It is simply inconceivable that China could go back to the kind of economic depravity as at the end of the Cultural Revolution. Culturally, however, China is far from having "risen" to a sustainable level. Whether China can successfully deal with its cultural challenge is not merely a matter of concern for the Chinese, but ultimately for the world as well. Here in this last chapter, I will discuss the cultural challenges facing China today and offer some personal reflections on possible ways forward. It would be advisable that such reflections start from pondering upon some of the cultural factors contributing to the economic rise of China.

THE RISE OF CHINA AND ITS CULTURAL FACTORS

Whatever you say about China today, one thing is true: China has gone through momentous changes during the so-called Reform Era of the last four decades. The economic rise of China has been a world spectacle. It is by no means an easy task for one fifth of the world population to get out of sheer poverty in the first place. There are many treatises on the economic rise of China, its causes and costs — it would not be possible, for instance, without the influx of global capital at the expenses of both human (labor rights) and environmental costs. I will spell out here, however, a few cultural factors related to the change.

1. Pragmatism

The city of Shenzhen, just across the border of Hong Kong and currently one of the four mega-cities (in addition to Beijing, Shanghai, Guangzhou) in China today, is quite symbolic of the new China under rise. Before the Reform Era, Shenzhen was an undeveloped "fishing village" bordering Hong Kong where many households were empty by the end of 1970s after several waves of "refugee escapees" flocked to the other side during the Mao Era. In May 1980, Shenzhen was declared as a Special Economic Zone, thus ushering in an era of "*gaige kaifang*" (reform and opening up). After a short suspension following the Tiananmen Incident of 1989, Deng Xiaoping made a "Southern Tour" in 1992, reaffirming the policy of reform and opening-up while upholding the exemplary role of Shenzhen, thereby recharging China's economy to the point of no return. Shenzhen had been on the forefront of reform and opening-up, enjoying many "firsts". In the early 1980s, the first high-rise building on mainland China — Guomao (International Trade Building) — was built, taking three days for each story; such speed was nicknamed the "Shenzhen speed," symbolic to the new era. The first McDonald's in China was opened in Shenzhen in 1990, and so did the Shenzhen Stock Exchange with much fanfare. But most importantly, Deng Xiaoping endorsed several catch-phrases that were related to Shenzhen and symbolic of a new ethos, such as "*shijian jiushi jinqian*" (Time Is Money), "*fazhan shi ying daoli*" (Development Is the Top Priority), "*rang yibufen ren xian fu qilai*" (Let a few get rich first).

This was the new ethos of pragmatism. Deng Xiaoping's "reform" did not project a new ideology. Rather, it resolutely shunned away from any ideology, including the Communist ideology of class struggle and "continual revolution." This was a crucial move without which China's "*gaige kaifang*" would not be possible at all. In other words, the Reform started with the "emancipation of one's mind" — to shake off the shackles of the stifling ideology of class struggle. Finally, a century of radical revolution, culminating in the disastrous Cultural Revolution, produced counter-effects, as a large number of Communist cadres had become victims of their own making and began to detest high-sounding extremism. Perhaps the guiding principle (if there was such a thing) for China's Reform was Deng Xiaoping's famous line: "Whether a white cat or a black cat, so long it catches a mouse, it is a good cat." And in the aftermath of the Cultural Revolution, there finally emerged a consensus about what it was for the cat to catch, namely, poverty. Deng Xiaoping's pragmatism, therefore, suspended any ideological debate: don't ask whether the economic reform measures are socialist or capitalist in nature; so long as it can alleviate poverty for China and make some Chinese get rich first, go ahead and do it.

Poverty was the biggest enemy facing China — that was actually the thesis put forward by Hu Shi in the 1930s. China had to go through the ordeal of revolutionary trauma to come back to this realization relying upon the legacy of pragmatism, arguably a Chinese cultural mechanism from Confucian to modern times. Pragmatism, after all, calls for attention to a reality check, compromise, a sense of proportions, as well as an emphasis on reasoning and reasonableness away from high-sounding utopian ideals. Particularly revealing was the notion "to let a few get rich first," which sounds downright politically incorrect in the Western context. But Western political correctness must understand that the Chinese practiced the Marxist ideology of class struggle to a devastating consequence, not only uprooting Chinese tradition, but turning the very reason into unreason and madness. To acknowledge social hierarchy is indeed a very pragmatic and down-to-earth recognition of humanity — an essential aspect of Confucianism as well. The revival of Confucianism in the Reform Era was not entirely a matter of political appropriation. It had its own *raison d'être* to a certain extent.

After three decades of orthodox Communist totalitarian rule, it was this pragmatic loosening of the grip that unleashed unprecedented energy of the Chinese people. The Chinese were allowed to open a shop, a restaurant, or to move between jobs, no longer "protected" for life as a cog in the machine in a working unit. People began to enjoy personal freedoms, and the whole society was on the move. The economic rise of China owes primarily to the unleashing of the Chinese people's energy having set the Chinese half free. On the other hand, however, such pragmatism is also the source for many of the problems China faces today. The Reform is full of paradoxes precisely because Deng's pragmatism only grants half freedom to the Chinese. It never forsook the party leadership. Who got to be the lucky few who were let to get rich first? In a state where the Party has supreme dominance in every aspect, it should not be a surprise that they turn out to be high (and low)-ranking Communist officials and their extended families *en masse*. It is true that China's economic rise saw the emergence of a middle class in China, concentrating in cities and coastal areas, quite a considerable number given China's population size. But it is also true that the gap between the rich and the poor is among the highest in the world (far greater than the old capitalist countries). The lives of the working class in both urban and rural areas have become much better compared to what it was four decades ago, but given the huge gap, they may not "feel better" at all. More importantly, the Reform was about making money by way of bracketing any ideological debates. That creates a spiritual vacuum along with the onslaught of commercialism. A material life is only half a life. Once one's stomach is full, one will have ideas and have a cultural life. No party or power can defy that logic, because it is human nature.

2. Education

As we have seen, Chinese emphasis on education has deep cultural roots. But the Communist revolution carried an anti-intellectual ideology. When this was carried out to its full extent during the Cultural Revolution, students were beating up teachers and those who failed in exams were hailed as "rebel heroes." Books were burnt and universities were closed down. The educated were disgraced in the society as "stinking No. 9" according to strict Communist class stratification.

China's economic rise would be impossible without bringing back the deeply rooted cultural ethic on education. A defining moment for the Reform Era was reinstituting the College Entrance Exam in 1977 and the opening up of universities again. Moreover, Chinese students were gradually allowed to go abroad to study, whether sponsored by the state or through private channels of their own pursuit. This was a game changer. The Chinese society would be changed significantly and irreversibly ever since. Just like the Civil Examination system in traditional China, the College Entrance Exam system ensured a fairly democratic way for entrance to the social elite class. By and large, all Chinese kids go to school at the age of six and enjoy free primary and secondary schooling. Then one centrally administered exam determines whether you can go to college and what kind of college, regardless of your family and regional background. A college degree is normally a passport to middle class status. One may very well question the defects of such "exam culture," but it is arguably the least corrupt and most democratic means of realizing one's potential.

Thus, education is back at the center of Chinese society. The youth again have the means for moving up the social ladder. Together with the one-child policy, Chinese parents are simply obsessed with their child's education, and will do everything for it. Competition usually starts in kindergarten. And parents compete for how many after-school clubs they have enrolled their children in. The days for the College Entrance Examination remain the most critical moments for examinees and their parents alike. Nowadays, however, the College Entrance Exam is no longer the only channel for stepping into a middle-class life. As the size of the middle class grows, more and more Chinese families can afford to send their children abroad for higher education. Chinese students are all over the world and they constitute the largest number of foreign students' group in many Western countries. It should be noted that Chinese students from rich families who do not care about tuition are still quite few, while majority of them are from middle class families, who usually have to save very hard to support their children's education abroad.

Chinese cultural obsession with education spreads to immigrant Chinese families as well. In Britain, for instance, ethnic Chinese students excel in school performances including GCSE (General Certificate of Secondary Education) and A-level exams way beyond the average and any other ethnic groups. There has been much discussion on the difference between Chinese style of rote-learning and Western style of creative learning, but this may be somewhat exaggerated, as some rote-learning is always necessary especially in primary schools. The real difference in approach is cultural: the Chinese simply attach overwhelming prominence to children's education and are committed in carrying it through. One can call this Professor/Take-away Model. Many Chinese new immigrants are highly educated, having come abroad to study in colleges in the first place, and they are usually eager to invest in their children's education. What is perhaps less known is that, for the other group of Chinese immigrants, uneducated and from villages in South China, many of them perhaps illegal, their main means of survival was to open a Chinese takeaway outlet and work extremely long hours all year around. Yet they are more eager to invest in their children's education by sending them to expensive independent schools. My daughter's best friend, in an English independent girls' school, is from a takeaway family, and she outshines my daughter in many aspects.

3. Family

I was in fact already talking about family in the context of education. In Britain, as in other western countries, some well-to-do families may help support their children's college education, but they belong to a minority. The cultural norm is that once you are eighteen, you are responsible for yourself — including your college education. Chinese families would never think that way, even though they would agree that you kind of come of age by eighteen (the other more traditional mark is that a man becomes a man after he gets married with children). The family bond is much closer, basically lasting a lifetime. Under the Communist ideology, however, family is something a revolutionary would gladly sacrifice for a higher and purer goal. During the Cultural Revolution, there were cases where family members split apart, even pitted against each other, in line with party politics. But even then, the family as an institution was largely intact. Even Mao Zedong could not destroy the family — perhaps the most elemental fabric of Chinese culture.

Family again played a significant role in the economic rise of China. I'll mention two functions here. It is often said that Chinese society is one of "*guanxi*" (connections), which starts with a big family, extending to relatives (sometimes very distant ones), then to hometown or village compatriots, and then all kinds of associates (school alumni, past colleagues from work or businesses, etc.) Chinese immigrant communities follow this family connections pattern closely and therein lies the preconditions for their success overseas (they still have to work very hard to make it). It was the same in China under the Reform. When you want to solve a problem, whether in starting a business or running a business, the first thing the Chinese think of is if they have a "connection" with someone who has the power to fix it. It is no wonder then who would actually get rich first — those whose family connections can boast of party officials, from the very top all the way down to the factory unit or village level, because they have unparalleled advantage in terms of access to policies and resources. A large majority of the "rich and powerful" in today's China obtained their wealth and power, thanks to such family connections. Therefore, you can say corruption in China is also very much cultural. Public exposure of the wealth and assets of officials can hardly serve as a credible anti-corruption measure, as officials' wealth may very well be hidden under the name of their cousins.

China under the Reform practiced a very crude type of capitalism, and in many ways the "survival of the fittest" became the norm. Competition inevitably produced casualties and misfits, and the society faced many severe challenges such as a growing ageing population. Most capitalist societies in the West are welfare states today, but the State in China is busy making money for itself, while the state-sponsored welfare net is almost negligible. It is the Chinese family that served as a kind of "free" welfare safety net. There are still hundreds and hundreds of "extremely filial sons" in China today. It is not uncommon, for instance, for a daughter to spend all her savings after her college education on her parents, sometime purchasing property for the parents. And after that, when they have their own children, they'll be worrying about purchasing property for their child. Chinese families help each other out for sure. But it is also true it may bring huge amount of anxiety among family members as well. For instance, whether to send ageing parents to care centers or not has become a major anxiety for many families. Chinese usually take care of their ageing parents at home at the sacrifice of some family members. Chinese culture will have to find a balance between individual dignity, caring for one another, self-sacrifice, and nepotism.

4. Work Ethic

The Chinese are probably some of the most hard working people in the world. The way the Chinese takeaway owners work, with no weekends no holidays, as mentioned above, are an example par excellence. But one can't take this trait for granted as a fixed cultural feature. Not long ago, during the Cultural Revolution, everybody was assigned a "work unit," usually for life. Whether you work hard or not, you won't be fired — the so-called "iron rice bowl." The Communist ideology imposed a fantasy world of equality in which "being better" or "earning more" was almost regarded as shameful. There is simply no incentive to work, and as a result, everybody enjoys a very poor standard of living.

The Reform shattered the "iron rice bowl." China's economic rise would be impossible without unleashing the freedom of work. Not only were urbanites able to change their "work units," but a large proportion of the rural population began to move to cities for work, as global capital came to China to open up factories. The whole society was on the move. A small number migrated overseas to almost all parts of the world running businesses such as Chinese takeaways. Majority of the migrants are internal, from rural areas to cities — these migrants are called "rural workers (*nongmin gong*)." China is now considered the "world factory," and many factories with global capital concentrate in the Pearl River Delta region in or near Shenzhen. The "rural workers" come from all over the country and provide the workforce. China's economic miracle is really the result of the sweat of these "rural workers." Among them, perhaps more than half are "working girls" (*dagong mei*) who work in all kinds of factories. Quite a few of them, however, become sex workers. They sometimes have to deal with bullying clients, but their real bully is the "law enforcement" from the government, as according to one of its notorious edicts, which have just been abolished at the time of my writing this passage, they could lock them up in detention centers at will. And they also have to bear the bad reputation as a "prostitute" from the public. More often than not, however, their income provides the whole family back in the countryside, for their brothers going to school, for instance. If a social survey is carried out properly, one would be amazed to find how many new houses that had been built in villages in Sichuan or Guizhou or other provinces were actually funded by these "working girls." I hope in the eye of their parents and brothers at least, they are real heroines.

5. Overseas Chinese

As mentioned above, Reform was forced upon the Communist regime, as hordes of mainland migrants flocked to Hong Kong, deserting villages in the border region. Instead of closing up the border, the Reformers decided to "open up" the country for overseas capitalist investment. The first investors who crossed the border were, alas, the Chinese from Hong Kong or Taiwan, many of them had fled the mainland earlier when the Communist regime took over. But culturally they are still Chinese, especially for the first-generation immigrants. This cultural attachment, incidentally, is not only specific to the Chinese. There was rampant sympathies and cultural attachment, for instance, from Japanese or German communities in America to fascist regimes in Japan or Germany during the prewar and wartime period. Overseas Chinese played a major role at different critical moments in modern Chinese history. Dr. Sun Yat-sen's Nationalist Revolution was not only funded by the overseas Chinese from the very beginning, but many of its prominent leaders were overseas Chinese. This time, overseas Chinese again played a critical role. It was they who first brought in not only the much-needed capital for investment — Hong Kong and Taiwanese businessmen are the major players in the Pearl River Delta and Yangtze River Delta regions, two most important economic mega-areas in China today — but more importantly, the technical know-how and business acumen for the economic takeoff. Just as the Chinese are not natural hard workers, they are not natural businessmen. We must dispense with these cultural essentialist ideas. One of the problems facing post-Soviet Russian economy was that after seventy years of Communist rule, Russians had simply forgotten how to run a business. The same happened to the Chinese at the end of the Cultural Revolution and at the beginning of the Reform era. But the Chinese were lucky to have a large population of overseas Chinese who could rekindle their knack for business. When I was in Hong Kong, I once asked a local contractor to do some home decoration at my apartment. He told me, somewhat nostalgically, that his peak time was in the early 1980s when he was hired as a headman by a big company for interior decoration work for a fancy hotel in Guangzhou. His job was to supervise a team of local Chinese workers and he had to literally coach them how to do any kind of work such as tiling the floor, as local Chinese workers knew nothing and couldn't do anything properly (after years of being told they were the "real masters of the country"). But now after a couple of decades, they were running their own companies (interior decoration is a huge business in China) and he was no longer needed in the mainland, so he had come back to Hong Kong, semi-self-employed, picking up some odd jobs here and there.

China's economic rise owed a lot to this Hong Konger and other overseas Chinese alike.

TO BE OR NOT TO BE A CHINESE: WHERE IS CHINA'S SOFT POWER?

By the end of the ninteenth century, the leading Chinese literati-official Zhang Zhidong lamented that Chinese culture was faced with an unprecedented crisis and attempted to identify Chinese-ness as upholding "Chinese learning as foundation." After more than a century, Chinese culture proved to be more resilient and flexible than Zhang might have thought. Its resilience is reflected precisely in its flexibility toward change as well as its inflexible tenacity to conserve. Chinese culture has gone through tremendous changes after its modernity experience for over a century now and has proved to be resilient and vibrant precisely through accommodating these changes, as the above cursory discussion of its role in the economic rise of China shows. On the other hand, Chinese culture today is still very much in a crisis of no less scale than a hundred years ago. Despite its economic rise, or precisely because of it, Chinese culture has no great appeal in the world, if not outright negative. An economic superpower has no soft power to speak of. Projects intended to enhance China's cultural soft power bring out counter-productive effects — a lot of money spent on helping foreigners to learn Chinese language and culture end up arousing much resentment, for instance. Being Chinese isn't something to be really proud of, aside from resorting to an irrational kind of nationalism. In fact, to be or not to be a Chinese is very much at the center of contention among overseas Chinese communities, particularly in Hong Kong and Taiwan.

One of the famous Confucius' sayings goes: "When people far away would not submit to you, you ought to improve your own civic virtues to attract them" (*The Analects* 16:1). This is still the most enlightening piece of wisdom for reflecting upon Chinese culture and its depravity of soft power today. When the majority of people in Hong Kong and Taiwan would not submit to you, and a significant portion of the people there would not even identify themselves as "Chinese," instead of resorting to condemnation based on a crude nationalism or even threatening with crude military prowess, the first step would be to do some self-examination: what is it in you that is not attractive, and most probably you will find the problem is indeed "within the wall," as Confucius would put it. In our global age where cultures meet and compete, it is clear where Chinese cultural deficit lies. In a nutshell, to be an individual Chinese is worth much less than an individual citizen in a democracy because Chinese culture is yet to afford an ordinary Chinese the right to freedom and its associated power for self-government.

As we know, to transform Chinese culture and usher it into modernity, the New Culture intellectuals put forward two slogans: Mr. Democracy and Mr. Science. The economic rise of China owes everything to a renewed and enhanced respect and emphasis on Mr. Science. But after more than a century of modernity experience, Mr. Democracy has still not arrived. For Chinese culture to overcome this deficit and to reset for the improvement of its "civic virtues," it is critically important to reflect upon its modernity experience. Sometimes, critical insight may very well lie in the opponent's argument. Let us approach the issue of Chinese cultural deficit from the counterargument of Gu Hongming (1857–1928),

Figure 18: Gu Hongming

perhaps the most eloquent critic against "Mr. Democracy" in modern Chinese intellectual scene.

In a seminal treatise titled "The Spirit of the Chinese People," Gu attempts to define what it really means to be a Chinese, or what he calls "the real Chinaman."[1] As this "real Chinaman" embodies "the Chinese type of humanity," it is also an inquiry into the essence of Chinese culture. The essay is in fact a defense of this Chinese type of humanity that, as Gu points out, was dying out and being replaced by a new progressive type of humanity as embodied by the "modern Chinaman." The real Chinese is special and distinctive because he lives a life of heart and yet has "a power of mind and rationality." In the West, by contrast, you have a religion that satisfies one's heart and a philosophy that satisfies one's intellect, but the two are constantly in battles. But the Chinese is a person with the happy union of heart and intellect. This is so because he is the product of a civilization that has made this happy union of heart and intellect possible — a culture that has both the functions of religion and philosophy. The secret to make this happy union possible is also the secret of the Chinese culture, which is also why the Chinese culture does not need religion in the Western sense and yet can serve as a replacement for it, as Gu explains. That secret is called "*ming fen da yi*," or the principle of honor and duty, which is the most important thing that Confucius taught the Chinese. The masses of the mankind feel the need of religion to find security and permanence against the mysteries of nature and cruelties and vicissitude of human life, and religion provides them with that sense of security and permanence in a refuge — the belief in a supernatural being and a future life. The Chinese on the other hand don't feel the need for religion because they have found the same sense of security and permanence in a Confucian "State Religion." The entire system of philosophy and morality taught by Confucius can be summarized

---

[1] Gu Hongming (Ku Hung Ming), *The Spirit of the Chinese People*.

as the "Law of the Gentleman" (*junzi zhi dao*) and Confucius weaved them into a State religion. At the core of this State religion is the principle of honor and duty — to the Emperor, an absolute loyalty to the Emperor. Confucius taught this in one of his latest works, *The Annals of Spring and Autumn*, chronicling the true history of the State of Lu and exposing the usurpations and treacheries, making "patricides and regicides scared." Under this "State religion," which was firmly tied up to the kernels of the family, hence "ancestor worship," the Chinese are not only taught to be a good person, but also a "good citizen" as his sense of security and permanence is closely associated with the various ethical relations — his relation to his children, to his wife, to his father, and ultimately to the Emperor. All in all, as Gu Hongming argues, this Chinese type of humanity as embodied in the Chinese person with the happy union of heart and intellect is very modern, as he quotes Matthew Arnold: "The poetry of later Paganism lived by the senses and understanding: the poetry of mediaeval Christianity lived by the heart and imagination. But the main element of the modern spirit's life, of the modern European spirit to-day, is neither the senses and understanding, nor the heart and imagination, it is the imaginative reason." The spirit of the Chinese people, concludes Gu, offers precisely this imaginative reason. Thus, Gu asks the world to appreciate the value of "the real Chinaman," to love him "instead of ignoring, despising and destroying it." As for the "progressive Chinese," who throws away the Code of Honor and forsakes the absolute loyalty and allegiance to the Emperor or Sovereign, "he is no longer a real Chinaman."

In defending "the real Chinaman," Gu Hongming steadfastly posits himself as a martyr. That may be heroic for Gu but not very productive for Chinese culture and its modern transformation. Gu may have very good reasons for lamenting the passing away of "the real Chinaman," but billions of Chinese still exist today after more than a century, and they are also real and will be actually existing for many centuries to come. The issue is what kind of Chinese we will all become as nurtured by what kind of Chinese culture in the twentieth, twenty-first centuries, and so on. The *Après moi, le déluge* approach is not only unproductive, but may very well be counterproductive. When, in 1915, Gu Hongming was taking a last good look at the "real Chinaman" endowed with an absolute loyalty to the Emperor, China was already a republic, and the emperor's head had already been cut off, so to speak. Reading Gu's treatise today, however, does give one an eerie sense when you reflect upon the modernity experience of the Chinese. After all, cultural traits don't change overnight. Even after the emperor's head had been cut off, it does not mean the Chinese cultural attachment to the emperor is gone — if the culture has not found something to replace it resolutely. Unfortunately, it came back in a monstrous transformation in the personality cult of Mao Zedong in twentieth-century China.

What Gu Hongming fails to understand is that Chinese culture won't disappear or die out so easily. It will transform and be transformed. The question is how and what shape it will take. There won't be any void after the "flood," either flowers or weeds will grow. If we want to make sure it is the former rather than the latter, we can find the clue in Gu's comparative cosmopolitan outlook, as Gu praises *The Annals of Spring and Autumn* in which "Confucius taught the divine duty of loyalty" as "the Magna Carta of the Chinese nation."[2] The link between Confucius' *The Annals of Spring and Autumn* and the Magna Carta is surprising but also illuminating, as they go precisely in opposite directions. The Magna Carta, or Magna Carta Libertatum (The Great Charter of Liberties) is of course generally acknowledged as the very foundation of modern liberal democracies. It was originally a charter of rights agreed between the King of England and his rebellious barons in the thirteenth century. It stipulates that the rebel barons have some rights *against* the King, such as protection for the barons from illegal imprisonment, protection of limited feudal payment to the King, and protection of church rights. When the barons have certain rights protected, it basically means the King has lost his "divine rights." The King cannot imprison any baron he dislikes at his will. This idea had a major leap forward in the enactment of *Habeas Corpus*, a series of acts that ensured the liberty of any free man. They stipulate that the King cannot put any of his subjects into prison at will without any proper scrutiny of the court, and the prisoner must appear in person at court to avoid "being disappeared." Starting from the Magna Carta and Habeas Corpus, through the English Bill of Rights of 1689, the American constitution and its associated Bill of Rights, English

---

[2] Gu Hongming (Ku Hung Ming), *The Spirit of the Chinese People* p. 41.

and American culture has found the cornerstone for a new system: the Man. This system not only provides a sense of security and permanence for ordinary people but also ensures their liberty. They are entrusted with a government not only for them, but also of them and by them. They are believed to be born equal and born with certain unalienable rights such as "Life, Liberty and the pursuit of Happiness." Of course, at the core of these rights is the political rights for self-government. To put such belief in the "Man" is a most audacious move on the part of human wisdom. And it did not happen overnight but rather developed over the centuries through many struggles. The nineteenth century basically saw this "Man" become classless: while the rights of man heavily tilted toward the noble and privileged class before, the working class finally gained equal voting rights through a series of reform bills in England. By early twentieth century, this "Man" also included women as they won major victories in universal suffrage. After the Civil Rights Movement in the 1960s, this "Man" finally crossed the race barrier and included the blacks and other non-white minorities. This idea of the rights of Man, originating from the Magna Carta, later developed in England and America, has now spread to and adopted not only in Europe but around the world with only very few exceptions, notably in the People's Republic of China and the Democratic People's Republic of Korea. That is why Chinese culture today has hardly any soft power to speak of despite its economic rise. An individual "Man" with these rights is worth a lot more than an individual Chinese without these rights. While economic well-being is certainly important, it cannot serve as the goal for itself. Once a Man is endowed with Liberty, nothing can take its place.

In order for Chinese culture to retain its appeal and exert its soft power, and for the Chinese people to be proud of being a Chinese wherever he finds himself in the world, it has no choice but to reconfigure itself so that one's faith and absolute loyalty is placed on the individual "Man" with Liberty and other unalienable rights — the alternative is an absolute loyalty to the Supreme Leader Kim Jun Un as practiced in the Democratic People's Republic of Korea. Gu Hongming was certainly wrong in assuming that either the Chinese culture sticks to its scheme with absolute loyalty to the Emperor or dies out. For the past century and more, the Chinese culture has gone through tremendous transformations.

From historical hindsight, it probably would have been far more benign if it had taken on the British model of constitutional monarch in which the rights of Man is at the center of its scheme while the monarch still remains as the nominal sovereign, exerting its various culturally symbolic functions. Chinese modernity, however, has been defined by ever more radicalizations and revolutions one after another, in pursuit of evermore illusive and twisted ideal of "progress." The end result was indeed a very destructive flood with a monstrous revival of the absolute loyalty to the Supreme Leader Mao Zedong or the party.

After more than a century of much traumatic modern experience, it should have made clearer to us that Chinese cultural rebirth could and should take on a different route that would make the Chinese culture appealing and attractive again, and make the Chinese proud of being Chinese again, by asserting the rights of Man at the center of its scheme. This is not only the most desirable and inevitable, but also eminently feasible. The binary approach of East versus West — you have the Magna Carta, we have *The Annals of Spring and Autumn* — is simply not helpful and is misleading. Confucianism has always been an open and cosmopolitan scheme, which in history has co-existed and co-opted with Taoism and Buddhism. When Western culture was brought to China after the Opium Wars, despite of its association with the opium trade and the gunboat power, the Chinese intellectual response was overwhelmingly one of accommodation and assimilation instead of resistance. What Gu Hongming called those "progressive Chinese" were all Confucian scholars and most of them had gone through the Civil Examination successfully. While Western missionaries played a major role in introducing new knowledge to China and opening up the horizon for the Chinese, it was ultimately the Chinese educated class who pushed for the reforms that ushered China into modernity. The first Reform movement was led by Kang Youwei and his talented disciple Liang Qichao. If their movement was successful, China would have been transformed into a constitutional monarchy. Even though they failed politically, their enlightenment ideas influenced a whole generation of Chinese youth at the time. The most representative and influential treatise was *New Citizen* by Liang Qichao, in which Liang called for the cultivation and emergence of a new type of Chinese who will be public citizens rather than private "familial men." Contrary to Gu Hongming's view, Liang sees the biggest challenge facing Chinese culture was the lack of public morality, and a people without a proper sense of public morality cannot really be called a "citizen." However, this insight is not to be seen as a binary break from the Chinese tradition. Liang does not see traditional Chinese culture, or the "Five Cardinal Principles," as "foundation" and any other ideas from the West as "foreign" and "utilitarian." In that sense, "progressive Chinese" were cosmopolitan in their world outlook. Another notable example was Guo Songtao (1818–1891), the first Chinese ambassador to Britain, who, as we noted before, developed a special friendship with Yan Fu when he was a student there. Guo rose to a prominent position in his early career by joining Zeng Guofan's Hunanese Army against the Taiping Rebellion, and was the first scholar-official to live and travel in the West in an official capacity. In Britain, he paid particular attention to its political system, and admired the people's genuine love of their king and the effective communication between commoners and authorities under the parliamentary system. Not only did he not see the constitutional monarchy in Britain as alien and "barbarian," but inferred that it would be precisely what Chinese sages like Confucius and Mencius would have liked to see. Gu Hongming was an eloquent defender of the Chinese in his English writings, but he could be sharply critical of the Chinese in his Chinese-language writings. On one occasion when Gu was criticizing the Chinese vulgarity in their behavior at theatres, he commented: "I once heard that, after the esteemed ambassador Guo Songtao had travelled in the West and seen the overwhelmingly good manner of the people there, he came back and said to his countrymen: 'I have been fooled by the teachings of Confucius and Mencious [In believing the Chinese are the most moral people in the world].' Mr. Guo can be said to be the real superior man who appreciates the good in the other while deliberately ignoring the good in his own."[3]

Thus, as Liang Qichao put it, "to be a new citizen does not mean that Chinese ought to abandon all that is 'old' and follow others. There are two

---

[3] Gu Hongming, *Zhang Wenxiang mofu jiwen*, p. 416.

connotations to the term 'new': to renovate what he already possesses and to adopt what he does not originally own."[4] To meet the modern challenge, it does mean that "old" Chinese culture needs to readjust itself. "To renovate what he already possesses" is eminently feasible. When looked at from the modern lens, we will value more the Mencian tradition in Confucianism with its emphasis on the government for the people as we explored in Chapter 2. In terms of "government by the people," Chinese culture had produced a civil administration through the Examination system, which was essentially a democratic institution based on education and merit. That is certainly beneficial in its transition to a real government by the people. Most importantly, Chinese culture is fundamentally one of humanism and it does not bear any religious burden on its path to modernity. Modernity in the Western context was largely a struggle against religious supremacy. It was the Reformation that made a breakthrough, which resulted, as Gu Hongming would say, a divorce between the mind and the heart. When modernity was forced upon other non-Western regions such as the Middle East, religious conflicts were usually at the core. Chinese modernity did not have such a concern (for better or worse). The key problem, as Gu Hongming rightly diagnosed, was to cut off the emperor's head or not. As modern Chinese experience has also demonstrated, even this task was not that difficult. The Qing Dynasty simply crumbled into pieces in the end. The Chinese loyalty to the Emperor proved to be skin-deep after all. Constitutional monarchy may very well be a better solution in terms of modern Chinese cultural transformation, but in reality, it seemed to be less feasible. The Mencian tradition in the belief of the Mandate of Heaven was undoubtedly at play here: Chinese emperors come and go, once you are deemed to have lost the mandate, you will be overthrown. The difference this time is that it proved almost impossible for any new emperor to emerge, unless he appeared in another form under disguise.

To prevent "fake emperors" from revival, then, Chinese culture must relocate its center of gravity that has been vacated. It has to be the Man (or to use the Chinese term: *ren*, a human being). Just as Chinese culture took on a new path of renaissance, thanks to the contribution of

---

[4] Liang Qichao, *Xin min shuo*, p. 54.

Confucius in terms of his compiling and editing the classics as well as his truth-telling in historiography, Chinese culture can take on a modern rebirth once this belief in the Man is established. It does not even take a Confucius to see the point. Many modern Chinese intellectuals have been advocating the central significance of the individual Man in a reconfigured cultural atlas. Unfortunately, the notion of the Man has been eclipsed in modern Chinese experience. Instead, a collective group notion (the "nation" for the Nationalists and the "people" for the Communists) has taken over. When Liang Qichao was offering a design for a new type of Chinese citizen, he was very clear the "rights of Man" would certainly be something the Chinese did not originally own and must now adopt. Liang lays out a series of attributes that identifies a "new citizen," such as public morality, patriotism, civic responsibilities, community spirit, aggressive and adventurous spirit, and rights and liberties. Ostensibly, the ideas of rights and liberty occupy a major place in his ideal of a new citizen. He adopts the notion that individuals are born with certain unalienable rights, and it is only just that the new Chinese are afforded with the same rights. He sees this as empowering the Chinese: "If you want the equality of rights between China and other countries, you must first endow each Chinese citizen equal rights, and you must first ensure the rights our citizens enjoy in China to be equal to the rights others enjoy in their own countries."[5] But here lies the problem: it turns out that Liang did not see the primordial centrality of the rights of Man, but rather, public morality and civic responsibilities were much more important as they would empower the nation. The most urgent thing to Liang was for the Chinese to develop a "social ethic" out of the "family ethic." Liang regroups the Confucian Five Cardinal Principles into "family ethic," "social ethic," and "state ethic," and finds that the old ethics quite deficient in the latter two. Therefore, he introduces two new ideas to form the basis for the "social ethic" and "state ethic": the ideas of the community (*qun*) and evolutionary progress. Liang's paradigm for the "new citizen" is heavily tilted toward a group identity with the ultimate aim to empower the state. Indeed, his *Discourse on New Citizen* is much more about what new Chinese ought to be: to possess public morality, to be patriotic, to have civic responsibilities, to be aggressive and adventurous,

---

[5] Ibid, p. 96–97.

and so on. And one way or another, they lead to strengthen the nation. Indeed, Liang's term for new "citizen" is *min* (people) rather than *ren* (Man). But a "state ethic" without the rights of Man as its absolute foundation is very shaky and can be dangerous. We have many lessons from modern Chinese historical experience. Nationalism certainly has its *raison d'être*, but the cost for the slippery move from the rights of Man to a group identity in whatever name is immense. After the traumatic experience of modern China, it is much more important to heed to Hu Shi's advice:

> Now some say to you: "Sacrifice your personal freedom to fight for the freedom of the nation!" But I say to you: "Fighting for your own individual freedom is fighting for the freedom of your nation! To fight for your own dignity is to fight for the dignity of the nation! *A nation of freedom and equality cannot be built by a group of slaves!*"[6]

Once Chinese culture resolutely endows the rights of Man at its core as a foundational cornerstone, just as Confucius reinterprets the classics by affording primordial significance to the loyalty to the Emperor, as Gu Hongming puts it, other parts and aspects of the culture can be readjusted or adopted anew, as Liang Qichao would have it. Within the new paradigm with the rights of Man at the center of gravity, Legalist principles will retain a surprising potency. As we noted before, the Legalist primary intention is to uphold the absolute authority of the Emperor. Now that the emperor's head has been cut off, a *fait accompli* in the modern transformation of Chinese culture, Legalist doctrines can be of great value as the main message is the equality of all, nobles, aristocrats, and commoners alike — everybody under the Emperor. Contrary to the Confucian scheme of government by the gentlemen, the Legalists propounded the government by law. As Lin Yutang puts it, "The Legalist system assumes every ruler to be a crook and proceeds to make provisions in the political system to prevent him from carrying out his crooked intentions... As Han Fei says, we should not expect people to be good, but should make it impossible for

---

[6] Hu Shi, *Hu Shi wenji*, pp. 511–512, original emphasis.

them to be bad. That is the moral basis of the Legalist philosophy."[7] When applied to everybody regardless of their social or educational status, the Man is an equal being among others. That is the spirit of the law. In replace of the family, the renovated Chinese culture must have the spirit of the law as its elemental fabric. Traditional Legalist thought could be an important resource.

Once reconfigured as such, however, it does not mean traditional Confucian values such as the family will simply die out. In fact, Confucianism can be revived as an important conservative force for Chinese culture today. This is first of all a crucial lesson from modern Chinese experience. The royal roads to Russia and its consequent human cost were in a sense due to the lack of a conservative force in modern China. The New Culturalists not only put forward the calls for "Mr. Democracy" and "Mr. Science," but also for an iconoclastic "re-evaluation of all values," which was quite effective. Just take the example of Gu Hongming. Ever since his own times, he has been stereotyped into a ridiculous and nonsensible person simply because even after the Qing Dynasty had been overthrown, he continued to wear his queue (*bianzi*) as a symbol of loyalty to the Emperor and to the spirit of the "real Chinaman." Few people ever read his works, which were mostly written in English and some in classical Chinese. But all kinds of biographies have been written on him based on sheer heresies portraying him as a clownish figure. But Gu was a true conservative — in the British sense. Gu Hongming and Yan Fu were contemporaries. In fact, Gu had been brought to a boarding school in Edinburgh and had just completed his study at the University of Edinburgh before Yan Fu embarked on his two-year study in Britain. While Yan translated and introduced Spencer, Huxley, and Stuart Mill — key proponents of liberal progressive thoughts — to China, Gu inherited another strand of important Victorian thinkers — Matthew Arnold, Thomas Carlyle, Ruskin, and Wordsworth, who emphasized the importance of "culture" in the modern transition. A healthy functioning of liberal democracy relies on the interplay of these two forces, generally referred to as "progressive" and "conservative." Being a conservative does not mean to go against every single progressive idea but may indeed mean to go against the very idea of

---

[7] Lin Yutang, "Han Fei As a Cure for Modern China," p. 54.

"progress." The problem for Chinese modernity was that progress was so overwhelming that there wasn't much conservative mechanism at all. Hence, the evermore increasing radicalization in competition to be "more progressive than thou" and the royal roads to Russia. Looking back at the trauma and horror that was brought to Chinese culture, we need to be more attentive to the conservative voice in the reconstruction of Chinese culture today.

In fact, when overseas Chinese are placed in the context of American or British political framework, an overwhelming majority of them are republicans or conservatives at least in terms of their social values. As we have discussed above, such conservative values as family, patriotism, and education have played a major role in the economic rise of China so far. Shifted into an Anglo-American context, these values also contributed a great deal of the overall success of the overseas Chinese — indeed, they contribute to the comparative advantage of the overseas Chinese. But of course, they would all have to be readjusted and realigned in the context where the rights of Man and the rule of law are cornerstones of its social fabric. There won't be any familism and big families as we know it before. Whether overseas or in China, Chinese family has truly become a nuclear family, but still with a much stronger bondage both within the nuclear family and between the nuclear family and extended family. This is on the whole not a bad modern transformation at all. In the Chinese case, the duty of a true conservative is perhaps not to emphasize the importance of family but continue to seek out a balance between traditional familism and modern progressive deconstruction of the family. Along with the family, the competitive advantage of the overseas Chinese in terms of education was also quite obvious. The Civil Examination was abolished more than a hundred years ago. Having an education no longer guaranteed a foot in the elite official class. In fact, twentieth-century China went so "progressive" as to label anybody with education as "stinking No. 9" and regard them as an enemy of the people. But the emphasis Chinese families attach to education remains outstanding, and a schoolteacher enjoys much more social prestige in China than her counterparts in the West. The problem with education for Chinese culture today is not whether education is valued or not, but rather with the kind of education imparted. In the traditional Confucian scheme, education was essentially a moral education based on Confucian classics (to be tested through the Examination), and it was an elitist education restricted mainly to a minority of boys. Nowadays, primary and secondary education has been made compulsory for all boys and girls, while the subjects have been opened up and tilted heavily toward "Mr. Science." The relative success of the "Mr. Science" project, particularly during the Reform period, has, however, produced another risk: emergence of the divorce of the head totally from the heart, much more than Gu Hongming saw about the Western modernity. Aside from political ideology, schools and universities in China are not much different from those in the West, which are manufacturing sites for knowledge that is barely concerned with one's heart.

But a Man cannot be amoral. Morality is central to human beings. Confucianism can still remain a major conservative force in a post-totalitarian Chinese society. Contrary to common misunderstanding, a government of the people, by the people, and for the people cannot be assured by the rule of law alone — particularly in the British model. The rule of law will protect the rights of Man, but it will not give you "Life, Liberty, and Happiness." Traditions and conventions as symbolized in the Monarch, as well as religious functionaries, still serve as culture-inspiring apparatus for the well-being of the nation. That is where Gu Hongming got his inspiration for appreciating the Great Principle of Honor and Duty in Confucianism. Honor and duty are indeed still very much the core values upheld by the British democracy. For Chinese culture to be reborn, Confucianism will have to find a way for revival and reinsert the Great Principle of Honor and Duty into Chinese culture — for Honor and Duty are what China is in most demand of today. A rise in living standards did not go along with the rise of one's moral standard. On the contrary, the depravity of morality and utter lack of sense of honor and duty have resulted in the society becoming truly deplorable. This does not mean that the Chinese are particularly amoral, not at all. This is the inevitable consequence of the totalitarian regime. A totalitarian regime is only concerned with power, and always enforces a twisted sense of morality to serve power. Living under such a regime for a long time where one cannot utter the truth for fear of dire consequences, one may become accustomed to "calling a deer a horse." This famous Chinese proverb is recorded in *The Records of the Grand Historian* as exactly what happened under the despotic rule of the First Emperor of Qin. After the First Emperor died, the actual power concentrated in the hands of the Prime Minister Zhao Gao because the Second Emperor was a weakling and good-for-nothing. Still,

> Zhao intends to usurp the crown and decides to test the loyalty of the ministers first. One day, he brought a deer to the court and told the Second Emperor: "Your Majesty, here is a horse for you." The Second Emperor laughed: "You must be mistaken, but this is a deer!" "No," replied Zhao, "it is indeed a horse. If you don't believe it, you can ask the opinion of your ministers." Among the ministers, some remained silent, some said it was a horse to demonstrate their submission to Zhao. For those who said it was a deer were all later purged and punished in the name of law with deliberately made-up false claims.[8]

The Confucianists should rejoice at the permanent removal of the Emperor in modern Chinese cultural transformation and strive to revive the Confucian principle of Honor and Duty by speaking truth to power. The Confucianists have a long tradition in that regard and can be proud of it. Instead of the Emperor or a monarchy, History can be a powerful mechanism to sustain and safeguard the Honor code. Just as Confucius has demonstrated, History will always find a way to haunt those despots who think they can twist one's sense of right and wrong so much by "calling a deer a horse."

In summarizing what Gu Hongming calls "the spirit of the Chinese people," he invokes what Matthew Arnold calls "imaginative reason": "Now the spirit of the Chinese people, as it is seen in the best specimens of the products of their art and literature, is really what Mathew Arnold calls imaginative reason."[9] We can also call this "imaginative reason" as shown "in the best specimens of the products of their art and literature" an Aesthetics of Life. Chinese culture — not just Confucian but combined with Taoist and

---
[8] Sima Qian, *Shiji*, p. 137.
[9] Gu Hongming (Ku Hung Ming), *The Spirit of the Chinese People*, p. 71.

Buddhist traditions — is certainly rich in resources in providing an aesthetics of Life and ways to Happiness, as we explored in Chapters 3 and 4. This is what Lin Yutang calls the "lyrical philosophy" of Chinese culture, which he interpreted so successfully to the world in the twentieth century. The best products of Chinese art and literature such as the works of Tao Yuanming and Su Dongpo convey a spirit of freedom, love of life, as well as an attitude of tolerant irony toward life. Underneath these features lies a fundamental philosophy of *daguan* (detachment) toward life "based on a sense of wise disenchantment." The key word here is "wise disenchantment." Disenchantment is a common term used by post-Enlightenment thinkers in the West to denote the sense of alienation in the modern man — what Gu Hongming calls the divorce of the heart and mind. By "wise disenchantment," Lin claims that Chinese culture has overcome this divide by raising from the level of tragedy to that of comedy. Chinese poets have understood the essential tragedy of life, and yet, instead of disenchantment alone, have turned the vicissitudes of life into laughter. Happiness and contentment are always a matter of tolerant irony. To be tolerant is to have a reasonable understanding so as to attain a free relationship with life's tragedies and farcicalities, which affords the Chinese a natural tendency to be forgiving and sympathetic. What Matthew Arnold calls "imaginative reason" echoes with what Lin interprets as the "Spirit of Reasonableness," which characterizes the humanistic tradition of Confucianism. Unlike Cartesian rationality, Confucian "reasonableness" is always imbued with a human touch. In that light, "the sage is no more than a reasonable person, like Confucius, who is chiefly admired for his plain, common sense and his natural human qualities, i.e., for his great *humanness*."[10]

A culture that prizes "humanness" above everything else should not wait for too long to rekindle itself by placing the rights of Man at its center and let Chinese enjoy the freedoms they deserve. Once Liberty is enshrined, along with a poetic aesthetic of Life and a reasonable philosophy of Happiness, Chinese culture may indeed show its own "civic virtues" to the world. By then, perhaps it will not be such a bad idea to be a Chinese in the world.

---

[10] Lin Yutang, *The Importance of Living*, p. 423.

Works Cited

Chen Duxiu. *Duxiu wencun* (Collected Writings of Chen Duxiu). Hefei: Anhui renmin chubanshe, 1987.
Chou, Chih-ping. "Introduction" in *A Collection of Hu Shih's Unpublished English Essays and Speeches*, edited by Chih-ping Chou. Taipei: Linking Press, 2001.
Cooper, Arthur. *Li Po and Tu Fu*. Translated by Arthur Cooper. Penguin Books, 1973.
Cui, Jie and Zong-qi Cai, eds. *How to Read Chinese Poetry*. New York: Columbia University Press, 2012.
de Bary, Wm Theodore, et al. eds. *Sources of Chinese Tradition*. Vol. 1, 2nd ed. New York: Columbia University Press, 1999.
Feng Guifen. *Jiaobinlu kangyi* (Timely Proposals). Zhongzhou guji chubanshe, 1998.
Gu Hongming (Ku Hung-Ming). *Zhang Wenxiang mofu jiwen* in *Gu Hongming wenji* (Collected Writings of Gu Hongming). Vol. 1, edited by Huang Xingtao. Hainan chubanshe, 1996.
———. *The Spirit of the Chinese People*. Peking: The Peking Daily News, 1915.
———. *Papers from a Viceroy's Yamen*. Shanghai Mercury Ltd., 1901.
———. *The Discourses and Sayings of Confucius—A New Special Translation, Illustrated with Quotations from Goethe and Other Writers*. Peking: Kelly and Walsh, 1898.
Hightower, James Robert. *The Poetry of T'ao Ch'ien*. Oxford: Oxford University Press, 1970.
Hu Hanmin. "Shu Houguan Yanshi zuijin zhengjian" (On Yan Fu's Recent Views), quoted in Pi Houfeng, *Yan Fu dazhuan* (A Biography of Yan Fu). Fuzhou: Fujian renmin chubanshe, 2013.

Hu Shi. *English Writings of Hu Shih*, Vol. 3, edited by Chih-ping Chou. Beijing: Foreign Languages and Teaching Press, 2013.

———. *The Personal Reminiscences of Dr. Hu Shih*. Beijing: Foreign Language Teaching and Research Press, 2012.

———. "Lest We Forget," in *A Collection of Hu Shih's Unpublished English Essays and Speeches*, edited by Chih-ping Chou. Taipei: Linking Press, 2001.

———. *Hu Shi wenji* (Collected Works of Hu Shi). Beijing: Beijing daxue chubanshe, 1998.

Huang Zongxi. *Waiting for the Dawn*. Wm. Translated by Theodore de Bary. New York: Columbia University Press, 1993.

Huxley, Thomas H. *Evolution and Ethics*. London: Macmillan and Company, 1893.

The Johannean. Vol. II, 1915–1916.

Kang Youwei. *Kang Youwei datonglun erzhong* (Two Books on Cosmopolitanism by Kang Youwei). Beijing: Sanlian, 1998.

Ku Hung Ming. See Gu Hongming.

Li Zehou and Liu Zaifu. *Gaobie geming* (Farewell to Revolution). Taibei: Tiandi tushu, 1995.

Liang Qichao. *Xin min shuo (Discourse on New Citizen)*. Zhongguo guji chubanshe, 1998.

Lin Yutang. "The Function of Criticism at the Present Time" in *The Little Critic: The Bilingual Essays of Lin Yutang*, comp. and edited by Qian Suoqiao. Beijing: Jiuzhou Press, 2012.

———. "Han Fei As a Cure for Modern China" in *The Little Critic: The Bilingual Essays of Lin Yutang*.

———. "Lianhebao chuangyong changyongzi de gongxian" (The Contribution of *The United Newspaper* in Launching Most Commonly Used Characters) in *Zhongyang ribao* (September 16, 1971).

———. "Yi leyin shi bashou" (Be Merry Poem), *Zhongyang ribao*, February 14, 1966.

———. *The Gay Genius: The Life and Times of Su Tungpo*. New York: The John Day Company, 1947.

———. "Singing Patriots of China," *Asia* XLI (February 1941): 70–2.

———. *The Wisdom of Confucius*. New York: Random House, 1943.

———. *The Wisdom of China and India*. New York: The Random House, 1942.

———. *A Leaf in the Storm*. New York: The John Day Company, 1941.

———. *The Importance of Living*. New York: The John Day Company, 1937.

———. "What Liberalism Means," *The China Critic* IV (March 931): 252.

———. "Tan zhuyin zimu ji qita" (On Zhuyin Scripts and Others) in *Jingbao fukan* (Jingbao Supplement). (December 5, 1924); *Yuyanxue luncong* (Essays in Linguistic Studies), Kaiming Bookstore, 1933.

———. "The Little Critic" (11 September 1930): 874.

———. "Lun Hanzi suoyin zhi ji xiyang wenxue" (On Chinese Character Index System and Western Literature) in *Xin qingnian* (La Jeunesse) 4, no. 4 (1918).

Liu, James J. Y. *The Art of Chinese Poetry*. Routledge & Kegan Paul, 1962.

Liu, Shi-yee. *Straddling East and West: Lin Yutang, a Modern Literatus*. The Metropolitan Museum of Art, 2007.

Lu Xun. *Diary of a Madman and Other Stories*. Translated by William A. Lyell. Honolulu: University of Hawaii Press, 1990.

———. *Lu Xun quanji* (The Complete Works of Lu Xun). Vol. 2. Beijing: Renmin wenxue chubanshe, 1981.

———. Lu Xun. "Tiansheng manxing" (Innate Obstinacy). *Lu Xun quanji*. Vol. 8, Renmin wenxue chubanshe, 2005.

Mengzi. *Mencius*. Translated by D. C. Lau. Penguin Books, 1970.

Platt, Stephen R. *Autumn in the Heavenly Kingdom: China, the West, and the Epic Story of the Taiping Civil War*. New York: Vintage Books, 2012.

"Proposal for a Liberal Cosmopolitan Club in Shanghai." *The China Critic* (13 September 1930): 1085.

Sima Qian, *Shiji*, edited by Wang Liqi. Xian: Sanqin chubanshe, 1988.

Snyder, Gary. *The Practice of the Wild*. North Point Press, 1990.

———. *No Nature*, New York: Pantheon Books, 1992.

Spence, Jonathan. *The Search for Modern China*, W. W. Norton & Company, 1990.

Sun Yat-sen. *Sources of Chinese Tradition*. Vol. II. Comp. by WM. Theodore de Bary et al. New York: Columbia University Press, 1960.

Waley, Arthur. *Monkey*. Arthur Waley trans. New York: John Day Company, 1943.

―――. *The Opium War Through Chinese Eyes*. George Allen & Unwin Ltd, 1958.
Watson, Burton. trans. *The Complete Works of Chuang Tze*. New York: Columbia University Press, 1968.
―――. *Han Fei Tzu: Basic Writings*. New York: Columbia University Press, 1964.
―――. *Selected Poems of Su Tung-p'o*. Copper Canyon Press, 1994.
Yan Fu. "Pi Han" (In Refutation of Han Yu), *Yan Fu ji* (Collected Works of Yan Fu), vol. 1. Beijing: Zhonghua shuju, 1986.
―――. "Yuan Qiang" (On the Origin of Strength), *Yan Fu ji*, vol. 1.
Zhang, Zhidong. *Quan xue pian* (Exhortation to Learning). Zhongzhou guji chubanshe, 1998.

Suggested Further Readings
(For Classroom Use)

General Sourcebooks (Chinese texts translated into English)

De Bary, W.T., *et al.* editors. *Sources of Chinese Tradition*, Second Edition: Vols I and II. Columbia University Press, 1999/2001.

Ebrey, Patricia Buckley, editor. *Chinese Civilization and Society: A Sourcebook*. Free Press, 1981.

Lin Yutang ed. *The Wisdom of China and India*. The Modern Library, 1942.

Chapter 1

"Biography of the Five Emperors". *Records of the Grand Historian* (*Shiji*) by Sima Qian (focusing on the story of Yao and Shun).

"The Life of Confucius" (translation of "Biography of Confucius" in *Shiji*). *The Wisdom of Confucius*, edited and translated by Lin Yutang, The Modern Library, 1938.

Chapter 2

Selected texts from *Hanfeizi* and *Shiji* on Legalist ideas ("Five Vermins," "Memorial on the Burning of Books"), and from *Mencius* on the idea of the government for the people.

Selected texts on the debate over Wang Anshi's Reform by Wang Anshi, Su Shi, Sima Guang, Zhu Xi, etc.

Chapter 3

Selected texts from *Analects* (focusing on the themes of *ren* [humanity] and *junzi* [gentleman]).

"Going Rambling Without a Destination," Chapter 1 of *Zhuangzi*.

Wu Cheng-en. *Monkey*, translated by Arthur Waley, John Day Company, 1943.

Chapter 4

Selected poems from *How to Read Chinese Poetry Workbook*, edited by Jie Cui and Zong-qi Cai, Columbia University Press, 2012.

Selected poems from *How to Read Chinese Poetry: A Guided Anthology*, edited by Zong-qi Cai, Columbia University Press, 2008.

Chapter 5

Gu Hongming (Ku Hung-Ming). "Defensio Populi Ad Populos, Or The Modern Missionaries Considered in Relations to the Recent Riots". *Papers from a Viceroy's Yamen*, The Shanghai Mercury, Ltd, 1901.

Lin Yutang. "The Birth of a New China". *My Country and My People*, 2nd ed., The John Day Company, 1939.

Lin Zexu. "Letter to the English Ruler". *Sources of Chinese Tradition, Second Edition: Vols II*. Columbia University Press, 2001.

Chapter 6

Selected texts from Kang Youwei's *Datong shu* (focusing on Kang's ideas on nation, class, race and gender). Thomson, Laurence G., *Ta T'ung Shu: The One-World Phhilosophy of K'ang Yu-wei*. George Allen and Unwin, 1958.

Sample, Joseph C. "Contextualizing Lin Yutang's Essay 'On Humour': Introduction and Translation". *Humour in Chinese Life and Letters*. Edited by Jocelyn Chey and Jessica Milner Davis, Hong Kong University Press, 2011.

Chapter 7

Lu Xun. "Diary of a Madman". *Diary of a Madman and Other Stories*, translated by William A. Lyell, University of Hawaii Press, 1990.

Gao Xingjian. *One Man's Bible*, translated by Mabel Lee, HarperCollins, 2002.

Chapter 8

Gu Hongming (Ku Hung-Ming). *The Spirit of the Chinese People*, The Peking Daily News, 1915.

Chinese Character List

Anyang 安阳

baihua 白话
Beijing 北京
Beiyang 北洋
bianzi 辫子
Bao Xuan 鲍宣

Cang Jie 仓颉
caoshu 草书
chan 禅
Chang'an 长安
Changzhou 常州
Chen Dong 陈东
Chen Duxiu 陈独秀
Chen Tianhua 陈天华
Chen Yinke 陈寅恪
Chen Zilong 陈子龙
Chenbao 晨报
Chiang Kai-shek 蒋介石
Chongqing 重庆
Chunqiu 春秋
ci 词
Cixi 慈禧

dagong mei 打工妹
daguan 达观
dalu 鞑虏

dangzheng 党争
Daodejing 道德经
Daoguang 道光
datong 大同
Datong shu 大同书
Daxue 大学
dazuo 打坐
De Xiansheng 德先生
Deng Xiaoping 邓小平
Dian 点
Dong Zhongshu 董仲舒
Dongguozi 东郭子
Donglin 东林
Du Fu 杜甫
dunwu 顿悟
Duxiu wencun 独秀文存

fazhan shi ying daoli 发展是硬道理
Fan Zhongyan 范仲淹
Feng Guifen 冯桂芬
fu 赋
Fuzhou 福州

gaige 改革
gaikai 改开
Gansu 甘肃
Gao Xingjian 高行健
Gaobie geming 告别革命

Gaoyao 皋陶
Gaozong (宋) 高宗
Gaozu (汉) 高祖
Gaozu benji 高祖本纪
gedi peikuan 割地赔款
geming 革命
gong'an 公案
gonghe 共和
Gu Hongming 辜鸿铭
guanhua 官话
Guangdong 广东
Guangzhou 广州
Guangxi 广西
Guangxu 光绪
guanxi 关系
Guanyin 观音
Guizhou 贵州
guo 国
Guo Songtao 郭嵩焘
Guomao 国贸
guoyu 国语
guqi 骨气

Hami 哈密
Han 汉 (朝)
Han Fei 韩非
Han Xin 韩信
Hanfeizi 韩非子
Hanshan 寒山
Henan 河南
Hong Rengan 洪仁玕
Hong Xiuquan 洪秀全
Hou Fangyu 侯方域
Hu Feng 胡风
Hu Hanmin 胡汉民
Hu Shi 胡适
Hu Shi wenji 胡适文集

Huai 淮
Huang Zongxi 黄宗羲
Huangdi 黄帝
Hui Neng 慧能
Huizi 惠子
Huizong 徽宗
Humen 虎门

jiaguwen 甲骨文
Jiang Qing 江青
Jiangnan 江南
Jiangsu 江苏
Jiangxi 江西
jiao 教
Jiaobinlu kangyi 校邠庐抗议
Jingbao fukan 京报副刊
jingcha 警察
Jinggao qingnian 敬告青年
jingji 经济
jingjie 境界
jinshi 进士
junzi 君子
junzi zhi dao 君子之道
juren 举人

kaifang 开放
Kaifeng 开封
kaishu 楷书
Kang Youwei 康有为
Kang Youwei datonglun erzhong 康有为大同论二种
Kangxi 康熙
keju 科举
kexue 科学
Kong Shangren 孔尚任
Kongzi 孔子

Kongzi zhi dao yu xiandai shenghuo 孔子之道与现代生活

Lao She 老舍
Laozi 老子
li 礼
Li Bai 李白
Li Bangyan 李邦彦
Li Gang 李纲
Li Hongzhang 李鸿章
Li Qingzhao 李清照
Li Shangyin 李商隐
Li Si 李斯
Li Xiangjun 李香君
Li Zehou 李泽厚
Liang Qichao 梁启超
Liang Shiqiu 梁实秋
Liang Shuming 梁漱溟
Lianhebao chuangyong changyongzi de gongxian 联合报创用常用字的贡献
Liji 礼记
lishu 隶书
Lin Yutang 林语堂
Lin Zexu 林则徐
Lingshan 灵山
Liu Rushi 柳如是
Liu Shaoqi 刘少奇
Liu Zaifu 刘再复
Lu 鲁 (国)
Lu Xun 鲁迅
Lu Xun quanji 鲁迅全集
Lun Hanzi suoyin zhi ji xiyang wenxue 论汉字索引制及西洋文学
Lunyu 论语

Mao Zedong 毛泽东
Mei Guangdi 梅光迪
Mei Yaochen 梅尧臣
Mengzi 孟子
min 民
Min 闽
Ming 明 (朝)
ming fen da yi 名分大义
Ming yi dai fang lu 明夷待访录
minquan 民权
minsheng 民生
minzu 民族
Mo Yan 莫言
Mozi 墨子

Nanjing 南京
neisheng 内圣
Nie Er 聂耳
nongmin gong 农民工

Ouyang Xiu 欧阳修

Pi Han 辟韩
Pi Houfeng 皮后锋
pinyin 拼音
putonghua 普通话
Puyi 溥仪

Qi 齐 (国)
Qian 钱
Qian Qianyi 钱谦益
Qian Suoqiao 钱锁桥
Qin 秦 (朝)
Qin Hui 秦桧
Qin Shihuang 秦始皇
Qing 清 (朝)
qing 情
Qinghai 青海
Qinzong (宋) 钦宗
qiwu 齐物

Qu Yuan 屈原
Quan xue pian 劝学篇
qun 群

rang yibufen ren xian fu qilai 让一
　部分人先富起来
ren 人
ren 仁
Ren Hongjun 任鸿隽

Sai Xiansheng 赛先生
sangang wuchang 三纲五常
Sanmin zhuyi 三民主义
shafa 沙发
Shandong 山东
Shang 商 (朝)
Shang Yang 商鞅
Shangdi 上帝
Shanghai 上海
Shangshu 尚书
Shanxi 陕西
Shenzhen 深圳
Shenzong (宋) 神宗
shi 诗
Shi Zhicun 施蛰存
Shiji 史记
shijian jiushi jinqian 时间就是金钱
Shijing 诗经
shizhe shengcun 适者生存
Shizhi 适之
shou zhu dai tu 守株待兔
*Shu Houguan Yanshi zuijin
　zhengjian* 述候官严氏最
　近政见
Shuihu zhuan 水浒传
Shun 舜
Shuowen jiezi 说文解字

Sichuan 四川
Sima Qian 司马迁
Sishi zixu 四十自叙
Song 宋 (朝)
Su Dongpo 苏东坡
Sui 隋 (朝)
Sun Wukong 孙悟空
Sun Yat-sen 孙逸仙
Sunzi bingfa 孙子兵法

Taierzhuang 台儿庄
Taiping Tianguo 太平天国
Taishan 泰山
Tang 唐 (朝)
Tang Yue 唐钺
Tao Yuanming 陶渊明
Taohua shan 桃花扇
Tian Han 田汉
Tiananmen 天安门
Tiansheng manxing 天生蛮性
Tian yan lun 天演论
tianxia 天下
tongshi 通事
Tongzhi 同治
Tongwen Guan 同文馆

Wang Anshi 王安石
Wang Fu 王弗
Wang Liqi 王利器
Wang Runzi 王闰之
Wang Shiwei 王实味
Wang Wei 王维
Wang Xian 王咸
Wang Xizhi 王羲之
Wang Zhaoyun 王朝云
Wanli 万历
waiwang 外王

Wei Zheng 魏征
Wei Zhongxian 魏忠贤
wen 文
wenhua 文化
Wenhui 文惠 (王)
wenyan 文言
Wu 吴
Wu Cheng'en 吴承恩
Wu Mi 吴宓
Wu Zetian 武则天
wu jing tian ze 物竞天择
Wudi (汉) 武帝
Wuhan 武汉
wuhua 物化

Xia 夏 (朝)
Xi'an 西安
Xianfeng 咸丰
Xiang 湘
xiangbin 香槟
xiaozhuan 小篆
xin 信
Xin qingnian 新青年
Xin Qingnian zui'an zhi dabian shu 新青年罪案之答辩书
xingshu 行书
Xinyue 新月
xiucai 秀才
Xiyouji 西游记
Xu Shen 许慎
Xu Zhimo 徐志摩
Xuan 宣
Xuanzang 玄奘

Yan'an 延安
Yan Fu 严复

Yan Fu dazhuan 严复大传
Yang Quan 杨铨
Yang Xiuqing 杨秀清
yangwu 洋务
Yangzhou 扬州
Yao 尧
yau tiao shu nu 窈窕淑女
yi 义
Yi leyin shi bashou 译乐隐诗八首
yi ziyou wei ben, yi minzhu wei yong 以自由为体，以民主为用
Yigeren de Shengjing 一个人的圣经
Yijing 易经
Yongzheng 雍正
you jiao wu lei 有教无类
youmo 幽默
Yuan 元 (朝)
yuan 缘
Yuan Qiang 原强
Yuan Shikai 袁世凯
Yuanmingyuan 圆明园
Yue 粤
Yue Fei 岳飞
Yuejing 乐经
Yueyang lou ji 岳阳楼记
yuluti 语录体
Yuyanxue luncong 语言学论丛

zawen 杂文
Zeng Guofan 曾国藩
Zeng Zi 曾子
Zhang Xueliang 张学良
Zhang Zhidong 张之洞
Zhao Gao 赵高
Zhao Mingcheng 赵明诚
Zhao Yuanren 赵元任

Zheng 郑 (国)
Zheng Xiaoxu 郑孝胥
zhi 智
zhi 质
zhi 志
zhong jun 忠君
Zhongyang ribao 中央日报
Zhongyong 中庸
zhongxue wei ti xixue wei yong 中学为体西学为用
Zhou 周 (朝)
Zhou Yang 周扬
Zhou Zuoren 周作人
zhuanshu 篆书
Zhuang Zhou 庄周
Zhuangzi 庄子
Zichan 子产
Zigong 子贡
Zilu 子路
Zixia 子夏
Zongli 总理
Zou Rong 邹容

Index

all under heaven (*tianxia*), 15, 34, 43, 54, 136
Annals of Spring and Autumn, The, 3, 10, 205–206, 208
Arnold, Matthew, x–xii, 151, 205, 213, 216–217

Babbitt, Irving, 151, 181
baihua (vernacular Chinese), 18, 21, 151–152, 157, 174, 176
Beijing, 16, 22, 51, 116, 119, 128, 131, 170, 182, 194
Boas, Franz, viii
Book of Change, The, 10, 20
Book of Poetry, The, 10, 20, 33, 85, 87, 89
Boxer Indemnity Fund, 153
Boxer's Rebellion, 16, 118, 122
British Empire, 14, 112
Buddhism, 5, 12–13, 28, 43, 56–57, 74–82, 105–107, 137, 208
Burke, Edmund, 151
burning books, 12, 20, 32, 169

Cang Jie, 18
Changzhou, 24

Chen Dong, 48–50
Chen Duxiu, 152, 174–176, 178–179
Chen Yinke, 51–52
Chiang Kai–shek, 128, 130–131
Chinese calligraphy, 25
Chinese characters, ix, 18–20, 22–25, 156, 159
Chinese Communist Party, The (CCP), 3, 17, 123, 128, 130–132, 174, 179–188
Chinese typewriter, 159
Chongqing bombing, 131
Civil Examination (*keju*), 13–14, 90, 112, 117, 122, 128, 140, 149–150, 153, 165, 167, 173, 197, 208, 214
Cixi (Empress Dowager), 118–119, 122, 172–173
Communism, 12, 15, 17, 117, 123, 128, 164, 178
Confucius, xi, 3, 5, 15, 38, 44–45, 66, 84–87, 110, 122, 136, 176, 203–206, 209, 211–212, 216–217
   life, 8–12
   on self-cultivation, 57–65
   on "education to all", 8, 38

cosmopolitanism, 12, 15, 137, 144, 164, 175
Cultural Revolution, The, 3, 22, 84, 183, 185–186, 188–189, 192 193, 195–196, 198, 200–201

dagong mei (working girls), 200–201
dangzheng (party contention), 41–42
Democratic People's Republic of Korea, The, 207
Deng Xiaoping, 17, 186–188, 192, 194–195
Dong Zhongshu, 30, 33–34, 37, 47
Donglin scholars, 50–53
Du Fu, 89, 95, 97–98

Eight Sample Movies, 187–188
equalization of things (*qiwu*), 68
Ever Victorious Army, 169

family-state, 29, 32, 34, 43, 47, 53–54, 124, 169
Fan Zhongyan, 39
Feng Guifen, 120, 138
filial piety, 8, 32, 44–45, 60, 126
First Chinese Educational Mission, The, 171
First Emperor of Qin (Qin Shihuang), 4, 12–13, 20, 23, 32–33, 43, 167, 169, 216
First Sino–Japanese War, The, 118, 120–122, 140, 166, 171
Five Classics and Four Books, 20
Four Cardinal Principles, 188–190
Foucault, Michel, xi

gaikai (reform and opening up), 192–193

Gao Xingjian, 189–190
Gaozu (Emperor), 34–35
gentleman (*junzi*), 16, 43, 57–65, 69, 87, 98, 205
Giles, Herbert, 25
Gladstone, William, 115
God (*Shangdi*), 4
Gordon, Charles George, 169
Great Union (*datong*), 137, 144, 147, 149–150
Gu Hongming, x, 34, 57, 88, 119, 182
    The Spirit of the Chinese People, 203–217
Guanyin, 75, 81
Guangzhou, 24, 117, 165–166, 194, 202
Guo Songtao, 140, 209

Habeas Corpus, 206
Han Dynasty, 3, 12–13, 20–21, 29, 34–37, 47, 74, 100
Han Fei, 5, 30–33, 212–213
Hong Kong, 18, 22, 25, 115, 189, 192, 194, 201–203
Hong Xiuquan, 117–118, 165–167
Hu Feng, 183, 185–186
Hu Shi, 144, 150–158, 174, 176, 181, 189, 195, 212
Huang Zongxi, 53–54
Huizi, 71–72
Huizong (Emperor), 26, 42, 48
Hundred Days' Reform, 118, 121, 144
Hundred Schools of Thought, 5, 12–13, 19, 29–30, 84
Huxley, Thomas, 139, 141–143, 213

iron rice bowl, 200

Jesus Christ, 8, 48, 117, 166
jiaguwen, 18

jinshi (advanced scholar), 37–39
juren (recommended man), 37

Kang Youwei, 141, 144–150, 171, 208
Kim Jun Un, 207
Kong Shangren, 52

Lao She, 187
Laozi, 5, 66–67, 73, 79, 84
    Laozi (Dao De Jing), 20, 66–67, 73
Law of the Gentleman (*junzi zhi dao*), 205
Left League, 180–183, 186
Legalism, 5, 29–30, 33–34, 65
Li Bai, 89, 91–92, 97
Li Hongzhang, 118, 168, 170–171
Li Qingzhao, 89–91
Li Shangyin, 89, 91, 93
Li Si, 20, 32
Li Xiangjun, 52
Liang Qichao, 141, 172, 208–212
Liang Shiqiu, 181
Liang Shuming, 185
Lin Yutang, xii, 11, 41–42, 51–53, 67, 97, 103, 107, 109, 133–135, 179, 181–182, 189, 212–213, 217
    as a cosmopolitan intellectual, 157–162
Lin Shu, 139
Lin Zexu, 112, 115
Literary Revolution, 21, 126, 151–153, 156, 158, 160, 173–174, 176, 181
Liu Rushi, 51–52
Liu Shaoqi, 3, 186
Lu Xun, 125–126, 144, 174, 176–178, 180–183, 186

Magna Carta, 206–208
Mandate of Heaven, 35, 44, 54, 165, 210
Mao Zedong, 3, 183–184, 186, 188, 190, 198, 206, 208
March of the Volunteers, The, 134
Marco Polo Bridge, 130–131
May Fourth Movement, The, 128
Mei Guangdi, 151–152
Mencius, 5, 44–46, 66, 122, 155, 209
    Mencius, 20, 46
Mill, John Stuart, 139, 141, 213
Ming Dynasty, 14, 50–51, 53, 74, 77, 111, 116–117
missionaries, 15, 25, 110–111, 115–119, 137–138, 167–168, 208
Mo Yan, 188–190
Mr. Democracy, 16, 128, 151, 157–158, 175, 203–204, 213
Mr. Science, 16, 128, 151, 157–158, 175, 203, 213, 215

nationalism, xii, 12–13, 15–17, 25, 110–111, 117, 120, 123–124, 127–129, 131–132, 136–137, 203, 212
Nationalist Party, The (Kuomintang, or KMT), 123, 127–131, 180
New Citizen, 208–209, 211
New Culture Movement, The, xi, 16, 21–22, 126, 128, 151–153, 157–158, 173–175, 178–179, 187
New Youth, The, 152, 174, 176
Nietzsche, Friedrich, xii, 153, 174

opium trade, 14, 110–112, 115–117, 121, 125, 137, 168, 208

Opium War, The, 4, 12, 114–118, 125, 132, 138–139, 164, 166, 169, 208
Ouyang Xiu, 39–41

People's Republic of China, The (PRC), 17, 132, 185, 207
Pound, Ezra, 19

Qian Qianyi, 51, 53
Qin Dynasty, 4, 12, 20, 26, 28, 34, 43
Qin Hui, 50
Qing Dynasty, 4, 13, 24, 28, 36–37, 43, 51–54, 89, 111–112, 115–119, 122–123, 127, 138, 140, 142, 167, 170, 172–174, 210, 213
    late Qing, 28, 36–37, 54, 137, 150, 152

Rape of Nanjing, 132–133
Republic of China, The (ROC), 17, 122, 154
Ricci, Matteo, 116

Sakyamuni, Gautama, 74
    Buddha, 74–77, 80–82
scholar–official, 36, 39, 41, 90, 112, 138–139, 165–166, 171, 173, 209
Self–strengthening Movement, 120–121, 170, 193
Shang Yang, 32
Shanghai, 22, 115, 131, 138, 154, 157, 158, 169, 174, 179–180, 184, 194
Shenzhen, 24, 192, 194, 200
Shi Zhicun, 182
Shun (Emperor), 4–8, 10, 30–32, 44

Sima Qian (Grand Historian), 2, 5–7, 11, 35, 216
    Shiji (*Records of the Grand Historian*), 3, 5, 32, 34, 215–216
Six Arts, 8, 37
Snyder, Gary, 70–71, 107
Song Dynasty, 13–14, 20, 26, 37, 39, 42–43, 48, 57, 90, 111
Spence, Jonathan, 114–115, 133
Su Dongpo, 39–44, 48, 90, 92–93, 95, 98, 106, 161–162, 217
Sui Dynasty, 37
Sun Yat-sen, 16, 122–123, 126, 128, 144, 172, 179, 201

Taiping Bible, The, 166–167
Taiping Rebellion, 117–119, 164–170, 171, 209
Taiwan, 17–18, 22–23, 25, 121, 123, 160, 189, 201, 203
Tang Dynasty, 21, 37, 46, 75–77, 89, 91, 97–98, 106, 137
Tao Yuanming, 98–105, 107, 217
Taoism, 5, 13, 56, 65–74, 208
Three Dynasties, 4, 10
Three Fundamental Obediences and Five Constant Virtues (*sangang wuchang*), 29, 190
Three Principles of the People, The (*sanmin zhuyi*), 123, 126
Tiananmen Square, 128, 188
Tongwen Guan, 138, 170
transformation of things (*wuhua*), 68

unification, 12–13, 25, 146

Wade, Thomas, 25
Wang Anshi, 41–43, 48
Wang Shiwei, 184–185
Wang Wei, 89, 106

Wang Xizhi, 26
Water Margins (*Shuihu zhuan*), 48
Wei Zheng, 46
Wei Zhongxian, 50–51
wenyan (classical Chinese), 18, 21–22, 151–152
Wu (Emperor), 36, 47
Wu Cheng'en, 77
Wu Zetian, 36, 43

xiucai (learned man), 37
Xu Shen, 21
Xu Zhimo, 181
Xuanzang, 75, 77–78

Yan Fu, 139–144, 150, 152, 154, 209, 213
Yan Hui, 58, 60
Yan'an, 180, 183–186, 190

Rectification Campaign, 184–186
Yang Xiuqing, 167
Yao (Emperor), 4–8, 10, 30–32, 40–41, 44, 69
Yellow Emperor (*Huangdi*), 2–4
Yuan Shikai, 126
Yue Fei, 50

Zeng Guofan, 118, 166–168, 170, 209
Zhang Zhidong, 118, 121, 123, 141, 171, 202
Zhao Yuanren, 25, 151
Zhou Yang, 183, 186
Zhou Zuoren, 182
Zhuangzi, 5, 66, 68, 71–72, 77
    Zhuangzi, 20, 66, 68–69, 77
Zilu, 58, 64

Made in the USA
Columbia, SC
02 January 2022